Upgrade
Your IBM® Compatible
and
Save a Bundle

Aubrey Pilgrim

Windcrest books are published by Windcrest Books, a division of TAB BOOKS Inc. The name "Windcrest" is a registered trademark of TAB BOOKS Inc.

Published by **Windcrest Books**
FIRST EDITION/FIRST PRINTING

Library of Congress Cataloging-in-Publication Data

Pilgrim, Aubrey.
    Upgrade your IBM compatible and save a bundle / by Aubrey Pilgrim.
      p.   cm.
   ISBN 0-8306-8468-9   ISBN 0-8306-3468-1 (pbk.)
    1. IBM compatible computers—Upgrading.   2. Microcomputers-
-Upgrading.   I. Title.
TK7887.5.P55 1990
621.39'16—dc20   89-29130
                                         CIP

TAB BOOKS Inc. offers software for sale. For information and a catalog, please contact TAB Software Department, Blue Ridge Summit, PA 17294-0850.

Questions regarding the content of this book should be addressed to:

Windcrest Books
Division of TAB BOOKS Inc.
Blue Ridge Summit, PA 17294-0850

Acquisitions Editor: Ron Powers
Technical Editor: Sandra L. Johnson
Production: Barry Brown

Contents

Introduction

To try to keep up, I subscribe to about 30 computer magazines, I attend many of the computer shows, and I work with several shops. But it is nearly impossible to keep up with all of the new hardware, new software, and new information.

I am going to tell you how to upgrade your older computer to bring it up to date with the new technologies. If you don't have an older computer to upgrade, don't let that stop you. Buy a used one and upgrade it.

Used Computers

The only trouble with buying a used computer is that you might have trouble finding one. I now live in the Los Angeles area, but when I check the classified ads for computers, I seldom see more than two or three IBM or compatibles listed.

About 20 million computers have been sold. Evidently everybody is holding on to them, or they are passing their old ones on to the kids or relatives. Many large companies are buying newer, bigger, better, and faster systems for the engineers and personnel who need them. But they don't get rid of the older ones. The companies just pass the old computers down the line to the personnel and departments who were doing without computers. Of course, an older PC or XT is better than no computer at all. Besides, many of those people, probably don't need the high power and speed of the 286s and 386s.

Perhaps one reason that you don't see too many used computers for sale is that computers are built primarily from semiconductors. If a system is designed properly, a transistor should last for several lifetimes. Of course, the disk drives, keyboards, and other components with moving parts will eventually wear out. But most of them can be easily replaced.

Buying a Used Genuine IBM

A used computer with a genuine IBM logo on it will probably cost more than two brand-new clones. This is pure snob appeal. There is no basic difference in the workings of the IBM and the clones. You can take anything out of the clone and plug it into the IBM and vice versa.

Some might argue that IBM is an American company so it has better quality. If you look inside an IBM, you will find almost as many ICs and components with foreign brands as you would find in a clone. As for quality, I have had quite a lot of experience with both IBM computers and clones, and I am convinced that the main difference between them is the IBM logo.

Beware of Used Mechanical Items

It is perfectly okay to buy anything electronic that is working. But I would strongly advise against buying a used printer, disk drives, or anything that is mechanical. As I said earlier, the semiconductors do not wear out, but the mechanical components have a finite lifetime and will eventually fail. According to Murphy's law, they will usually fail at the most inopportune time.

Of course, if you find a mechanical component that is almost new, and you get a good buy on it, then go ahead.

Buying a Bare-Bones Unit

Only one used computer store advertises in the classifieds every day in the L.A. area. You might check the area you live in. If you can't find a used one, then you might consider buying a bare-bones system and building it up yourself. You can still save money, and you will have put together your own computer. If it doesn't suit you, then you will have only one person to blame.

Compatibility

Some computers and some software are more IBM-compatible than others.

In the early days of computers, you didn't have too many hardware and software choices, so it wasn't much of a problem for them all to be very similar and compatible. Now, about six or seven billion dollars worth of software and about the same amount of available hardware are available. One of the most basic principles of sales is to make your product a bit different and better than the competition. Many of the clone products have been made better than even IBMs. Certainly, there are a lot more clone products than IBM. So with whom should you worry about being compatible?

I will say it again and again, what you put into your computer or add to it should depend primarily on what you want it to do. In most cases, it will be at least 99 percent compatible. But if it does what you want it to do, it doesn't really matter even if it is only 50 percent compatible.

Organization of the Book

One of the problems in writing a book is that you don't know how much your readers already know. If you make it too simple, it will discourage the old pros. If you make it too technical, it will be over the heads of the newcomers. I try to take the middle ground throughout the book.

This book is primarily about hardware and components that you can add to your system to make it bigger or better. I discuss the options and choices at the beginning of each chapter, and then go into more detail later for those who might want more information.

I have used plain English throughout this book and tried to avoid using computer jargon unless it is absolutely necessary. In some cases, there is no other way. I have included a comprehensive glossary in the back of the book. If you come across something that is unfamiliar, check for a definition in the glossary.

The Future

I am sure that you have all heard of the fantastic new Intel 80486. Figure I-1 shows 1.2 million transistors in this small chip. The chip measures .414 inches by .619 inches. (I can remember when a single transistor was bigger than this chip.) In contrast, Fig. I-2 is a 386 chip with only 275,000 transistors in it. It measures approximately .380 inches × .380 inches.

Fig. I-1. The 486 chip with 1.2 million transistors. The chip measures .414" × .619".

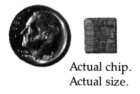
Actual chip.
Actual size.

Fig. I-2. A 386 chip with 275,000 transistors. The chip measures about .375″ × .375″.

But the 486 is not "the ultimate chip." Even at this moment, Intel is working on an 80586. Motorola and several other companies, especially the Japanese, are also working to improve and develop larger and better chips. You can be sure that faster, more powerful, and more useful computers will be on the market by the time you read this, but that doesn't mean that you should wait for the newest development. Remember, there will always be newer ones out tomorrow.

You Can Do It

Despite all my assurances, some of you may still have doubts or fears that you cannot do an upgrade yourself. Don't worry. It does not require a lot of expertise. It requires no soldering or board assembly. Please believe me, you can do it. Be confident.

The author. I hope you enjoy this book.

1

Upgrade To Prevent Obsolescence

Computer technology is advancing and changing faster than any other technology. By the time you walk out of a store with a brand new computer, and get it home, it will probably be obsolete. If your computer is three or four years old, it belongs to the dinosaur age. But not to worry. Your computer, no matter how old, can be upgraded to take advantage of all the latest and greatest. This book will show you how you can do it yourself.

Power Strip

If you have not done it already, one of the first things you should do is buy a power strip so that all of your equipment will be plugged into one source. You might have five or six power cords from your computer, your monitor, printer, lamps, and other devices plugged into various outlets and extensions. This can be messy and potentially dangerous.

Some older or less expensive equipment might have only two-wire cords. It is possible to plug these devices in so that there is a voltage potential between them. This could cause grounding problems. Check the prongs on the plug. One prong should be wider than the other. This is the ground side. The wider blade should be plugged into the wider slot in the receptacle.

You should be able to buy a power strip with six outlets and switch for $10.00 to $15.00. Some companies advertise very expensive strips with filtering. In most cases, they only have a cheap capacitor and a varistor that filters some spikes from the voltage source. But ordinarily there is not that much need for filtering. If you do need a filter, make sure that the unit has a good electronic filter that should include coils and more electronics than just a capacitor and a varistor.

Uninterruptible Power Supply

While the San Francisco and Los Angeles areas have very few electrical storms, you might live in an area where there are storms and power outages. Then you might consider buying an uninterruptible power supply (UPS). This is essential if you do any critical work on your computer. Any time the power goes off, you can lose any data that you are working on. A UPS would take over and keep your computer going if the power is interrupted.

I like WordStar 5.0 because it can be set to save your files to disk automatically every so often. That way if the power is accidentally switched off or interrupted, most of your file will still be on your hard disk. The set of utility programs called Mace Gold has a Power-Out Protector, that can be set to save database files, spreadsheets, or any other file to disk at predetermined intervals. It can undelete a file, unformat, defragment, and has many other valuable utilities. Mace Gold is available from most software houses for about $80.00.

The highest voltage that your computer uses is 12 volts. The power supply in the computer takes the 120 volts alternating current, (AC) and converts it to direct current (DC) that the computer needs. Several UPS techniques provide uninterruptible power. Most use rechargeable batteries, some even use automobile batteries. The cost of the systems depend primarily on the amount of wattage that is needed.

There are a large number of companies. Most advertise in computer magazines. Here are just a few:

Alpha Technologies	(206) 647-2360
American Power Conversion	(401) 789-5735
Best Power Technology	(800) 356-5794
Brooks Power Systems	(215) 244-0624
Clary Corporation	(818) 287-6111
Computer Power Products	(213) 323-1231
Sola Corporation	(312) 439-2800
Tripp Lite Corporation	(312) 329-1777
UPSystems	(213) 634-0621

Some of the Ways To Upgrade

Here is an overview of some of the things that you can do. Specifics about each item are in the following chapters.

1. *New plug-in board.* About six billion dollars worth of hardware has been developed for the IBM PC and compatibles. Because of the open architecture, these computers can be configured to perform thousands of applications. Many boards have been designed for these applications. They can be plugged into one of the slots in the motherboard for a very easy upgrade.

2. *Accelerator boards.* Several companies have developed accelerator boards that can be plugged into your old motherboard. The more popular of these boards have newer CPUs such as the 386. Just plug one of these boards into your computer, and you transform your old XT or 286 into an amazing 386 machine.

3. *New motherboard.* The motherboard is the main board in your computer. It has the CPU, the memory, the BIOS, the bus, and many other components on it. It has slots so that other boards can be plugged into it. If you have an XT or an older 286, you can remove the motherboard and replace it with a late model 286 or a 386. Depending on your needs and what you want to spend, you can get a faster motherboard, one with more memory, more built-in functions, and other goodies.

4. *New power supply.* You will probably want to install a new power supply also. The original PC had a 63 watt power supply. That is not nearly enough for a decently configured computer today. You should have a minimum of a 150 watt supply, or preferably, a 200 watt supply. The power supplies are very easy to install; just slip it in and install a couple of screws. Then plug in the power to the main board and to the disk drives.

5. *New floppy drives.* The 1.2Mb floppy drives can read, write, and format both 360K disks and the 1.2 Mb. They cost only a few dollars more than a 360K drive, but a 1.2Mb can store over three times more data. I don't know why anyone would buy a 360K drive nowadays. The 1.44Mb $3^1/2$ inch drives can read, write and format both 720K disks and the 1.44Mb. The 1.44Mb drives cost only a few dollars more than the 720K drives but allows you to store twice as much data. You should not buy an obsolete 720K drive.

6. *New hard disk.* I assume that you already have a hard disk. If you do not, then by all means you should get one. If you have an older one that is less than 30Mb, you should probably get a second one or a larger one. You might even want to consider an SCSI or ESDI system.

7. *Backup devices.* You will want to make sure that your hard disk is backed up at all times. You never know when it might fail, or you might accidentally erase a critical file. There are several good backup software programs available. One of them comes free with your copy of DOS, the BACKUP and RESTORE commands. Others cost a bit of money, but their speed, versatility, and convenience make them worthwhile. Many hardware systems such as $1/4$ inch tape, videotape, and other disk systems can be very good backup methods.

8. *More memory.* My first computer, a little Morrow CP/M machine, had a whopping 64K of memory. That was plenty for the few applications that were then available. But programs were soon developed that required many times more than this. The new OS/2 will require

about 2Mb in order to run smoothly. The new Lotus 1-2-3 Release 3 also requires about 2Mb.

You might want to add more memory, especially if you have less than 640K on the motherboard. Depending on what you are using your computer for, you might also want to add a few megabytes of expanded or extended memory.

9. *New monitor.* New monitors have been developed with much greater resolution than the early CGAs. And the prices have come way down. A good high-resolution VGA color monitor costs about the same as a monochrome did a few years ago. The VGA will be the new standard. There are many options and choices available.

   Some people will spend four or five thousand dollars on a computer system, then install a low-cost monochrome monitor. Monochrome monitors can give excellent resolution, but most people like color. Even if I do nothing but word processing, I am willing to pay a few dollars more for color. In many applications color is essential.

10. *New BIOS.* The Basic Input/Output System (BIOS) is on plug-in chips on the motherboard. As the name suggests, it controls the input and output of data to the computer. In the early days, they were fairly simple because not too many applications were available. The original IBM PC didn't even support hard disk drives. BIOS chips have improved to meet the needs as applications have proliferated.

    If you have an older machine, then you probably need a new BIOS. I have an ancient 286 that was designed and built in 1984. I had problems with several new programs and applications until I installed a new BIOS.

11. *New modem.* A modem is almost essential to a good computer system. It is your link to the rest of the world. You can communicate with other computers, with bulletin boards and on-line services, even do your banking with it. Downloading software from a bulletin board can more than pay for the modem in a very short time.

12. *Fax and scanners.* Facsimile machines have been around since the early 1950s. They are a fantastic tool for communicating. Plug-in boards have been developed with the fax machine on them. So it is very easy to add a fax to your computer.

    Also, you will need a scanner if you want to send graphic images along with your fax. A scanner is necessary for most types of desktop publishing (DTP).

13. *New keyboard and mouse.* If you use your computer very much, then you know the importance of the keyboard. It is the primary method of data input. If the keys are too soft or they don't suit your typing style, then you should consider upgrading. Keyboards are now very inexpensive.

You might have to buy a keyboard if you upgrade from a PC or XT motherboard to a newer one. The PC and XT keyboards might look exactly like the 286 and 386 keyboards, they even have the same connector, but if you plug one into a 286 or 386, it will not work. Some later model keyboards have a small switch underneath that allows them to work with both systems.

One of the biggest selling points of the Apple Macintosh is the fact that it is so easy to use a mouse and point and click. More and more software is being developed for the IBM and compatible world that uses the mouse and icons. A mouse can make life in the computing lane a lot easier.

14. *New printer.* If you have an old 9-pin dot matrix printer, you might be unhappy with the quality. New printers can deliver near-letter-quality type. Most of them are fast and comparatively inexpensive. Even the new laser printers are coming down in price to where they are affordable.

15. *New DOS and other software.* Depending on your applications and needs, you will probably want to move up to DOS 3.3 or 4.01. You may even want to move up to OS/2 and Presentation Manager or to Unix.

About ten billion dollars worth of software has been developed for the IBM PC and compatibles. New programs and improvements are being introduced daily. This software can give you great versatility, utility, and capability.

This is not a complete list. There are many other things that you can do to improve and enhance the performance and capabilities of your computer. One reason the list is not complete is that new devices, hardware and software are being developed and introduced every day. We could never have a complete list.

Figure 1-1 shows some of the parts that make up a 386 computer. Except for the motherboard, most of these parts are the same as those found in a PC, XT, or 286.

Tools Needed

You will not have to do any soldering or use any electronic meters or instruments. All of the parts are connected together with cables and plug-in boards. The motherboard, power supply, and disk drives will be secured with a minimum number of screws. The cover will also be secured with five screws.

The only tools you will need are a couple of screwdrivers, one Phillips and a flatblade. It would help if the screwdrivers are magnetized. Some of the screws are small and go in places that are difficult to reach.

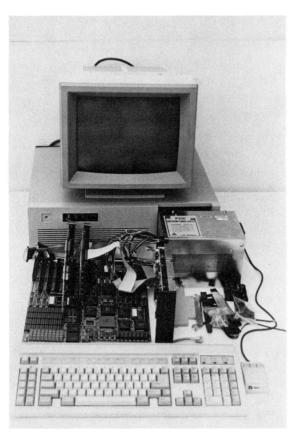

Fig. 1-1. The parts needed to make a 386. Note that, except for the motherboard, these are about the same parts found in a PC, XT, or 286.

A magnetic screwdriver can hold the screw until you get it started. You can buy them already magnetized, or you can magnetize them yourself by rubbing them on a strong magnet. A pair of longnose pliers might also help. I also use a small penlight quite often for peering inside my computer when I want to change something. See Fig. 1-2.

I bent a small screwdriver so that it is very handy for prying out chips from their socket. The metal blank covers for the back panel openings are also a great tool for lifting out chips as you can see in Fig. 1-3.

Why You Should Do It Yourself

There are shops, and several mail order stores, who will do the upgrading for you. Of course, these stores cannot stay in business unless they make a profit, so it can be a bit expensive. It can also take a lot of time and cause a considerable amount of problems. If you take it to a shop, you have to find someone who will do it for you. Then you have to lug the computer down to the shop, usually during business hours, fight traffic, and find a place to park. Or you can package it up and send it off to a mail order store.

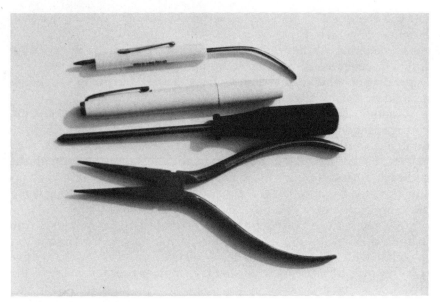

Fig. 1-2. Helpful tools.

Fig. 1-3. The metal filler for the slot openings on the back panel is a good tool for lifting out chips.

If you send it to a mail order store for an upgrade, there can be a problem of communications. Just what do you want done to your computer? How much do you want to spend? How busy is the shop or mail order store? How reliable is the shop? Can you get a firm price for the total cost and a date as to how soon they can get it back to you? How long can you wait for it? If the shop is very busy, it might take longer than promised to get it out.

Considering all the trouble and expense, you might think that it would be better to sell your old computer for scrap and buy a new one. Depending on what you have, and what you want, scrapping it or selling it might be a viable alternative.

Another alternative might be to donate it to a church or to a charitable organization. You might not be able to sell the computer for what you think it is worth. The computer that you paid $2500 for a few years ago may not be worth $500 today. Or you might not want to go through the bother and hassle of advertising and selling it. Depending on your tax situation, you might come out ahead by donating it and deducting it as a gift on your income tax return.

You might then consider buying a completely new system. You might even consider the true blue IBM if you have a lot of money. A model 30, with a single $3^1/2$ inch floppy disk drive and a 20Mb hard drive will cost over $2000. This is not too bad. But one disadvantage of the model 30 is that it does not have a $5^1/4$ drive and no room to add one internally. So there may be a problem if all of your previous data is on $5^1/4$ disks. If you have been using a computer for a while, you probably have lots of disks filled with programs that have been accumulated over the years.

For that same $2000, you could buy a clone 286 with a $3^1/2$ inch drive and a $5^1/4$ drive. You could also get at least a 30Mb hard drive, which is the minimum that anyone should consider nowadays. You would also get several other goodies that you would not get on the IBM. But that logo means more to some people than the extras that you can get with a clone.

You could buy a barebones XT clone for about $250 or a barebones 286 for about $500. You can then upgrade it yourself. If you are on a budget, you can skimp a little on the grocery money each week and do it a little at a time.

If you are lucky, you might be able to buy a used computer and upgrade it. But I live in the Los Angeles area now, and I look at the want ads each day and never see more than one or two used computers for sale.

If you work for a large company, chances are that they are in the process of buying new more powerful systems to meet their added business needs. (Another law, based on Parkinson's laws, is that the need for more and larger computer systems grows in a logarithmic fashion each year that the company is in business whether or not the business increases.) Try to find out what the manager of the computer procurement department is doing with the old computers. Some companies pass them down to secretaries and other people who are low on the totem pole. Many companies will sell them to their employees for a good price. Talk to the manager and remind him how much goodwill that such a practice can buy for the company.

Even if you have a brand new computer, there are all kinds of things you can do to upgrade it. And you can upgrade it yourself. You don't need to send it out to have it done. If you are not too familiar with the innards of your computer, you might be afraid to tackle a project like this. But it is very easy to do. No offense intended, but I have seen people who are absolute klutzes do it. So I know that you can do it. I am going to show you how you can do it yourself and save a bundle.

There are an endless number of applications and things that you can do with a computer. Because I don't know what your applications or needs are, I will talk about several alternatives and options in the following chapters.

Sources

One of the better sources for information about computers and components is computer magazines. There are at least 100 of them being published today. Most are filled with ads because ad revenue is the thing that makes them possible. I have listed several magazines in Chapter 17.

I also talk about mail order in Chapter 17. It might be one of your better alternatives for components and supplies.

Another good source is computer shows and swaps. If you live near a large city, there will probably be one going on every weekend. I enjoy going to them even if I don't need anything. It is almost like a circus atmosphere.

Of course, whenever possible you should patronize your local computer dealer. His prices might be slightly higher than the mail order houses or the prices at computer swaps. But he might be able to give you help and support and answer questions if you have problems.

You should also join a user group and attend meetings. You will find people at these meetings who can help you and exchange ideas with you. Most groups also are able to acquire public domain software and other goodies at a discount.

If you have a modem, you can access bulletin boards, download public domain software and usually get help for any problems.

New Business Opportunity

After you finish this book, I think you will agree that it is very easy to upgrade a computer. Once you see how easy it is, you might even want to go into business. There are over ten million older computers that could be upgraded. Many of them are owned by large companies. Some companies are buying new computers because they don't realize how easy and inexpensive it is to upgrade their older ones, which is a terrible waste of money and good resources.

2

A Few Minor Upgrades

If you have been putting off replacing a board in your computer because you were afraid, don't wait any longer. There is really not much that you can do to harm your computer or yourself. If you know which end of a screwdriver to use, you will have no trouble upgrading your computer. And you can save a bundle.

Installing a New Board

You might have decided that you need to add a new board to your computer. Adding a new board is one of the most common and easiest ways to upgrade. Maybe you need a modem so you can access some of the bulletin boards. Most of them are crammed full of public domain software and other goodies. You can buy a board with an internal modem for less than $100. A single public domain program might be worth more than that to you.

Or maybe you need to install an adaptor board for a new color monitor or a graphics monitor that you have bought. Or a multi I/O (Input/Output) board to give you extra ports for your printer or an external modem. It is a very simple task. Anyone who knows how to use a screwdriver can do it.

Removing the Cover

In order to take advantage of the goodies that are available, the first thing you have to do is remove the cover. There are five screws that hold the cover on, one at the top and bottom of each corner in the rear. There is also one in the center at the top in the rear. These five screws are the only ones that should be removed. You may find other screws on the rear panel but you should not remove them. Some of these screws hold the power supply in place and others might be for connectors. See Fig. 2-1.

Fig. 2-1. *The five screws that hold the cover on are located at each of the four corners and with the fifth one at the top center on the back panel.*

Just remove the five screws, slip the cover off, and plug in your new board. Some computers have a flip-top case. With these you need only press the two buttons on the side and the top of the case can be raised much like the hood of an automobile.

The Inside of Your Computer

The inside of your computer is safe. Except for the power supply, which is completely enclosed, the highest voltage in your computer is only 12 volts. But of course if you are going to open your computer and add or change anything, there won't even be 12 volts in it. Because the very first thing that you should do, even before you start to take the cover off, is to unplug it.

CAUTION!!! *Never* plug in or unplug a board, cable or any component, while the power is on. The fragile transistors and semiconductors on these boards and components can be easily destroyed. It only takes a second to turn off the power or to remove the power plug.

The second thing that you should do if you are going to remove any boards or change any cables or switch settings is to make a drawing or diagram of the original setup. Many cables and connectors can be plugged in backwards or into the wrong receptacle. It only takes a minute to make a rough diagram. It might save you hours of agony in trying to solve a problem if you plug something in backwards or into the wrong receptacle. Or you could possibly burn out an expensive component.

Your computer, whether it be a true-blue IBM XT, AT, or a clone XT, 286, or 386, will have eight slots on the motherboard. (Some baby 286 and 386 motherboards might have only seven slots. The early IBM PC had only five slots.) These slots, or *connector receptacles*, are for the various boards that you might want to use. Plug-in boards have an edge connector with copper etched fingers that contact the spring loaded contacts of the motherboard slot connectors.

One of the major differences between the XT, the 286, and the 386, is the motherboard. Figure 2-2 shows an XT motherboard on the left, a 286 in the center, and a 386 on the right. The plug-in slots are at the bottom in the photos. Notice that the 286 has six extra 36-pin slots above the standard eight 62-pin slots. The 386 motherboard has four extra 36-pin slots and two extra 62-pin slots.

Fig. 2-2. From left to right, comparison of an XT, 80286, and 80386 motherboards.

The standard 62 pin slots on all of the motherboards are 8-bit slots. Boards developed for the XT are 8-bit boards. Boards specifically developed for the 286 are 16-bit boards and those for the 386 are 32-bit boards. Notice that all of the 8-bit 62-pin slot connectors are separate from the extra 16 bit and 32 bit connector slots.

As you have probably deduced, an 8-bit board designed for the XT can also be used in a 286 or 386 computer. They are compatible. But a 16-bit board designed for a 286 cannot be plugged into an XT. However, it can be used in a 386. And of course a 32-bit board designed for a double 62-pin slot cannot be used in a 286 or XT.

Check the manual or documentation for your board. It might have some switches or shorting bars that must be set to configure the board to your system, or to whatever it has to do.

After you have set any necessary switches, look for an empty slot and plug your board in. It doesn't matter which slot. The slots are all connected to the standard bus. If you look closely at the motherboard, you can see etched lines that go across the board to the same pin on each slot connector. The pins on one side of the connector are numbered A1 to A31. On the other side they are numbered B1 to B31. Pin B1 on every connector is ground. B9 on every connector is +12 volts. The connections on the A side are I/O and address lines.

In most cases, it is physically impossible to plug a board into a slot backwards. But you should make sure that it is plugged in all the way. Some slot connectors are very tight, and it may be difficult to get the board to seat properly. If you press down too hard you could flex and damage the motherboard. The motherboard sits on standoffs so there are areas beneath it where there is very little support.

After you are satisfied that the board is seated properly, install a screw in the bracket to hold it in place. It helps if you have a magnetized screwdriver to hold the screw while getting it started. If you don't have a magnetized screwdriver, you can magnetize one by rubbing it vigorously against any strong magnet. (If you have a stereo system, your large speaker will have a strong magnet around the voice coil.) You should be careful not to place the magnetic screwdriver, or any magnet, near any of your floppy disks because it could partially erase them.

If you are upgrading an XT or PC, you might have to reset the dual in line (DIP) switches on the motherboard. The PC has two, the XT only one of these DIP switches that are set for various configurations. See Fig. 2-3. Here are the settings for the XT at various configurations:

1 is usually set to OFF
2 is OFF without an 8087, ON with an 8087 coprocessor
3 OFF, 4 ON if only 128K memory on motherboard
3 OFF, 4 OFF if 256K or more on motherboard
5 ON, 6 OFF for color monitor
5 OFF, 6 OFF for monochrome monitor
7 ON, 8 ON if only one floppy drive
7 OFF, 8 ON for two floppy drives

As long as you have the cover off, check to make sure that the openings in the rear panel above any empty slots have blank covers installed. Those little electrons that represent bits of data don't make any noise at all when they go racing around through the semiconductors in your computer, but they can get hot. Heat is an enemy of all semiconductors. What you hear when you turn on your computer is the cooling fan located in the power supply.

The power supply fan draws air from the front of the computer, pulls it over the boards and components, and forces it out through the rear opening of the power supply. To make it work efficiently, all of the openings in the rear panel should have blank covers installed. There should

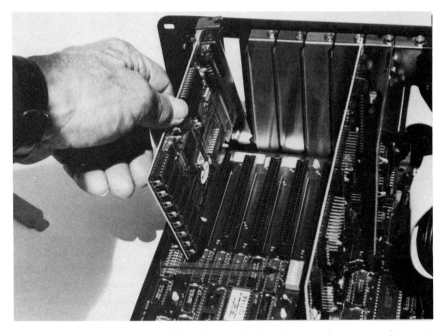

Fig. 2-3. The dip switch on an XT. It has 8 switches that must be set to configure the computer.

be no obstruction in the back or the front of your computer that would interfere with the flow of air through the power supply.

Once you have installed your new board, check it to make sure that it is completely seated in the slot and that everything is proper. Then connect the power, the keyboard, and the monitor, and try it out before you replace the cover. There have been times when I installed new parts, then replaced the cover, turned on the power, and it didn't work. It was usually some small thing that I had not done, or had done improperly. So I would end up having to remove the cover again. It doesn't hurt at all to run your computer without a cover. I have several computers. I am constantly running tests, evaluations and trying out new boards and products on my computers. Most of the time I don't even bother to replace the covers on them.

One reason to have a cover on your computer is to shield and prevent it from radiating TV and radio interference. The FCC gets very concerned about this, but in most cases, the interference from a computer will not affect a TV set unless it is within a few feet of it.

Adding a Clock

Almost all of the 286 and 386 motherboards have a built-in electronic clock. The clock is in a chip and is powered by batteries so that the time is kept even when the computer is turned off. If you have a PC or an XT, you might not have a clock. Every time you boot your computer up, it will ask for the time and date. If you type in the time and date, the computer will keep excellent time right down to the hundredth of a second as long as the computer is turned on. Any file that you create will be stamped with the time and date. Any time you are at the DOS prompt >, you can type TIME or DATE and it will pop up instantly and ask you to input new time and date.

If you don't have an installed clock and you hit return, it will go to its BIOS chip and use the time and date that was burned into the chip when it was designed. If you create a file without an on-board clock, it might be stamped with a date such as 01-01-85 01:31a.

Several multifunction boards have such things as extra memory, parallel and serial ports, print spoolers, and a clock. Some include game ports, have floppy disk drive controllers, video display adapters, or other goodies. The boards are very easy to install. An excellent feature is that several functions can be included on one board that requires only one of your precious slots. Several companies offer different versions of the multifunction boards for various prices. The Liuski Company (located in California, (818) 912-8313) offers several versions costing from $30 up to $79.

Another way to add a clock is to use a no-slot clock that can be plugged into a 28-pin ROM socket. Most motherboards have an empty ROM socket alongside the BIOS chip. If you don't have an empty ROM socket, you can take the BIOS ROM out, plug in the clock, then plug the BIOS into the built-in socket on the no-slot clock. Several dealers carry them. (One dealer is the Central Computer Products: (800) 456-4123.) The cost is $49.

Another slotless clock is the dClock II. It plugs into the back of the floppy disk drive. It is available for $49.95 from the Arrick/Microsync Computer Products, (800) 543-0161.

If you have an empty slot and don't have a full 640K of memory, or you need an extra port or some other function, you would probably be better off buying a multifunction board. For about what it would cost for one of the no-slot clocks, you could get several other functions on a plug-in board.

Installing a Coprocessor

If you do a lot of heavy number crunching or large spreadsheet work, then you could probably benefit from a coprocessor. Depending on the program that you are running, a coprocessor can speed up the operation from 5 to over 100 times faster.

Almost all of the motherboards are designed with an empty socket alongside the CPU for a coprocessor. Most computers are sold without this chip because not all programs can make use of them and they are rather expensive. The coprocessor chips all have an 87 at the end of their chip designation; for the 8088 family it is 8087, for the 286 it is 80287, and for the 386 it is 80387. (The new Intel 486 CPU will have the coprocessor built into the chip, somewhere among the 1.2 million transistors within the chip.)

The coprocessor chips are priced according to the speed at which they are designed to operate. For instance an 8087 designed to operate at the standard 5 MHz is about $95. For an 8087-1 that operates at 10 MHz, the price is about $175. An 80287-6 for 6 MHz systems costs about $140, an 80287-10 for 10 MHz will cost about $240. An 80387-16 for 16 MHz will cost about $350, an 80387-20 for 20 kHz will cost about $450 and a 25 Mhz 387 chip will cost about $550. There are many dealers who offer the chips. Here are just a few:

Quick Peripherals	(800) 333-4072
DSI's Computers	(800) 284-4374
Leo Electronics	(800) 421-9565
SDI, Inc.	(800) 759-0148

Steps to Install a Coprocessor

Step 1. Remove the cover of the computer. If you have a PC or XT, look for the 8088 CPU. It is a long, narrow chip with 40 pins. It will probably be located near the motherboard power supply connector at the back of the board. There should be an empty socket alongside the 8088.

You might have to disconnect the power supply cables or remove some of the plug-in boards. Make a diagram of the boards and cables before you disconnect them.

If you are installing an 80287 or 80387, look for the 286 or 386 CPU, a square chip of about 1¹/₂ inches. It will probably be located near the center of the board. There should be an empty socket nearby.

Step 2. Note the orientation of the 8088. There should be a small U-shaped notch at one end of the CPU which indicates pin one. The empty slot should also have some sort of indication or outline on the board that would indicate the orientation of the chip.

The 286 CPU chip is square, but the 80287 coprocessor has the same long shape and 40 pins of the 8087. The 80387 has 128 pins and fits in the square socket near the 386 CPU. It can only be plugged in one way.

The NEC V20 for Extra Speed

If you have a PC or XT, there is a very inexpensive and easy way to speed it up and increase its performance by as much as 30 percent. Just remove your 8088 CPU, and install an NEC V20. This chip is a direct replacement for the 8088, but its internal construction is such that it handles some types of data at a much faster rate.

The chips are available at most electronic stores for $7 to $12, depending on the speed of your system. JDR Microdevices, at (800) 538-5000, lists the 8 MHz NEC V20 for $6.95, the 10 MHz for $11.95.

Speeding Up an AT

The XT uses a 14.31 MHz crystal which is divided by one-third down to 4.77 MHz for the system clock. Several clone makers installed an additional 24 MHz crystal and upped the clock frequency to 8 MHz. When IBM introduced the new PC-AT, it used a 12 MHz crystal which was divided in half so that the system operated at 6 MHz. Many people soon discovered that they could replace the 12 MHz crystal with a 16 MHz crystal and up the speed to 8 MHz. Unlike the PC and the XT, the AT comes with two separate crystals. It is a very simple matter to change the one that controls the clock speed. Almost all of the clone ATs came with three crystals and a method of switching so that the frequency could be changed. This option was provided because some of the older software programs, mostly games, would not run properly at 8 MHz. Many of the newer ATs now operate at 10 MHz and some go as high as 20 MHz.

If you have an older AT or 286 that operates at the snail's pace of 6 MHz, you can buy and install a 16 MHz, 18 MHz, or even a 20 MHz crystal. You might have some problems if you go above 18 MHz. But the crystals cost less than $2 each, so you could buy them all and try them for the highest speed. If you have problems, just plug in a lower frequency.

The crystal is a small rectangular cylinder that plugs into a socket. Most manufacturers locate them near the rear of the motherboard, others might locate it anywhere on the motherboard. Most electronic parts houses such as JDR Microdevices at (800) 538-5000 can supply the crystals.

About Upgrading

If you have an IBM computer or a compatible clone, you have a machine that is quite versatile. There is about eight billion dollars worth of boards and peripheral hardware that can be used with your computer. With this hardware an IBM or clone can be upgraded or configured to do almost anything that you can imagine.

3

Installing an Accelerator Board

The standard IBM PC and XT operates at 4.77 MHz. They process data in 8-bit chunks. But 8-bits is only a single byte. Some programs have several thousand bytes that have to be manipulated. This can be painfully slow when it comes to handling large spreadsheet files, number crunching, and CAD and graphics programs. You will have to sit there and twiddle your thumbs while your computer is redrawing the screen for a CAD program, or off somewhere in never-never land manipulating the data on a large spreadsheet. It is almost like the feeling you get when you're trapped in a five o'clock traffic jam.

Most of the clone manufacturers designed motherboards that could operate at a turbospeed of 8 Mhz to 10 Mhz. This helped considerably, but it is still very slow compared to the 16-bit 286 and 32-bit 386 systems.

You might have an emotional attachment to an older PC or XT and might not want to get rid of it. It might do almost everything that you need to do. Still, it would be nice to have something a little bit faster or more powerful. But maybe you don't want to pay the high price for a 286 or 386. You could install a new motherboard, but you might not want to go to that much trouble. (It really isn't much trouble. The next chapter tells you how.) You might have an AT&T, Zenith, or one of the other compatible systems whose case would not accept a new motherboard.

To help solve the speed problem, several manufacturers developed speed-up or accelerator plug-in boards for PCs and XTs. Some accelerator boards can push a PC up to as high as 12 MHz to 16 MHz. It is something like putting a 12-cylinder Ferrari engine in a Volkswagen.

Different Types

There are basically two types of accelerator boards. One type uses a 286 CPU which essentially turns your PC or XT into a 286. The other type uses a 386 CPU to turn a PC or XT into a 386. There are also 386 accelerator boards that can be plugged into a 286 to turn it into a 386. A 286 CPU chip costs about $50, and a 386 CPU goes for about $300 or more depending on the speed. You can see why the 386 accelerator is going to cost more than the 286. The 286 accelerator might cost from $350 up to $700. The 386 accelerator boards will cost from $600 up to $1700.

Installing an accelerator board is a very easy and relatively inexpensive way to move up to the 286 or 386 world. Simply remove your computer cover and plug an accelerator board into an empty slot on a PC, XT, AT&T, Zenith, Compaq, portables, or almost any compatible. Most of them also require that you remove your present CPU and plug a cable from the accelerator board into the CPU socket.

None of the accelerators will give you all of the versatility and flexibility of a real 286 or 386. The computer will still be a bit slower than a real 286 or 386. When accessing your motherboard RAM or the hard disk, you will still be going through the 8-bit bus. To get around this bottleneck, some accelerator boards use a *cache* memory system. The cache system stores data that is most used in high-speed memory. This can cut down considerably on the number of times that the system has to run out to the hard disk or to your RAM.

Some boards, such as the Intel Inboard 386/PC can have 1Mb of memory on board. Another 4Mb can be added by using piggyback boards which attach to the Inboard 386/PC.

One disadvantage is that you will not be able to use the 16-bit 286 or 32-bit 386 boards since your motherboard has 8-bit slots. Also, you will not be able to use some software and utilities.

But you might not need all of the capabilities of the 286 or all of the awesome power and speed of the 386. You must decide what you need. For a fairly reasonable price and very little trouble, you can get almost all of the benefits of the 286 or 386.

AT Accelerator Boards

I am going to list a few of the boards that can make your old PC or XT sit up and purr like a 286. The following is not a complete listing. Look through the computer magazines for other companies who manufacture them.

The Breakthru 286 company has two versions, one that operates at 8 MHz for $395, and one that operates at 12 MHz for $595.

Another option is from SOTA (for State of the Art). They manufacture a plug-in board that they call the Mothercard. It has an 80286 CPU that runs at 8 or 10 MHz. It comes with a real-time clock, 1Mb of memory, an optional 80287 coprocessor and an optional daughter board for additional memory up to 16Mb. The list price is $995.

Here are the addresses of a few companies:

Breakthru 286 $395 and $595
PC Support Group
11035 Harry Hines Blvd. #207
Dallas, TX 75229
(214) 351-0564

Univation Dream Board $512
Univation Co.
1037 N. Fairoaks Av.
Sunnyvale, CA 94089
(408) 745-0180

Orchid PC-Turbo 286e $1195
Orchid Technology
47790 Westinghouse Dr.
Fremont, CA 94536
(415) 490-8586

Mothercard $995
SOTA Technology
657 N. Pastoria
Sunnyvale, CA 94086
(408) 245-3366

One of the nice things about the PC Support Group (PCSG), the company that makes the Breakthru, is that they will allow you to use it for 60 days, then if you are not satisfied, you can return it. That is exactly what I did. I ordered it for evaluation on an XT. But I use an AT most of the time, so I decided I did not really need the Breakthru. So after 45 days, I returned it for credit.

The prices quoted above will have probably changed by the time you read this. These prices were listed for purposes of comparison only. Check with the vendor before ordering any advertised component.

You should be aware that none of these boards will give you all of the power and benefits that is possible with a true AT. These plug-in boards do not provide a 16-bit data bus, so there are many AT type boards that cannot be used with these systems.

If you can find one at a reasonable price, you might be better off if you buy a baby AT motherboard and use it to replace your PC or XT motherboard. Again, the prices of the baby AT motherboards can vary considerably, all the way from $250 up to $800. By all means do some comparison shopping.

Moving Up to the 386

There are several companies who make plug-in boards that can essentially turn a PC, XT, or AT into a 386 machine. For certain applications, this is the least expensive way to go. These boards may cost from $595 up to $1995.

Most of the boards come with a comprehensive manual and instructions for installation. The installation is usually fairly simple. Some of the boards replace the 8088 CPU in the XT by plugging a cable into the CPU socket. The 8088 in an XT is the long chip at the back of the motherboard, near the connector for the keyboard. It can be removed with one of the chrome slot covers that fit over empty slots on the back of the computer.

Most of the AT accelerator boards are installed the same way as the PC or XT. On most, you must remove the 286 CPU and plug in a cable. The accelerator board then plugs into one of the XT or AT slots.

Most of the boards come with software with utility and configuration programs. The XT or AT then becomes a 386 for most applications.

One drawback is that the XT motherboard only has an 8-bit bus. There are some boards that have been developed for the 286 and the 386 that you will not be able to use. But you will be able to process large spreadsheets, CAD programs, and other CPU intensive programs at the speed of the standard 386.

Having to use the XT 8-bit bus can be a bottleneck for access to the hard disk and to on-board memory. To get around this problem, many of the boards provide the capability of adding 4 to 16Mb of memory on the accelerator board. That way the data can be processed on the board with minimum use of the 8-bit bus. Many of them also have cache systems so that the need to access the hard disk through the 8-bit bus is reduced.

Because the AT or 286 motherboard is a 16-bit board, not much speed is sacrificed. Besides, at this time, not too many available programs can take advantage of a 32-bit bus. Most of the boards designed for the AT use the same type of on-board memory and caching used by the XT boards.

Quadram has developed an 80386 accelerator board for the PC or XT. Their Quad386XT board shown in Fig. 3-1 runs at 16 MHz, has 1Mb of memory on board, and sells for $896. Up to 8Mb of memory can be added by using daughter boards. The board is easy to install and use; just remove your 8088 CPU and plug in the special cable. It is also necessary to plug in an 8087 adapter module chip in the coprocessor socket.

The Intel Inboard 386/PC shown in Fig. 3-2 lists for $895. But I have seen ads from discount houses for as little as $599 with 1Mb of memory on board, or $1249 with 4Mb.

AOX, Inc., manufactures a 16 MHz and a 20 MHz accelerator card for the AT or 286. The AOX Master 386 shown in Fig. 3-3 works without removing the 286 CPU. Users can switch back and forth between the 286 and the 386 if the need arises. The AOX Master 386 can double or triple the overall speed of a standard 286. The price of this board is only $795. Optional 32-bit memory expansion boards can be installed in adjacent 16-bit slots and connected to the AOX Master by cables.

Fig. 3-1. A Quad386XT accelerator board. This board can turn your XT into a 386.

Fig. 3-2. An accelerator board from Intel, the Inboard 386/PC. (Photo courtesy Intel Corp.)

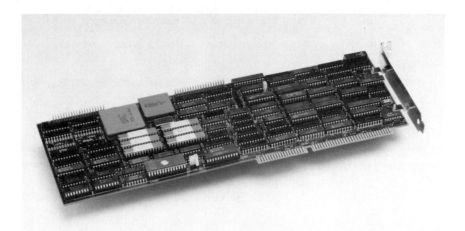

Fig. 3-3. An accelerator board for the AT, the AOX Master 386. (Photo courtesy AOX Corp.)

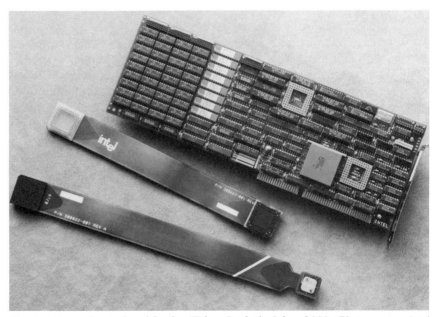

Fig. 3-4. An accelerator board for the AT from Intel, the Inboard 386. (Photo courtesy Intel Corp.)

Intel also makes the Inboard 386 board for the AT, as shown in Fig. 3-4. It lists for $1795 with 1Mb of memory. A discount house lists it for $945. To install this unit, the 80286 CPU is removed, and a cable from the accelerator board is plugged into the CPU socket.

If you think an accelerator can satisfy your needs, a short list of vendors is given in Table 3-1.

Table 3-1. A Short Listing of Accelerator Vendors.

Company	Telephone	Board Name	Cost
PC and XT Boards			
Applied Reasoning	(617) 492-0700	PC Elevator 386	$1795
Intel Corp.	(800) 538-3373	Inboard 386/PC	895
QuadRam	(404) 923-6666	Quad 386XT	896
AT Accelerator Boards			
American Computer	(714) 545-2004	386 Turbo	$1199
Aox, Inc.	(617) 890-4402	Master386	795
Cheetah International	(800) 243-3824	CAT386	1495
Intel Corp.	(800) 538-3373	Inboard 386	1595
Orchid Tech.	(415) 683-0300	Jet 386	1299
PC Technologies	(800) 821-3086	386 Express	995
Seattle Telecom	(206) 820-1873	STD-386	1995

Alternatives

Once again, accelerator boards cannot give you all of the benefits of having a motherboard with the 32-bit bus and other options.

Several companies have developed baby 386 motherboards that will fit in an XT case. I discuss them in more detail in the next chapter.

Considering the price of most of these boards and the limitations of an accelerator board, you could probably replace the motherboard in an AT for about the same cost. This approach would also give you much more versatility and true 32-bit processing.

No matter how you do it, if you move up to the 386 world, you will find that the added speed, power, and versatility of the 386 is well worth it.

4

Installing a New Motherboard

If you have an old PC or XT, you might tell your spouse that you need a new computer. If your spouse is in charge of the purse strings, you might be asked, "Why in the world do you need a new computer? You haven't worn out your old one yet."

You can say then "Well how about if I just replace my motherboard?" Your spouse will probably go along with that.

This is a biggie. A new motherboard can give you all of the benefits of a new system at a fairly reasonable cost. Just pull out your old motherboard and install a new baby 286 or baby 386. Or, if you have an older standard 286, you can easily move up to a 386. Even if you are moving up from an old PC or XT, you will still be able to use most of your old components such as the plug-in boards and disk drives in your new system. You can probably even use your old memory chips.

You might not be able to use your old keyboard. Although the XT and AT keyboards look exactly alike and have the same connector, the XT keyboard will not work on the 286 or 386 because the XT keyboard has a different scanner frequency. Some of the keyboards have a small switch on the back side that allows them to be switched from one type to the other.

Of course if you decide to install a fast and powerful new 386 board, you might not want to use your old monochrome or CGA monitor. You might also want to move up to larger-capacity hard drives and newer floppies. But if you are on a tight budget, you can always use your old components until you can afford the new goodies.

Deciding What To Buy

One of the first things that you will have to do is decide what you want. Or, if you are like me, decide what you want at a price you can afford.

I subscribe to several computer magazines. Most of them have articles and reviews of software and hardware. And of course they have lots of ads from stores that sell by mail. The ads give me a fairly good idea of the prices so that I know what I can afford. Mail order may be one of the better ways to purchase your parts, especially if you don't live near a large city.

Usually, the larger cities have lots of computer stores. The San Francisco Bay area and in the Los Angeles area have hundreds, and computer swaps go on every weekend. If I need something, I will go to one of the swap meets and compare the prices at the various booths. I often take a pad along, write the prices down, then go back and make the best deal that I can. Sometimes you can haggle with the vendors for a better price, especially if it is near closing time.

Upgrading a PC or XT to an XT Turbo

The original PC and XT used the 8088 central processing unit (CPU). This CPU has about 29,000 transistors and operates at 4.77 MHz. Computers perform their operations by moving blocks of data in precise blocks of time. The PC and XT can cycle 8-bit blocks of data at 4.77 million times per second. That sounds fast, but it takes 8 bits to make a single byte. It also takes 8 bits to create a single character of the alphabet. And it takes a whole lot of bytes if you are using graphics. It can be painfully slow if you have to run a CAD program or a large spreadsheet. The turbo XTs have been souped up so that they can operate faster than their normal 4.77 MHz. Most have a "high gear" so that they can be shifted up to 8 MHz or even up to 10 or 12 MHz. Of course the faster the speed, the more the board will cost.

You might see a turbo XT motherboard advertised for about $65. The ad will probably say 0K memory. This does not mean that it has okay memory. It means that it has zero memory. It would be very difficult to run most software today without at least 640K of memory. At the present price of chips, 640K of 120 ns memory costs about $125. Faster chips such as the 100 ns and 80 ns will cost more. (Read more about memory in Chapter 9.)

If you have an original true-blue IBM PC, it will only have five slots, so the case or chassis has five openings on the back panel. The XT has eight slots with eight openings in the back panel. Almost all motherboards now have eight slots. Your old PC case with the five openings in the rear panel will not accomodate the eight-slot motherboards. Your best bet is to scrap the old case with the five-slot openings, and buy a new case. It would only cost about $30 for a new one. But if you are in love with the IBM logo and want to keep the old case, a few companies who make special motherboards for the old five-slot PC. However, buying one of these special five-slot motherboards will cost more than what a new case and an eight-slot motherboard would cost. It would be much better to buy a new case, rip the IBM logo off the old case, and tape it to the new one.

If you are upgrading a PC, you should also buy a new power supply. The original PC had a puny 63 watt power supply. The XT and later models had 135 to 150 watt power supplies. A 150 watt power supply will cost $60 to $75.

So by moving up from 4.77 MHz to a turbo, you can double or even triple your processing speed for a cost of $200 to $250.

Of course, to really improve it, you should consider adding or replacing your old floppy drive with a 1.2Mb. This would add about $120 to the project for the drive and a new controller. But this would allow you to read and write to all of your old 360K floppies. And you can use the forty-nine cent high density 1.2Mb floppies to store $3^1/3$ times more data on each floppy.

You might also want to install a 30Mb or 40Mb hard disk to the system. This could cost an additional $350 to $500. But if you do much computing at all, it is well worth it.

More about floppy and hard drives in the following chapters.

Upgrading a PC or XT to an 80286

The IBM AT (for *Advanced Technology*) uses the 80286 CPU. It has 125,000 transistors and is a 16-bit system. The original IBM AT operated at a very conservative speed of 6 MHz, but many of the 286 clones now run at 12 MHz, 16 MHz and even up to 20 MHz.

An 80286 CPU handles data in 16-bit chunks, just twice that of the 8088. A 286 operating at 10 MHz would be more than four times faster than an XT operating at 4.77 MHz. Because it handles twice as much data per cycle, the 286 will still be twice faster even if the XT is operating at the same 10 MHz.

The standard size AT or 286 is a bit larger than the XT. The XT is 5 inches high, $19^1/2$ inches wide and $16^1/2$ inches deep. The AT is 6 inches high, $21^1/2$ inches wide, and $16^1/2$ inches deep. By combining several chips into single very large scale integrated (VLSI) chips, the clone builders soon developed a "baby" 286 motherboard that was about one inch longer than the XT, but it still fits in the XT case. Figure 4-1 shows a baby 286 motherboard. The baby 286 and baby 386 motherboards are the same size. Figure 4-2 shows a baby 386 motherboard alongside an XT motherboard.

One early problem was that several companies had developed 16-bit plug-in boards for the larger size AT that were about one inch wider, or higher, than the 8-bit XT boards. So these wider 16-bit boards cannot be used in the smaller XT-size case. But, with the advancing technology, most new plug-in boards are now very small so the size is no longer much a problem.

Fig. 4-1. A baby 286 motherboard.

Fig. 4-2. A baby 386 motherboard on the left and an XT motherboard on the right. Note that the 386 is about one inch longer.

Many people still prefer the original standard size 80286, but it has no real advantage over the baby size. Besides, the standard size 286 is 2 inches wider than the XT. That doesn't sound like much, but if your desk is as cluttered as mine, it wastes a lot of desktop real estate.

If you are upgrading an XT to a 286, then look for the baby 286 motherboard. The cost of a baby 286 motherboard will depend on several options. Most of them have built-in clocks, calendars, and serial and parallel ports. Some even have built-in EGA monitor drivers. The speed of the CPU will be a cost factor, and so will the amount of memory. If you choose a system that runs at 12 MHz or less you might be able to use your old memory chips. Depending on the options, a baby 286 motherboard might cost from $200 up to $800.

You might be able to get by with your power supply if it is 150 watts. But if you expect to install a couple of hard drives and fill all eight slots with boards, then maybe you should buy a heavier power supply.

Upgrading a PC or XT to an 80386

The 386 systems use the Intel 80386 CPU. The CPU has 275,000 transistors and can handle data in 32-bit chunks. The standard 80386 motherboard is the same size as the original AT motherboards. Again, using VLSI chips, baby 386 motherboards have been developed that are about one inch longer but still fit in the XT case. See Fig. 4-2 for an XT and 386 motherboard comparison.

There are also several options available for the baby 386 motherboards. Speed of the CPU, on-board RAM memory, cache memory, built-in serial and parallel ports, EGA monitor drivers, and other options are available at added cost. Of course, the more goodies that you can get that are already built into the motherboard, the more open slots you will have. Besides, a utility that is built-in such as EGA, will cost less than buying an EGA board.

You should be able to use all of your old plug-in boards and peripherals. But you probably will not be able to use your old memory chips unless they are 100 ns or faster. You will also probably need to buy a power supply with greater capacity.

The 386 systems are much more complex than the XT or the 286 so the motherboards are more expensive. Depending on the options chosen, the 386 motherboard might cost from $900 up to $1800.

OK Memory and CPU

You have to read the ads closely. Almost all of the motherboards and bare-bone systems are advertised with 0K memory. I recently saw an ad for 386 motherboards for only $465. When I called, they told me that this price was without memory or the CPU. You can buy 80386 CPUs with different rated frequencies, 16 MHz, 20 MHz, 25 MHz, and 33 MHz. Of course, the higher the frequency or speed, the higher the cost.

Intel Corporation is the only company who manufactures the 80386 CPU. A standard 16 MHz unit costs from $250 to $299. One that has been selected, tested, and proven to be able to run at 20 MHz will cost $350 to $599. The 25 MHz and 33 MHz units sell for prices ranging from $1000 and up per unit. Because they have no competition, it is not likely that the prices will come down very much. Intel has their factories going night and day, and are selling all of the 386 chips that they can produce.

My Upgrade

After checking several sources, I decided to buy a DTK baby 386 motherboard. DTK is a well-known name, and from the specifications of the board, it appeared to have all of the functions and goodies that one could want. Also, it was offered at a very good price of less than $1300.

I ran into the problem of the boards developed for the 286 and 386 being wider than those of the PC and XT when I upgraded my old XT to a baby 386. Many of the baby 386 motherboards do not have enough space for on-board memory, so they use a plug-in memory card. This is usually a special board that is designed for that motherboard only. The memory board that came with my motherboard was about one inch wider than my other boards. I could not get my case cover back on.

I had to make a choice. I could send the whole system back and look for another board, or I could run my system without a cover. I didn't want to send the boards back because I really liked the system, and I got a very good price on it. Computer cases are very reasonable so I spent a whopping $30 and bought a new case for my new system. I now have an extra XT case and motherboard. I will probably build it back up for evaluating various products.

My DTK baby 386 motherboard and case cost me a little over $1300. I had to buy 1MB of 80 ns memory for it. But I used my old disk drives and boards. Altogether, I spent a little over $1500 on my upgrade. If this same machine had an IBM logo on the front panel, it would have cost about $6000.

Upgrading a 286 to a 386

If you have a standard size 286 it will be very easy to move up to the faster and more powerful 386. The motherboards are the same size, and there should be very little trouble using your old plug-in boards. Depending on the speed of the 386 that you want and the speed of your old 286, you might have to buy new memory.

Upgrading a 286 to a 386SX

Intel developed the 386SX, a 16-bit version of their 32-bit 386. Compaq, IBM, and several other large companies have developed machines that use the 386SX. However, the 386SX has not taken off as expected, so very few clone motherboards have been developed for it. It doesn't seem to offer a large enough advantage over the 286 to make it worthwhile.

Because it is a 16-bit chip, some clone vendors have developed a 386SX adapter board that is a circuit board about 3 inches square with a 386SX CPU and several other chips mounted on it. Pins on the bottom side correspond to the pins of the 286 CPU. The 286 is removed, and the 386SX board is plugged in. The cost of these adapter boards is $600 to $1000.

Upgrading an AT&T 6300 or Zenith-151

These computers have a different type of case. You should be able to use most of your present components, but to add a new motherboard, you will have to buy a new case.

Installing the Motherboard

Now that you have bought a new motherboard, you can easily install it in a few simple steps. The following procedures can be used for installing any motherboard.

1. Remove Cover. The first thing to do is to remove the cover from your old computer. Unplug the power and remove the screws at each corner on the rear panel and the one at the top center. Refer to Fig. 2-1 in Chapter 2. Slide the cover off.

2. Remove plug-ins. Make a rough diagram of the cables and the board where they are connected. You might even take pieces of tape or a marking pen and mark each board and cable with a number. Notice that the ribbon cables have one wire that is a different color. This indicates pin one. Pay close attention as to how the connectors are oriented. On most boards that have vertical connections, pin one is towards the top. If the connection is horizontal, pin one is usually toward the front of the computer, but this is not always so. Check the boards for a small number or some indication as to which is pin one. Note the colored wires on the ribbon cables, and record their positions on your diagram. If possible, leave the cables from the disk drives connected to the plug-in boards when you remove them.

Note that the connectors from the power supply are connected so that the four black wires are in the center. When reconnecting the cables, it is possible to replace the cable connectors upside down or backwards, or on the wrong connector. Be sure that your diagram is complete before disconnecting anything.

Remove all of the plug-in boards, the keyboard cable, and other wires and cables that are connected to the motherboard. If at all possible, leave the cables connected to the disk controllers. Just pull the boards out and lay them across the power supply. It should not be necessary to remove the disk drives or the power supply.

3. Remove the motherboard. Depending on the type of computer you have, you might have nine standoffs holding the motherboard off the chassis. If so, there should be nine small nuts on the bottom of the chassis. The standoffs might also be plastic inserted in the holes. If they are plastic, they will be held in place by flared portions of the body of the standoff. Use a pair of pliers to press the flares together so that the standoff can be removed. With the XT motherboard removed, it should look like Fig. 4-3.

Fig. 4-3. The chassis with the motherboard removed.

4. Install memory chips. If you got a board without memory, it might be possible to use the chips from your old motherboard; it depends primarily on how fast your new board operates. For the older 4.77 MHz PCs and XTs, 200 ns was plenty fast enough. You will probably need at least 150 ns for 8 MHz. If it operates faster than 12 MHz, then you will probably need 120 ns or faster chips. Some systems use wait states so that you can use slower memory chips. The size and speed of the chips are usually marked on the top along with the vendors name and other information. The zero will be left off, so you might see something like 64-15 or 256-12, which would indicate 64K at 150 ns and 256K at 120 ns.

If you are going to use your old memory chips, you will need a small screwdriver or some other tool to pry them out of their sockets. The blank fillers on the back panel, where there are no boards installed, are a very good tool for lifting chips out of their sockets.

The memory chips will be located at the left front quarter section of the motherboard. There will be four banks, or rows, of chips with eight chips in each row. If you have 640K, then you should have two rows of 256K chips which equals 512K, then two rows of 64K which equals 128K for a total of 640K. If you have 1Mb capacity, then each of the four rows will have 256K chips.

You should get some kind of diagram or information with your motherboard that tells you where the 256K and 64K chips should be installed. Be very careful when inserting them so that they are all oriented in the proper direction. The chips should have some kind of notch or dimple that indicates pin one. The board should have a marking of some kind that indicates how the chips should be oriented. Ordinarily, most of the chips on the boards will all be oriented in the same direction. Be careful not to bend the legs, and make sure that all of the legs are inserted.

Some 286 and 386 motherboards will have the *single inline memory module* (SIMM) chips. This will be an assembly of nine miniauture chips that make up a whole bank. See Fig. 4-4.

Fig. 4-4. SIMM memory chip modules.

Some of the baby 386 boards use a separate plug-in board for memory.

5. Install the new motherboard. Most of the new boards use a standoff system that is different than that used in the old PCs and XTs. Most of the new ones have raised channels on the floor of the chassis. The channels have holes with elongated slots. Plastic standoffs with rounded tops and a thin groove fits in the holes. The standoffs are pressed into holes in the motherboard. See Fig. 4-5.

The board is then placed so that the standoffs fit into the holes in the raised channels. See Fig. 4-6. The board is moved to the right so that the grooves slide into and are locked in the narrow elongated slots. Then one screw at the back center of the board and one at the center front locks the board in place.

6. Replace the boards and cables. You are now ready to start replacing your components. Reconnect the power to the board from the power supply. Make sure that it is oriented so that the four black wires are in the center as shown in Fig. 4-7.

Replace your plug-in boards and any cables that were disconnected. See Fig. 4-8. Make sure that they are connected properly. If you made a diagram before you removed them, you shouldn't have any problems.

Fig. 4-5. The white plastic standoffs on the bottom of the motherboard.

Fig. 4-6. Position the motherboard so that the standoffs drop into the holes in the chassis, then slide it about a quarter of an inch to lock it in. A screw is then installed in the front center and one in the rear center of the board.

7. The smoke test. You are now ready to turn it on and try it before you replace the cover. Of course you hope that you do not see any smoke, but if you do, turn the power off quickly.

If every thing was done properly, then you should not have any problems. If so, you are now ready to replace the cover on your new computer.

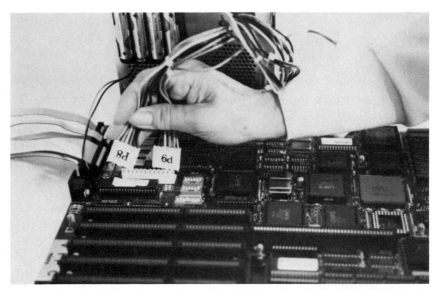

Fig. 4-7. Plugging in the power to the motherboard. Note that the black wires will be in the center.

Fig. 4-8. Reinstalling the plug-in boards.

New EISA Boards

The IBM PS/2 systems use the proprietary Micro Channel Architecture (MCA). This more advanced system has several advantages over the standard AT bus system. It allows faster data interchange between the peripherals, the bus, and memory and can recognize the settings of DIP switches on the plug-in boards. The PS/2 system is compatible with the older AT system software, but the MCA plug-in boards are incompatible.

None of the billions of dollars worth of AT type boards can be used in the PS/2 system.

In an instance of rare cooperation, a group of IBM compatible clone manufacturers got together. They devised the EISA system bus standard that can do everything the MCA can do. In addition, the new EISA standard is designed so that the older XT and AT boards can still be used. This new board has unique connectors that are about twice as deep as the standard type. The connectors have cross keys. The EISA plug-in boards have matching slots so they can be inserted to the full depth, while the older standard boards can only be inserted to the depth of the cross keys.

Only a few manufacturers are offering EISA motherboards and plug-in boards, but before long more 386 and 486 boards will be on the market.

486 Motherboards

The 1989 Fall COMDEX had only a few 486 motherboards. More companies are planning to have boards on the market, but they are still very expensive. The 486 chip alone costs over $1000 and a 486 motherboard costs about $4000. But as more vendors enter the market, the price should come down a bit. A 486 system, depending on the memory, hard disks, and other options, will cost from $10,000.00 and up.

Many of the 486 systems shown at COMDEX used the standard AT type bus. But again, by the time you read this, most of them should have the new EISA standard motherboards. Some of the sources for 486 motherboards are:

AMI
1346 Oakbrook Dr., Suite 120
Norcross, GA 30340
(404) 263-8181

Micronics
935 Benecia Ave.
Sunnyvale, CA 94086
(800) 234-4386

Wave Mate
2341 205th St. #110
Torrance, CA 90501
(213) 533-5940

United Computer Technology (A 486 on a plug-in board)
26460 H Camino De Vista
San Juan Capistrano, CA 92675
(714) 240-3458

Fountain Technologies
12k World's Fair Dr.
Somerset, NJ 08873
(201) 563-4800

DCM Data Products
610 Tandy Center
Fort Worth, TX 76102
(817) 870-2202

ICC
8 East Lawn Dr.
Holmdel, NJ 07733
(201) 946-3207

Fujikama
14145 Proctor Ave. #3
City of Industry, CA 91746
(818) 330-9733

Soyo USA
148 8th Ave. #H
City of Industry, CA 91746
(818) 330-1712

Caliber Computer
1635 McCandless Dr.
Milpitas, CA 95035
(408) 942-1220

Artek Computer Systems
750 Montague Expressway #203
San Jose, CA 95131
(408) 433-9208

AOX Incorporated
486 Totten Pond Rd.
Waltham, MA 02154
(617) 890-4402

Interphase Corp.
2925 Merrell Rd.
Dallas, TX 75229
(214) 350-9000

VIPC
384 Jackson St. #1
Hayward, CA 94544
(415) 881-1772

5

How to Install Floppy Drives

Installing high-density floppy disk drives is a very useful upgrade that is relatively inexpensive and easy to do. The $5^1/4$ high-density drives can read and write to both the 360K and 1.2Mb formats. The $3^1/2$ inch high-density drives can read and write to both 720K and 1.44Mb formats.

If you have an older computer, then no doubt you have a $5^1/4$ inch 360K floppy drive, or maybe two such drives. If they are very old, they may be full height, or about $3^1/2$ inches high. If they are original IBM drives, then they probably have a rubber "O" ring for a drive belt from the motor to the disk spindle. The rubber "O" ring deteriorates and stretches with time and will cause problems. Most of the newer drives use direct drive motors.

Advantages of High-Density Drives

Even if you have fairly new half-height 360K drives, it is well worth the cost and the effort to replace them with high-density drives.

I have about 500 360K floppy disks that are full of programs. They take up quite a lot of space, and I sometimes have a difficult time finding what I need at the moment. Someday I am going to get around to transferring them all to high-density disks. If I used 1.2Mb floppies, it would only require 150 of them to store all the data on the 500 360K disks, or only 125 of the $3^1/2$ inch 1.44Mb floppies.

I have several hard disks that must be backed up constantly. It would require over 50 360K floppies to back up 20Mb. It only takes about 17 of the 1.2Mb or about 13 of the 1.44Mb floppies to back up 20Mb.

One of the disadvantages of using the high-density disks is that they cost considerably more than the standard floppies. But there is a way to use the 720K $3^1/2$ inch disks as high density. I explain that in the next chapter.

Where to Buy the Drives

As I said earlier, if you live near a large city, lots of stores should be nearby. And also computer shows and swap meets. If you don't live near a good source, then the next best would be a mail order house.

Again, lots of computer magazines are full of ads. Space for these ads is rather expensive, so quite often the vendors use abbreviations. Floppy disk drives are usually listed as FDD. Before I go to a computer show or to a store to buy something, I usually check out the ad prices in the magazines to get an idea of what the price should be. In some cases, the store price might even be lower than the magazine price. The magazine ads have to be made up a month or so before it is published and because the computer business is so volatile, often the prices change in the meantime. The computer business is about the only business where the prices of components tend to go down. If you are ordering something by mail, you might call first to see if the price is still the same.

The 1.2Mb and the $3^1/2$ inch 720K drives have been around for some time. But the 1.44Mb $3^1/2$ inch drive is still fairly new. It was rather expensive when it was first introduced, but it has now come down to a reasonable price.

Because the 1.2Mb and the 1.44Mb drives will read and write to all formats, the 360K and the 720K drives are obsolete. But you will still see ads for the 360K and the 720K drives alongside those for the 1.2Mb and the 1.44Mb drives. The 1.2Mb and the 1.44 may cost from $70 to $100. These prices are usually only $10 dollars or so more than the prices listed for the obsolete 360K or 720K drives. I would not advise that you buy the 360K or 720K drives. Figure 5-1 shows a $5^1/4$ inch 1.2Mb drive on the left and a $3^1/2$ inch 1.44Mb in the center. They are shown connected to floppy disk controller. Because the $3^1/2$ inch drive is much smaller, it is mounted in an extension housing that allows it to be mounted in the standard $5^1/4$ inch bay.

Several large companies manufacture the floppy drives such as Sony, Toshiba, Fuji, Teac and others. Each company's prices are within a few dollars of the others. Most of them are fairly close in quality but there may be minor differences. For instance, I have two 1.2Mb drives made by Toshiba, one slightly newer than the other. The older one is much quieter and operates much more smoothly than the newer one.

Disk drives have two motors. One motor drives the spindle that rotates the disk. Then a stepping motor, or *actuator*, moves the heads to the various tracks. On my older Toshiba drive, a fairly large stepping motor is used to position the heads. A very small stepping motor is used on the newer one, so it is very noisy when it searches for tracks. Otherwise, both have worked perfectly. Figure 5-2 shows portions of the two drives. The one on the right has a large stepper motor in the top right corner, but the drive on the left has a very small motor in the same area.

Fig. 5-1. A 5¹/₄ inch 1.2Mb floppy drive on the left, a 3¹/₂ inch 1.44Mb drive in the center, and a controller on the right.

Fig. 5-2. Two Toshiba 1.2Mb floppy drives. The drive on the right has a large head, or actuator motor (top right corner). The one on the left has a small motor in the same area.

Floppy Disk Drive Controllers

You might have to buy a new floppy disk controller (FDC) for your new drives. The older FDCs operated at a data transfer rate of 250 kHz. The high-density drives operate at a rate of 500 kHz. A new FDC may cost from $40 up to $95 or more.

If you are just installing a 1.2Mb floppy, you can get by with DOS version 3.2. But if you are installing a 1.44Mb, then you will need DOS version 3.3 or later unless you use a special software driver. You can buy DOS 3.3 for about $65 or DOS 4.01 for about $95.

You might also need to upgrade your BIOS so that it can recognize the high-density drives. BIOS upgrades are available from AWARD, Phoenix, AMI, Quadtel, DTK, and other manufacturers, but they do not sell to individuals. You will have to go through a dealer. A BIOS for an XT might cost $25 to $40 and from $50 to $75 for a 286. (More about BIOS upgrades in Chapter 10.)

Available software systems provide drivers for high-density drives. With these drivers installed, you won't have to buy a new BIOS, and you can get by with an older version of DOS. The Liuski Company sells a software driver from the BASTECH Company:

Liuski Company
18025 Courtney Ct.
City of Industry, CA 91745
(818) 912-8313

It comes on a 360K floppy disk and only costs $16. It is copy protected so that you can make only five copies of it. Each time it is installed onto a hard disk or other floppy disk, the count is reduced by one. However, if you decide to reformat your disk, it can be uninstalled. When copied back to the original disk, the count will go back to five.

One of the disadvantages of drivers is that they usually change your drive letters. If you have two floppies and a hard disk, the floppies would be drive A and B and the hard disk would be C. (DOS checks to see what is installed and automatically assigns drive letters.) But if you use a driver.sys for a 1.44Mb floppy in drive B, the driver.sys would probably change it to drive D. You probably would not be able to format or do several other routines unless you used the driver.sys software. This can create a problem at times.

Some floppy disk controllers, such as Compaticard, come with driver software. Compaticard is a fantastic board that works with almost any machine. It can be the only floppy controller in the system, it can work in conjunction with another one, or it can control up to four floppy disk drives. Compaticard costs about $90 and is available from:

Micro Sense Company
5580 La Jolla, Blvd., # 313
La Jolla, CA 92037
(619) 589-1816

Fig. 5-3. A Compaticard floppy disk controller attached to a 1.2Mb drive. It will control all types of floppy drives.

Figure 5-3 shows a Compaticard connected to two drives.

Some FDCs come with an on-board BIOS that installs a driver.sys each time the system is booted up. The Liuski Company sells a Magitronic controller that works well with an XT, 286, or 386. It does not change the drive letter and everything functions just as if it were a normal A or B drive. The driver, shown in Fig. 5-4, sells for about $40.

Many of the hard disk controllers have integrated floppy disk controllers onto the same board. These are usually advertised as HDC/FDC. Some of them were designed soon after IBM introduced the AT with its 1.2Mb floppy. At that time, the 720K $3^1/2$ inch floppy was in use, but the 1.44Mb had not been developed.

I have a 40Mb hard disk so I bought one of the Western Digital HDC/FDC controllers. It is a RLL controller that allows me to store over 60Mb on my 40Mb hard disk. (More about RLL in Chapter 7.) It can control two hard disks and two floppies. Figure 5-5 shows a Western Digital HDC/FDC.

I bought a 1.2Mb and a 1.44Mb floppy drives for my system. The controller worked fine on the 1.2Mb and 720K, but it would not let me read or write to the 1.44Mb. It took me a lot of time and trouble but I finally found that the reason was that my ancient 286 had a 1984 BIOS that didn't know about 1.44Mb drives. I installed a new AMI BIOS and now the controller works great with all formats.

Fig. 5-4. A Magitronic floppy disk controller. It will control all types of floppy drives.

Fig. 5-5. A Western Digital hard disk and floppy disk controller. It can control two hard disks and two floppy drives of any type.

Several HDC/FDC boards on the market work great with all formats. They cost from $100 to $200; look through the computer magazines or visit a local computer store.

Installing Your New Drives

To install your drives, you will need a Phillips and a flat blade screwdriver. (It helps if they are magnetized.) You might also find it helpful to have a pair of long-nosed pliers.

You should have received some sort of documentation with your drive. The drive will have jumpers that have to be set depending on the type of system with which it will be used. Check the documentation and set the jumpers before you install the drive.

I once overlooked the setting of a jumper on one of the 3¹/2 inch drives that I had installed in one of my 386 machines. It seemed to work fine, but if I typed DIR, it would display the directory of whatever disk that was in the drive. If I removed that disk, inserted another and did another DIR, it would display the same directory from the first disk. The other drive on my system worked fine, so I knew something was wrong with the new drive. When I got out the documentation and checked the jumper settings, I found I had not set one of the jumpers properly.

The documentation that comes with most of the drives and other components is often very poorly written and organized, and might have trouble understanding it. Your dealer might not be able to help you, especially if you bought it from a mail order house. This is a good reason why you should belong to a good user group if possible. Such a group can be a tremendous help if you have problems.

The 3¹/2 inch drives are much smaller than the standard 5¹/4 inch. The 3¹/2 inch drives usually come with an installation kit that includes an expansion bracket that allows the drive to be mounted in any standard 5¹/4 inch drive bay. Usually, four screws mount the drive to the bracket as shown in Fig. 5-6. If the drive is to be used in an XT, the bracket assembly has threaded holes for mounting in the XT drive slots. If the drive is to be used in a 286 or 386 chassis, then you must also install the two plastic slide rails on each side of the bracket assembly.

Fig. 5-6. Installing an expansion bracket on a 3¹/2 inch drive.

You are now ready to install the drive in the system. The first thing to do, of course, is to unplug the power. Then remove the cover by removing each of the screws in the four corners and the one screw in the top of the back panel. Slip the cover off.

Once the cover is off, make a rough diagram of the cables and how and where they are connected. Pay close attention to the position of the colored wire on each ribbon cable. Now you can remove your old drives. If you are going to use the same controller, leave the cable plugged into them.

Mount the drives in the chassis. If you have a 286 or 386 chassis, your drives will have plastic slide rails on the sides. You will probably have to attach them. There are several holes on the sides of the drives and the rails. Install a rail with just one screw. Try the drive in the bay to see if you have selected the right holes. If so, then install the other rail.

The ribbon cable to the drives should have three connectors as you can see in Fig. 5-7. The one on the end will have a split and twist in some of the wires. This connector goes to drive A; see Fig. 5-8. This will be your boot drive. In most cases, this should be your 1.2Mb or 5^1/4 inch drive. The middle connector goes to the B drive, and the end connector plugs into the controller (see Fig. 5-9).

Fig. 5-7. A 34-wire ribbon cable with three connectors. The connector on the left has some twisted wires and goes to drive A. The connector in the middle goes to drive B if you have one. The end connector goes to the controller.

CAUTION! The connectors can be plugged in backwards. Note that the edge connector on the drives will have a narrow slit between contacts 2 and 3. That end of the board has contact number 1, the colored wire on the ribbon cable that goes to pin 1 of the connector. You might also see a number etched on the board. All of the even numbers of the contacts are on top of the board, and the odd numbers are on the back. You might see a small number 2 near the narrow slit and a 34 on the other end.

Fig. 5-8. *Installing the cable to drive A. Note the slot on the drive's edge connector and the colored wire on the ribbon cable. Pin one should be near the slot. The colored wire side of the cable goes to pin one.*

Fig. 5-9. *Connecting the ribbon cable to the controller. Note that the colored wire side goes to pin one on the board.*

The power to the drives is a four-wire cable from the power supply. As seen in Fig. 5-10, this cable can only be plugged in one way.

Fig. 5-10. Connecting the power plug to the drive. It can only be plugged in one way.

If you are installing the drives in an XT, line them up to match the holes in the bracket and install the screws as shown in Fig. 5-11. You can also install a couple of screws from the bottom of the case to hold the drives, but it is not really necessary.

Fig. 5-11. Installing the drives in the brackets of an XT.

After you have installed your drives, try them out before you replace the cover. Try formatting a blank disk, then writing a file to it, and reading it back.

Congratulations! You can now format, read and write to all floppy formats.

New Ultra-High-Density Drives

Brier Technology and several other companies are developing new floppy drives that can store as much as 50Mb on a $5^1/4$ inch floppy. These drives use sophisticated technologies such as embedded servo tracks and advanced controllers. Many of them will be available by the time you read this.

6

Floppy Disks

I am sure that you will agree that floppy drives and disks are a very important part of the personal computer. It would be very difficult to operate a personal computer without them. (Although Steve Jobs' NeXT machine does not have one.) Can you imagine trying to load programs onto a hard disk or doing backups without floppies?

The last chapter covered high-density drives. With 1.2Mb and 1.44Mb drives, you can read and write to all formats. The one disadvantage is that the 1.2Mb disks are selling at discount houses for as little as 49 cents apiece while the 1.44Mb high-density disks cost from $4 up to $10 each.

Some discount mail order houses are advertising the standard double-density 720K disks for as little as 59 cents each. If you have several hard disks that must be backed up frequently, or use a lot of $3^1/_2$ inch disks, you could save a lot of money. For instance, I bought a box of ten high-density disks for $52. A hundred would have cost me $520. I bought a hundred of the 59 cent disks for only $59, a difference of $461.

I can store 14.4Mb on the 10 high-density disks, and 72Mb on the 100 double-density disks. That is quite a difference.

Some people have claimed that there is not much difference in the high-density and the double-density disks. Except for a small square hole in the rear right corner on the high-density disks, they are about the same as far as performance characteristics go.

Several companies have developed punches that can be used to punch a square hole in the 720K disks. These low-cost disks can then be used to store 1.44Mb.

It sounds too good to be true. Does it really work? What is the real difference in the disks? If these disks are equivalent, why is there such a difference in cost? Will my data be safe? Will it still be there six months from now?

I ordered one of the punches and tried it. It seems to work. But I still had questions, so I wrote to over 20 manufacturers. Most of them did not bother to answer my letters, so I called several of them. I talked to one engineer. When I told him I had written the company and had gotten no response, he asked to whom I had addressed the letter. I told him the marketing manager. He said, "Well, that explains it." He asked not to be quoted by name.

I will talk later about some of the answers that I got to my questions. But first, here a few disk basics.

Some Floppy Disk Basics

Floppy disks are made from a plastic material called polyethylene terephthalate which is coated on each side with a thin layer of magnetic material. The magnetic coating is made primarily from iron oxide, or powdered rust. Bits of cobalt and other materials are added to give it special characteristics. The finished product is similar to the tape used in audio cassettes and video tape recorders.

A disk is similar in some respects to a phonograph record. However, a record has only one track that starts at the outer edge and winds toward the center. A 360K floppy has 40 single concentric tracks on each side. The 1.2Mb and the $3^1/2$ inch floppies have 80 tracks on each side. The 360K and the 720K are formatted so that each track is divided into 9 sectors. Each of the 80 tracks of the 1.2Mb high-density floppy is divided into 15 sectors, and 18 sectors per track on the 1.44Mb. Each sector holds 512 bytes.

When data is recorded, it is written in the first empty sector that it finds. The location of that particular data is then recorded in the directory section of the disk. Because each track and sector is numbered, the location of any data on the disk can be easily found and read back.

A $3^1/2$ inch standard floppy drive can store 360K per side, or 720K total, on a double-sided double-density (DSDD) disk. A $3^1/2$ inch high-density drive can store 720K per side, or 1.44Mb total, on a double-sided high-density (DSHD) disk. The 720K floppy is actually 1Mb before it is formatted. The 1.44Mb is 2Mb unformatted. Some vendors advertise them as .5Mb per side or 1Mb per side.

The 40 tracks of a 360K are laid down at a rate of 48 tracks per inch (TPI) so each of the 40 tracks is $1/48$th of an inch wide. The 80 tracks of the high-density 1.2Mb are laid down at a rate of 96 TPI, so each track is $1/96$ of an inch. The 80 tracks of the $3^1/2$ disks are laid down at a density 135 per inch or $1/135$th of an inch per track.

The $5^1/4$ inch drives have a conical spindle that centers the disk. The plastic material that the disk is made from is subject to environmental changes and wear and tear. The conical spindle might not center each disk exactly so head-to-track accuracy is difficult with more than 80 tracks.

Most of the 360K disks use a reinforcement hub ring, but it probably doesn't help much. The 1.2Mb floppies do not use a hub ring. Otherwise, the two formats look exactly the same.

The 3$^1/_2$ inch floppies use a metal hub for centering the disk. Although the tracks are narrower and greater in density per inch, because of the metal hub, the head tracking accuracy is much better than that of the 5$^1/_4$ inch systems. Hard disks have very accurate head tracking systems and can have a density of well over 1000 tracks per inch.

Formatting

The tracks and the sectors must be formatted on a disk before it can be used. If the A drive is a high-density drive, to format a 360K disk with the 1.2Mb drive, type:

    FORMAT A: /4

To format to 1.2Mb you only have to type:

    FORMAT A:

or you may have to type:

    FORMAT A: /T:80 /N:15

To format a 720K disk on a high-density drive, type:

    FORMAT B: /T:80 /N:9

To format a 1.44Mb disk, just type:

    FORMAT B:

or you might have to type:

    FORMAT B: /T:80 /N:18

When formatting 3$^1/_2$" disks, the drive checks for the hole on the rear right before it formats to the high density. If it does not find the hole, the computer sits there a minute, then gives this message INVALID MEDIA OR TRACK 0 BAD. You get the same message if you try to format a 1.44Mb disk as a 720K.

I have made up four batch files that save me a lot of time in formatting disks. Here is how I made my batch files:

```
COPY CON FMT36.BAT
C: FORMAT A: /4
^Z
COPY CON FMT12.BAT
C: FORMAT A: /T:80 /N:15
^Z
COPY CON FMT72.BAT
C: FORMAT B: /T:80 /N:9
^Z
```

```
COPY CON FMT14.BAT
C: FORMAT B: /T:80 /N:18
^Z
```

The ^Z is made by pressing F6 or you can use the ^ over numeral 6 and the Z. With the batch files I only have to type fmt36 for a 360K, fmt12 for a 1.2Mb, fmt72 for a 720K, or fmt14 to format a 1.44Mb floppy.

Differences in Double-Density and High-Density Disks

The main difference between the 5¹/₄ inch 360K double-density and the 1.2Mb high-density disk is that the 360K has an Oersted (Oe) of 300, the 1.2Mb floppy has an Oe of 600. The 3¹/₂ inch 720K double-density has an Oe of 600, the 1.44Mb has 700. The Oe is a measure of resistance to magnetization. (More about Oe later.)

One of the differences in the double-density (DD) 720K and the high-density (HD) 1.44Mb is that the 1.44Mb has two small square holes at the rear of the plastic shell, while the 720K has only one. In Fig. 6-1, the disk on the left is a 1.44Mb, the one on the right is 720K.

Fig. 6-1. The disk on the left is a 720K and the one on the right is a 1.44Mb. Notice the extra square hole in the lower left corner of the 1.44Mb.

The hole on the left rear of the shell has a small slide that can be moved to cover the hole. A small microswitch checks the hole when the disk is inserted. If the hole is covered, then it can be written on. If it is open, then the disk is write-protected. The 3¹/₂ inch write-protect system is just the opposite of the system used by the 5¹/₄ inch disks. The 5¹/₄ inch disks have a square notch that must be covered with opaque tape to prevent writing or unintentionally erasing the disk. (Incidentally, you must use opaque tape. The 5¹/₄ system uses a light to shine through the square notch. If the detector in the system can see the light through the notch, then it can write on the disk. Some people have used clear plastic tape to cover the notch with disastrous results.)

On most of the $3^1/_2$ inch drives capable of 1.44Mb, a small micro-switch checks for the hole on the right rear side of the disk. If you insert a disk and the drive finds a hole in the right rear area, it will allow you to format, read, and write the disk as a 1.44Mb.

Differences in 720K and 1.44Mb Floppies

A reader wrote to the editors of a popular computer magazine and asked what the difference is between the 720K and the 1.44Mb. The editor replied that there was a substantial difference—the price.

Of the few companies who answered my letters, all said that there were considerable differences. They all said that one would be risking the loss of data by using the 720K disk as a high-density 1.44Mb. They did not offer any kind of proof or evidence that any tests had actually been done. The main differences that they cited were that the 720K disks have a coercivity or Oe of 600, whereas the 1.44Mb has an Oe of about 700. Another difference is that the 720K has a minimum bits-per-inch packing density of 8,717 and the 1.44Mbs has 16,000 to 17,000 BPI. Another major difference is that the media thickness on the high-density is about half the thickness of that on the 720K.

The specifications mentioned by the vendors are according to the ANSI specifications. All of the vendors I talked to agreed that ANSI specs were a minimum and that their products exceeded the specs in most categories.

One engineer pointed out that there is an ANSI specification for the $3^1/_2$ inch disks, but there is no ANSI specs for the $3^1/_2$ inch drives. The ANSI specs are concerned primarily with minimum performance of such things as signal amplitude, resolution, bits-per-inch packing density, and mechanical dimensions. ANSI does not tell the manufacturer how to make the disk. The Oersted value, the media thickness, and several other parameters are left up to the manufacturer just so long as the product meets minimum specs. So there will be slight differences from different manufacturers.

Coercivity and Bits-Per-Inch Density

The coercivity of the media determines to some extent the packing density to which the floppy can be magnetized. The higher the *coercivity*, the more the media resists becoming magnetized or demagnetized. To record data, a current is passed through the head and switched on and off to represent 0s and 1s. This magnetizes spots on the track beneath the head. A higher recording current is needed for the higher coercivity.

A higher coercivity usually allows a greater packing density of bits-per-inch. The $5^1/_4$ inch 360K disks have a nominal coercivity of 300 Oe. A packing density of up to 6000 BPI can be stored on a 300 Oe disk. (NOTE:

Some companies use bits per radian (BPR) instead of bits per inch (BPI). A radian is equal to 57.2958 degrees or 6.28 radians in 360 degrees. I think they probably do this deliberately to confuse people like me. The 360K disk can support 7958 BPR or 6000 BPI). The 1.2Mb disks have about 600 Oe, the same as the 720K $3^1/2$ inch floppies. They can be recorded with a density up 9869 BPI per ANSI, or 1152 more BPI than the 720K using the same media.

Several of the manufacturers that I spoke with said that if the recorded BPI is too high on a low coercivity disk, the data bits will be so tightly packed that they will tend to demagnetize the bits near them. The bits may be repelled or attracted to each other and migrate one way or the other. This could cause data to be lost.

Using the ANSI specifications, a 360K disk with 300 Oe can handle 6000 BPI. The outer diameter of the disk is $5^1/4$ inches, but because of the cover and edge margin, the head sees an outer diameter of about $4^3/4$ inches. If you could take an outside track from one of these disks and stretch it out straight, it would measure about 15 inches long. (You can determine this by multiplying the diameter, 4.75 inches by pi or 3.1415). Each track is divided into 9 sectors, so each sector would be 15 divided by 9 = 1.66 inches. The inner track would be much shorter, about 9.9 inches long, with each sector about 1.1 inches long. Some similar rough calculations for the other formats and tracks are in Table 6-1.

Table 6-1. Comparison of Floppy Disks.

Drive Type	360K	1.2Mb	720K	1.44Mb
Tracks/side	0-39	0-79	0-79	0-79
Sectors/track	9	15	9	18
Track 0 length	15 in.	15 in.	10 in.	10 in.
Sector length	1.66 in.	1 in.	1 in.	.55 in.
Inner track length	9.9 in.	9.9 in.	6.5 in.	6.5 in.
Sector length	1.1 in.	.66 in.	.73 in.	.37 in.
Oersteds (Oe)	300	600	600	700
Pack density BPI	6000	9869	8717	16000

To DOS, a sector is a sector is a sector. DOS stores 512 bytes in a sector, whether it is on a 360K, 720K, 1.2Mb, 1.44Mb, or hard disk. Eight bits make a byte, so 4096 (8 × 512) bits are stored in a sector. If a 720K disk rated at 8717 BPI is formatted as a 1.44Mb with 18 sectors per track, it would have no trouble at all with the outer track sectors. The .55-inch-long sectors (× 8717 BPI) mean it could store 4794 bits. The length of the 18 sectors of the innermost track is .37 inches, so it could store 3225 bits (.37 inches × 8717 BPI) in each sector. According to the ANSI BPI specifications, the 720K disk would not have enough space to store the minimum 4096 bits per sector needed for 512 bytes. However, the inner tracks of the 1.44Mb at 16,000 BPI × .37 = 5920 would.

The ANSI specification of 8717 BPI for the 720K appears much too conservative. This specification was based on the early Sony 720K disks introduced about seven years ago. But the technology has changed tremendously since then. The newer drives, controllers, and disk media are much more improved and sophisticated but the old ANSI specification has not been changed to reflect the improvements.

How To Convert a 720K to a 1.44Mb

If you would like to convert a disk, it is very easy to do. To convert a 720K to a 1.44Mb, just add a second hole on the right rear side. It will then format, write, and read at the 1.44Mb capacity.

At this time, about 100,000 punches, selling for $20 to $40 have been sold. But you don't need to buy one of those punches. The hole does not have to be square, and the size is not too critical. A quarter inch drill, a hot soldering iron, or a plain old pocket knife will do fine.

The first thing to do is to mark the location for the new hole. Take two disks and slide the write protect tab so that the square holes are open. Place the two disks so that the metal hubs are facing each other. Line them up so that all of the edges are equal. Use a scribe or a thin pencil to trace the outline of the write protect square hole onto the opposite disk.

You might notice that the shell or plastic casing for the floppy is made of two pieces of plastic. You need only drill through the bottom layer, the side that has the metal hub, to make an indentation. You might also use a hot soldering iron to melt a hole in the location, or a pocket knife. Make a hole or indentation, then try it. If it works, fine; if not, enlarge the hole. Figure 6-2 shows a disk that has been converted. The one on the bottom right was drilled part way through.

Fig. 6-2. A 720K disk on the right that has been converted to a 1.44Mb by drilling a hole on the lower left corner of the disk. The disk on the left has not been converted.

It doesn't hurt to have the hole a bit large. I bought a box of 10 brand-name 1.44Mb floppies for $52. I was surprised to find that several of them would not format. I was about ready to take them back, but I decided to compare them with some other disks. I placed one of the disks on top of another brand and noticed that the square holes did not line up. I enlarged the holes on the disks and they now work fine.

You might have a 720K drive such as those in most laptops, so you might want to use the disk as a 720K. All you have to do is put a piece of tape over the depression or hole. Covering the hole allows you to format and use a converted disk, or a real 1.44Mb high-density disk, as a 720K.

Incidentally, you can format a 360K as a 1.2Mb. There will probably be several bad sectors that cannot be formatted. Because these sectors are locked out during formatting, you can actually store more than 1Mb on a 360K floppy. But because of possible loss of data due to the close packing and data migration, I would not recommend it.

Although you can format a 360K as to 1.2Mb, you cannot format a 1.2Mb high-density disk as a 360K. The 360K drive does not provide enough head current to be able to format the 600 Oe media.

Summary

All of the vendors that I talked to were very eager to help me. But in a single voice, all of them said that a person would be taking a chance with their data using the 720K as a 1.44Mb. None of the vendors offered any proof that they had actually done any tests to format and use the 720K as a high density.

Over 100,000 punches have been sold, and the punch vendors claim that they have had very few complaints. Thousands of people have formatted and used the 720K DSDD disks as 1.44Mb. I have formatted and tested several just to try them out. I used them to record and store non-critical data. Some of the vendors claim that the data could disappear over a period of time due to bit migration or peak shift. I have periodically checked the disks with Nortons DISK TEST utility. I have some disks that were written about 6 months ago and not updated since except to test them with Norton's DISK TEST. I have some others that I have used daily to back up my daily files. (But just in case, I also use a high-priced disk for backup.) So far I have not had any problems, but maybe I have been lucky.

When I started this section, I had hoped to gather some definitive facts as to whether it was safe to use the 720K as a 1.44Mb. I have spent many hours and talked to a lot of people, but I am sorry to say that I still don't know.

The bottom line seems to be, it depends on what you are going to use the disks for. If it is critical data, then use the best. If it is something not so critical, then buy lots of 720K and use two of them to store 1.44Mb.

Apparently, there is little difference in the manufacturing process and materials of the DD and HD floppies. I find it difficult to see how they can justify charging up to ten times more for the 1.44Mb. One spokesman agreed that they were overpriced, and he pointed out that the high-density 1.44Mb is still fairly new. He says that they will be coming down very soon because of the greater demand. Within six months, you might be able to buy the high-density disks at a more reasonable price.

Sources

Again, the cost of high-density 1.2Mb disks is about 49 cents each. The cost of 360K disks, in 100 lots, is about 25 cents each. The $3^1/2$ inch high-density floppies at this time cost from $4 up to $10 each. The double-density 720K cost 59 cents each from the MEI/Micro Center.

Here are just a few companies that sell disks at a discount. There are several others. Check computer magazines for ads.

MEI/Micro Center	(800) 634-3478
The Disk Barn	(800) 727-3475
Americal Group	(800) 288-8025
MidWest Micro	(800) 423-8215

7

Choosing and Installing a Hard Disk

If you have been doing without a hard disk, how in the world did you ever get anything done? Believe me, it is a lot easier with a hard disk.

You need to choose what type and size of disk to buy. Of course, that will depend on what you need to do with your computer and how much you want to spend. Some of the following factors might influence your decision. At the end of the chapter, I include some of the more basic details.

Factors To Consider

Capacity. Buy the biggest you can afford. Don't even think of buying anything less than 20Mb. Even better would be 30Mb minimum. New software programs are constantly growing. OS/2 will require about 2Mb. Even some of today's word processors require about that much. Also, you probably have lots of software on $5^1/4$ disks that are always hard to find when you need them. I used to waste hours looking for a particular program, now I have hundreds of them at my fingertips on my hard disk. It is very convenient, but it is amazing how fast those little bytes multiply and fill up a disk, all according to Parkinson's Law.

You might not have heard Parkinson's Law. This law is like Murphy's Law that anything that can possibly go wrong, will; and usually at the most inopportune time. Parkinson's Law also covers several areas. It says that the time needed to finish a project will always expand and exceed the time allocated, or the cost of a project or an endeavor will always expand and exceed the cost that was allocated or budgeted. (This law also applies to the cost of upgrading your computer or to buying a new system, a new car, house, or almost anything.)

So according to Parkinson's Law, the need for hard disk storage will always exceed that which is present, so it is best to get the biggest disk that you can afford. Someone once said that you could never be too thin or have too much money. Add to that: you can never have too much hard disk storage.

You should also be aware that the capacity of a hard disk can be stated as unformatted capacity or formatted capacity. Unformatted, a disk might have a capacity of 24Mb, but only 20Mb of usable storage after it is formatted. You have to read the ads closely.

Speed. This depends on what you are going to use it for and what you are installing it on. An 85 Ms hard disk is fine for a slow XT. A 28 Ms might not be fast enough for a 386. For most normal uses, 28 Ms to 40 Ms will be fine.

Type of drive: stepper or voice coil. Most of the less expensive drives use a stepper motor to move the heads. The voice coil types are quieter and a bit more reliable, but of course more expensive. Voice coil drives can be recognized because they have an odd number of heads. (One head and platter surface is used as a servo control for the heads.)

Type of drive, MFM, RLL, ESDI, SCSI. The *Modified Frequency Modulation* (MFM) has been the standard method for disk recording for years. This method formats several concentric tracks on a disk and stores data at a rate of 17 sectors per track, with 512 bytes in each sector. They usually have a transfer rate of 5 megabits. The MFM method can be used with drives from 5Mb up to several hundred megabytes. Cost will vary, but the price in one ad from the Computer Shopper for a Seagate ST251 40Mb, 40 Ms drive is $329. The MFM drives might even be a bit lower when you read this.

The *Run Length Limited* (RLL) drives, when used with a RLL controller, format 26 sectors per track, which allows 50% more data than on a MFM drive. For instance, a 20Mb would store 30Mb, a 40Mb would store 60Mb. They have a transfer rate of 7.5 megabits, 50% faster than MFM. Not all drives are capable of running RLL. Seagate uses an R after the model number to denote the RLL drives. One advertisement shows a Seagate RLL drive ST277R, which is actually a 42Mb, 28 Ms drive that formats to 65Mb with a RLL controller. The ad price is $379.

The Small Computer Systems Interface (SCSI, pronounced "scuzzy") is an interface that works with certain drives. SCSI can be daisy chained to control up to seven devices which can include a tape drive, an optical drive, or other hard disks. It allows up to 36 sectors per track and has a transfer rate of 10 megabits or more. These systems can be expensive also, especially the high-capacity drives. A high-capacity SCSI drive such as a 350Mb system might cost over $4000, but many companies are also making smaller capacity drives. Seagate adds an N to their model numbers to denote SCSI. An ad for a Seagate ST277N shows basically the same 42Mb drive as the ST277R and the ad price is $449. SCSI seems to be one of the better systems and is expected to eventually become the standard.

The Enhanced Small Device (or Disk) Interface (ESDI, pronounced "ezdy") drives have their controller built onto the drive, but they still require an interface card. An EDSI system can format to 34 sectors per track, so they can store twice as much data as the MFM. They have a very fast access speed, usually 15 Ms, and a data transfer of 10 megabits or more. These systems are fairly expensive and are usually used on very large systems. A 150Mb ESDI system, with cables and interface, costs about $1400.

Physical size. Today the most common size of the 20 to 40Mb hard disk is the half height $5^1/4$ inch size. But because the smaller size generally uses less power and is faster, many companies are now making $3^1/2$ inch drives with up to 100Mb or more. Most of the very high-capacity drives are full height $5^1/4$ inch.

Hard cards. Some companies have developed hard disks on plug-in cards. These cards have the disk on one end of the card and the controller on the other. You simply remove the cover of your computer and plug the card in. The most common capacities are 20, 30, and 40Mb. Typical speed is 40 Ms, but since they are small, many of them are rated at 28 Ms and less. Some are available with up to 80Mb. Some models overlap the adjacent slot so that they require two slots. But most of the models are arranged so that the disk is toward the front of the computer and the controller portion, which is much thinner, is to the rear. Therefore a short card could be used in the adjacent slot. The hard cards cost from $250 up to $500. The Hardcard 40 from Plus Development shown in Fig. 7-1 is a 28 Ms 40Mb drive is very thin and occupies only one slot.

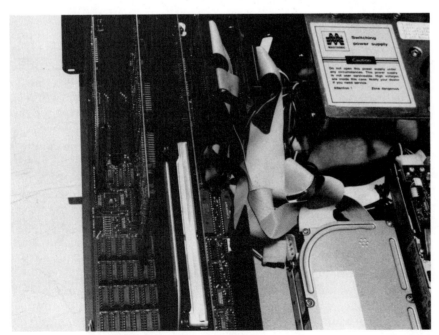

Fig. 7-1. The Plus Development Hardcard 40 (the slim bright colored card near the left). Note that it takes up only one slot space.

Removable media. The IOMEGA Corporation has a high capacity Bernoulli box floppy disk system. Their system allows the recording of up to 20 Mb on a floppy disk. They are ideal for confidential data. Each person in an office can have a 20Mb floppy which can be removed and locked up. This system is also great for backing up a hard disk system. They have had the field to themselves for several years, so the Bernoulli box has always been a bit expensive at about $1500 for a drive and about $70 for each disk. But Kodak, Brier, and several other companies are now giving them some competition with new very high-density systems. You should soon see prices that are quite reasonable on the very high-density floppy disk systems.

The Plus Development Corporation, who developed the first hard disk on a card, has developed a removable 40Mb hard disk. The disk and drive motor are all one slim unit which plugs into a fixed housing. The housing can be mounted internally in a floppy disk drive bay, or externally. It is very quiet and fast. The list price is about $1200 for the total system. Additional 40Mb hard disk cartridges are about $600 each. Figure 7-2 shows the drive, controller card, and housing.

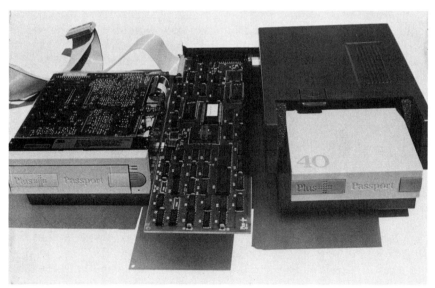

Fig. 7-2. A removable 40Mb hard cartridge from Plus Development. On the left is the housing, the controller board in the center and a storage case on the right.

Mean Time Before Failure (MTBF). Every disk drive will fail sooner or later. Manufacturers test their drives and assign them an average life time that ranges from 20,000 to 50,000 hours. Of course, the larger the figure, the longer they should last (and the more they cost). But these are average figures, much like the figures quoted for a human lifespan. The average man should live to be about 73 years old, but some babies die at less than one year and some men live to be 100. Some hard disks die very young, but some older ones become obsolete before they wear out. However, be assured that they will all fail eventually, so you should always have them backed up.

Controllers. Hard disks need a controller card that plugs into one of the slots in the computer. There are several controller companies, but very few of the hard disk companies make controllers for their disks.

Many types of hard disk controllers (HDC) are available. Some were developed specifically for 8-bit systems and others for the 16-bit AT type systems, which includes the 286 and 386. An 8-bit controller can also be used on a 16-bit machine, but a 16-bit cannot be used on an 8-bit. Many of the companies who make 16-bit controllers have integrated the HDC with the floppy disk controller (FDC) onto the same FDC/HDC board. This saves space and is very convenient. Most of these new FDC/HDC boards will control 360K, 1.2Mb, 720K, and 1.44Mb disk drives as well as two hard disks.

Several companies manufacture controllers. The major ones are Western Digital, Adaptec, Scientific MicroSystems, and DTK. Most of them also manufacture interface boards for the ESDI and SCSI systems.

The MFM controllers are generally less expensive than the specialized ones such as SCSI and ESDI. When they were first introduced the RLL controllers were significantly more expensive than the MFM, but now there is very little difference. Many people didn't trust them at first, but the technology has improved. I have used them for over three years with no problems. Remember that MFM divides each track into 17 sectors of 512 bytes each; RLL divides each track into 26 sectors of 512 bytes each. You must buy a disk that is certified, but with a bit of judicious shopping, you can put together a system that will store 50 percent more for only a few dollars more. RLL controllers have been developed for 8-bit and 16-bit machines. Most of the 16-bit ones have an integrated floppy controller that can control all types of floppies.

Perstor Systems manufactures a controller that allows a disk to be formatted to 31 sectors per track as you can see in Fig. 7-3. Perstor has both 8-bit and 16-bit controllers. The 8-bit works on XTs as well as the ATs, 286s, and 386s. The 16-bit can only be used with ATs, 286s, or 386s, but it also controls all types of floppy drives. I have used both the 8-bit and the 16-bit for almost two years on different drives, and I have not had any problems.

The Perstor controller might not work with some drives. But they are constantly testing drives. Write them or call them for a list and for the prices of their controllers. Their address is:

Perstor Systems
1335 S. Park Lane
Temple, AZ 85281
(602) 894-3494

Fig. 7-3. A HDC/FDC card from Perstor. It can control two hard disks and two of any type of floppy drives. The controller almost doubles the capacity of a hard drive.

The controller is a bit expensive, but it is less than an ESDI or SCSI interface. My 16-bit controller cost $245. I am using it on two Seagate ST251 40Mb drives. I paid $400 each for the drives. (They are less now.) For $1045, I have 156Mb of storage. For this much storage, other systems would cost $1500 to $3000.

The Konan Corporation also manufactures a unique controller called the TENTIME. Shown in Fig. 7-4, this controller has a built-in cache system that makes it very fast. The cache system stores frequently used data in very fast RAM memory. If the requested data happens to be in the memory cache, it is read from there instead of from the disk.

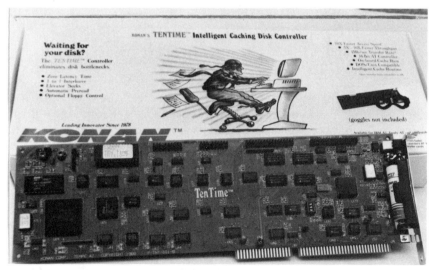

Fig. 7-4. The Konan TenTime hard disk controller. It uses a cache system to speed up the disk access time.

They manufacture two 16-bit controllers. One model controls hard disks only, and the other model controls hard disks and all types of floppies. Write or call them for their latest information and prices at:

Konan Corporation
4720 South Ash Avenue
Tempe, AZ 85282
(602) 345-2829

Note that the advertised price of most disk drives does not include the controller or the necessary cables. An 8-bit controller may cost as little as $40 for a no-name clone. A brand-name 16-bit FDC/HDC might cost from $120 to $150.

A Software Approach

SQUISH Plus is a software approach to storing more data on a disk. This software automatically compresses data, then writes it to the disk. It then uncompresses it when the data is read back. It does not have much effect on .COM or .EXE files, but word processing, database, spreadsheet, and many other files can be compressed up to 50 percent or more.

You use the software to create a SQUISH disk from a portion of your hard disk, or even on a floppy. Then it is accessed, written, or read just like any other disk. You can set the size of the disk that you want. If you set it for 400K, then do a CHKDSK, it will say that there is 800K available.

The list price of the software is $99. This is the least expensive method that I know of to almost double the size of a hard disk. SQUISH PLUS was developed by:

Sundog Software Corporation
264 Court St.
Brooklyn, NY 11231
(718) 855-9141

Sources

Local computer stores and computer swap meets are a good place to find a disk. At least you can look them over and get some idea of the prices and what you want. Mail order is a very good way to buy a hard disk. There are hundreds of ads in the many computer magazines.

Installing Your Hard Disk

Below are the steps to install a hard disk.

Step 1. First we have to remove the cover. Refer to the procedure outlined in Chapter 2.

Step 2. Check the instructions that came with the disk and set any jumpers that might be required. Unless you are installing a second hard disk, you probably will not have to set any.

XT Installation

If you are installing the disk in a XT, place the disk in an open bay and mount into the brackets with screws. If it is a half height size and you only have one floppy disk drive, you might want to install it in the lower bay on the right beneath your floppy drive. If you have two floppy drives, or you are installing a full height drive, then you should install it in the left hand bay. If you are installing a $3^1/2$ inch drive, it is not absolutely necessary, but you might want to mount it in an expansion frame so that it fits in the bay just like a $5^1/4$ inch drive. The threaded holes in the side of the disk should line up with the holes in the bracket. Start all the screws, then tighten them. Be careful because it is easy to strip the threads. There are also threaded screw holes on the bottom of the drive. The bottom of the case has openings for access to these screw holes. If you have a magnetized screwdriver for this operation, it helps. Unless I am going to be moving the computer around a lot, I seldom install the screws in the bottom. All of the access holes in the bottom of the case, and all other holes, should be covered with some kind of tape before the computer is put into use. The fan in the power supply should draw air only through the vents in the front of the computer. It then passes this air over the components to cool them. If there are additional openings in the case, it cuts down on the efficiency of the cooling system.

AT, 286, or 386 Installation

Check the instructions to see if there are any jumpers that should be set. Unless you are installing a second drive, there probably will not be any.

If you are installing a $3^1/2$ inch disk, then it should be mounted in an expansion frame. Install the plastic rails on the sides of the disk with one screw. There are several holes in the side of the disk. The easiest way to determine which ones to use is to try them. The tapered end of the rail should go toward the rear. Insert the disk in the bay, and check for the proper fit. If you are lucky and have started them in the right holes, then install the rest of the screws in the rails.

Installing Controller and Cables

Now that you have the drives installed, you need to check any instructions that might have come with your controller. Set any switches and jumpers on the controller board as necessary. Plug the board into an empty slot, preferably one near the disk drives so that the cables will not have to be draped over other boards.

You should now attach the cables to the drives. Figure 7-5 shows different types of ribbon cables. There will be two flat ribbon cables, one with 20 wires, the other with 34. One edge of the cable has a different colored wire to indicate pin one. It is possible to plug the connector in backwards. The disk drive edge connectors have a slit in the board

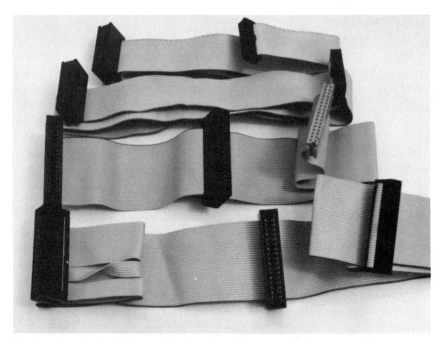

Fig. 7-5. Some typical ribbon cables that are used to connect drives to controllers.

between pins 2 and 3, the colored wire goes to this side of the connections. See Fig. 7-6.

If your controller can handle both floppies and the hard disk, you will have one 34-wire ribbon cable from the floppies and one from the hard disk. The controller will have two sets of pins for the attachment of the 34-wire cable connectors. Your controller instructions should tell you which cable goes to which row of pins. Ordinarily, the row of pins in the center will be for the hard disk, and the one toward the rear will be for the floppy. The connectors can be plugged in backwards, so be sure to check the board for a small number 1 or some indication as to which pin is number one. Then plug the connector so that the colored wire goes to that end. If the pins are in a horizontal row, pin 1 will usually be oriented so that pin 1 is toward the front. See Fig. 7-7. If vertical, then pin 1 is usually toward the top of the board. If you determine the orientation of one connection, all of the others should be the same.

There will also be two sets of 20-wire pins. The row closest to the hard disk 34-wire connector will be for hard disk number 1. If you install a second hard disk, the 20-wire cable will plug into the second set of pins, those usually toward the bottom if oriented horizontally, or toward the front if vertical.

Install Drive Power Cables

The power cables for the drives are four wire cables from the power supply. They can only be plugged in one way; see Fig. 7-8.

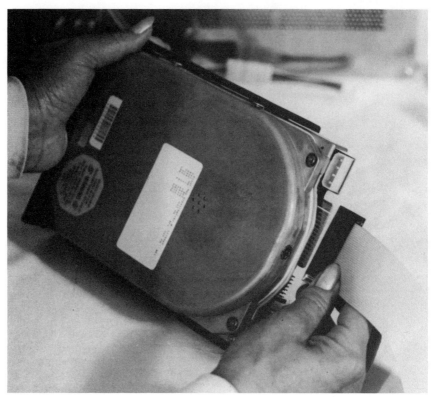

Fig. 7-6. Connecting a 34-wire ribbon cable to a hard disk. Note the slit in the edge connector. Pin one will be near that end. The colored wire on the ribbon cable goes to pin one.

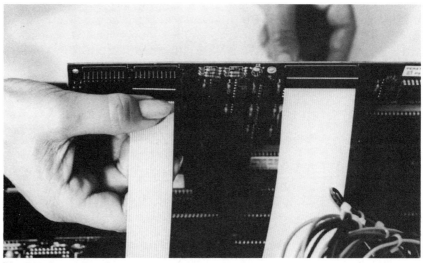

Fig. 7-7. Connecting the 34-wire and 20-wire ribbon cables to the controller. Make sure that pin one on the cable and the board match up. Note that the 20-wire cable goes to the set of pins nearest the 34-wire connector.

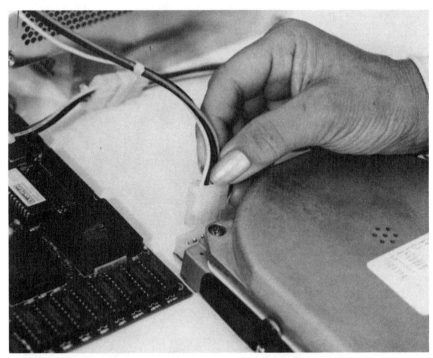

Fig. 7-8. Connecting the power to the drives. It can only be plugged in one way.

Floppy Drive Connections

If you are installing floppy drives at this time, or the cable has been disconnected, the end connector with the twisted wires should be connected to the A drive as shown in Fig. 7-9. I like to have my A drive in the top right bay. Again, this connector can be plugged in backwards. Look for a number near the edge connector or for a slit between two and three of the gold contacts. If you have a B drive, the middle connector attaches to it. Make sure that the colored wire goes to pin one of the disk edge connector.

Installing a Second Hard Disk

Most controllers can control two hard disks, so it is easy to add a second hard disk. Some controllers will allow you to use different types and sizes. Others will only control a second drive if it is the same type and size as the first one.

If you are installing a second hard disk, follow the instructions that came with it. It should have a terminating resistor pack which should be removed; see Fig. 7-10. It should also have a row of pins with a jumper so that it can be configured as drive number 2. If you have a ribbon cable with no twisted wires at the end connector, this should go to disk number 1, which should have its pins jumpered for disk 1. (NOTE: Some systems call the first disk 0 and the second disk 1.)

Fig. 7-9. Connecting the 34-wire cable to the A drive. Note the split and twist in the cable.

The 34-wire ribbon cable will have a connector on each end and one near the center. The cable might have some twisted wires at the end connector and look very much like the cable used for the floppy drives. If the cable has a twist, the number one drive and the number two drives will both be jumpered as drive 2. Again, you should have received some instructions with your drive.

Formatting

Now that the drives are installed, you are ready to reconnect the power. You should try them before you put the cover back on to make sure that they will operate properly.

Formatting organizes the disk so that data can be stored and accessed easily and quickly. If there was no organization in the way the data is recorded, it would be very difficult to find an item on a 30 or 40Mb disk. So tracks and sectors are numbered and recorded on the disk. The location of each track and sector is then recorded in the *File Application Table* (or FAT).

Fig. 7-10. Configuring two hard drives. Note that the terminating resistor pack has been disconnected on the drive on top. The pens are pointing to the pins and shorting bars.

A disk organization is similar to that of a developer of a piece of land. He would lay out the streets and create blocks. He would then partition each block into lots and build a house on each lot. Each house would have a unique address. A map of these streets and house addresses would be filed with the city. A track is analogous to a street and a sector number would be similar to a house number.

Each time data is recorded on a disk, the location of that data, by track and sector number, is recorded in the FAT. If the data needs to be retrieved, the computer goes to the FAT and reads the data location, then directs the head to the exact track and sector where the data is written.

Formatting is not something that is done every day, and it can be rather difficult in some cases. There is very little literature on the subject. Unless you are fairly knowledgeable, try to have your vendor format your hard disk for you.

One reason the disks do not come from the manufacturer preformatted is that there are so many options. There are also many different controller cards. The controller cards are usually designed so that they will operate with several different types of hard disks. Most controller cards have DIP switches that must be set to configure your particular hard disk. Usually, some documentation that comes with the hard disk controller. But like most other manuals and documentation, the instructions are sometimes difficult to understand, especially if you are a beginner.

Low-Level Format

A floppy disk is formatted in a single procedure but a hard disk requires two levels of format, a low level and then a high level.

You should have received some sort of documentation with your hard disk and controller. Chances are that it has not been low-level formatted. Ask your vendor. If it has been low-level formatted you can type FDISK, and it will allow you to partition the disk. If it does not allow you do FDISK, or if you are using a controller other than MFM, then you must do a low-level format. If it has not been formatted, use whatever software or instructions that you might have received with the disk.

With many controllers you can use the DOS DEBUG command. Type DEBUG and when the hyphen - comes up, type G=C800:5. It would look like this:

```
A>DEBUG
-G=C800:5
```

This message will be displayed, This is a FORMAT routine. It will DESTROY any existing data on your disk! Press <RET> if you wish to continue or <ESC> to abort...

Bad Sector Data. If you press Return, it will ask you several questions. One question it asks is if you want to input any bad sector data. It is almost impossible to manufacture a perfect hard disk. The disk usually comes with a list of bad sectors that the manufacturer discovered during his testing. If they are very bad, your controller might detect them, but if they are marginal it might not. When you input the list of bad sectors, DOS marks them so that they are not used. There may be as many as 100K or more space in bad sectors, but that will be a small percentage compared to the disk's capacity.

Interleave Factor. It will also ask you to choose the interleave factor that you want to use. This is an important item so I go into a bit of detail about it.

The interleave factor determines to a great extent the speed at which data can be read from a hard disk. You might have the fastest disk in the world, but if the interleave is not set properly, you would have to sit there and twiddle your thumbs while waiting for data.

The interleave factor depends on the disk and its electronics, the controller, and the system into which it is plugged. With the hard disk spinning at 3600 RPMs, data can be read much faster than many systems can handle. For instance, it takes a finite amount of time to read the data from track one, sector one. After it is read, it must be assembled and transmitted to the system. Unless you have a very fast system, by the time sector one is read and transmitted, the disk has spun around past sector two, so it has to wait for a complete revolution in order to read sector two. Again, once sector two is read, sector three has already passed, so again it must wait for the disk to spin around. Because a standard track has 17 sectors, the disk would have to spin around 17 times to read one track. Most files would be spread over several tracks. A long file could take a considerable amount of time to read.

In the example above, by the time sector one is read, assembled, and sent to the system, the disk might have spun around to where it is over sector four. So if you move sector two over to where sector four normally would be on the track, you could skip over the next two sectors, then read sector two immediately after you have read sector one. You could then skip the next two sectors and read sector three and so on around the track. With this arrangement, you could read six sectors in one revolution. This is a 600 percent increase over the example above when you could only read one sector per revolution. The inner circle of Fig. 7-1 shows how the sectors would be arranged for an interleave of 3:1. The outer circle shows consecutive sectors for 1:1 transfer.

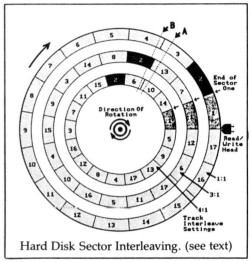

Hard Disk Sector Interleaving. (see text)

Fig. 7-1. Showing various interleave settings. (Drawing Courtesy Gibson Research.)

Interleave factors should be set to match the speed of the system. The interleave factor is set during the low-level format of the hard disk. Disks that run on an XT are fairly slow because of the system clock speed of 4.77 MHz. They need an interleave of about 6:1. Most XT Turbos that run at 8 MHz can get by with 4:1. Some of the newer systems that run on the 286 and 386 can handle interleaves of 1:1 or read directly.

The interleave is set during the low-level format. The only way to change it, or experiment with different settings, is to completely format the disk, both low-level and high-level, and then try it. (If the disk is already in use, all data on it must be backed up or copied onto disks, before any formatting is done. The formatting process erases everything on the disk when it lays down its new tracks.)

Here is a short batch file that I made that can do a rough check of the speeds. I called it TST.BAT. It uses the clock in the computer to measure time. It measures in hundredths of a second, so it is quite accurate. WordStar comes with a thesaurus called WordFinder. I copied the the-saurus synonym file, WFBG.SYN which was 325,330 bytes, into my C drive. I then typed in the following:

```
C> COPY CON TST.BAT
ECHO | MORE | TIME
COPY WFBG.SYN \MYFILE
ECHO | MORE | TIME
^Z
```

The ^Z is made by pressing F6. It signifies the end of the batch file. Ordi-narily when you ask the computer for TIME, it displays the current time, then says Enter new time:. The computer will pause until a new time is entered or the Enter key is pressed. The ECHO | MORE | TIME causes the computer to continue without the need to press the Enter key.

You should have a fairly large file that you can copy from one part of the hard disk to another. Don't copy more than two or three files, otherwise the beginning time will scroll off the top of the screen. Here is what it would look like:

```
C>TST
C>ECHO | MORE | TIME
Current time is 10:04:11.57
Enter new time:
COPY WFBG.SYN \MYFILE
     1 File(s) copied
C>ECHO | MORE | TIME
Current time is 10:04:16.90
Enter new time:
C>
```

You can then subtract the beginning time from the ending time. In the example above, it would be 10:04:16.90 − 10:04:11.57 = 5.33 seconds to copy 325,330 bytes. I used this test on my two 40 Ms disks and my 28 Ms. They all tested very close to 6 seconds. This little batch file can be rewritten and used for many other things where you need an accurate elapsed time count.

To check your interleave, copy a file of about 300K from a floppy onto the hard disk. It should be one long file. Then use the batch file above. Write down the time. Then reformat the disk for low level, change the interleave up or down, reformat at high level, and run the TST batch file again. You should see a difference in the time.

Perstor controllers. The Perstor controller is nonstandard, so it comes with software that allows you to low-level format your drive easily. A built-in feature automatically checks for the optimum interleave factor. It tests the disk and displays the data transfer rate at interleaves of 1:1 up to 6:1. It will then be obvious which factor allows the fastest transfer.

Other utility packages. Several hard disk utility packages check the interleave factor for the optimum value for your system. They will even let you change the value without having to reformat your disk. These programs copy a track into memory, reformat that track, then copy the information back to the track from memory, then proceed to the next track. Here are a few companies who provide this type of software:

Spinrite
Gibson Research Corp.
Box 6024
Irvine, CA 92716
(714) 830-2200

Disk Technician
Prime Solutions
1940 Garnet Ave.
San Diego, CA 92109
(619) 274-5000

Optune
Gazelle Systems
42 N. University Ave., Suite 10
Provo, UT 84601
(800) 233-0383

Mace Utilities
Paul Mace Software
400 Williamson Way
Ashland, OR 97520
(503) 488-0224

Depending on your type of drive, you might hear a distinct step or click as the drive formats each track. You might not be able to hear a voice coil type. The light on the front should also come on and might blink with each step. Depending on the capacity and speed, it can take 10 to 20 minutes to format a drive.

High-Level Format

After you have completed the low-level format, you can now proceed to the high level. Boot up from your floppy disk drive with a copy of DOS and type DIR C:. If the message comes up, Invalid drive specification, put a copy of DOS in drive A that has the FDISK command on it.

When you type FDISK, this message will be displayed if you are using DOS 3.3:

Fixed Disk Setup Program Version 3.30
(C)Copyright MicroSoft Corp. 1987

FDISK Options

Current Fixed Disk Drive: 1

Choose one of the following:

1. Create DOS partition
2. Change Active Partition
3. Delete DOS partition
4. Display Partition information

Enter choice: [1]

Press ESC to return to DOS

If you choose 1, and the disk has not been prepared a screen like this comes up:

Create DOS Partition

Current Fixed Drive: 1

1. Create Primary DOS partition
2. Create Extended DOS partition
3. Create logical DOS drive(s) in the Extended DOS partition

Enter choice: [1]

Press ESC to return to FDISK Options

If you want to boot from your hard drive (I can't think of any reason why you would not want to), then you must create a *primary* DOS partition and make it active. Because DOS can only handle 32Mb, if the disk is larger, you can create *extended* DOS partitions. Then you must choose option 3 above to have DOS create logical DOS drives in the extended partition. For instance if you have a 60Mb drive, the first 32Mb would be drive C; DOS would then assign the rest of the disk as drive D.

After the FDISK options have been completed, return to drive A and high-level format drive C. Because you want to boot off this drive, you must also transfer the system and hidden files to the disk as it is being formatted. Use a /S to transfer the files. Type:

FORMAT C : /S

DOS will display a message that says:

WARNING, ALL DATA ON NON-REMOVABLE DISK DRIVE C: WILL BE LOST!
Proceed with Format (YN)

If you press Y, the disk light should come and you might hear the drive stepping through each track. After a few minutes, it will display:

Format complete
System transferred
Volume label (11 characters, ENTER for none)?

You can give each partition a unique name, or volume label if you wish.

You can test your drive by doing a warm boot; press CTRL, ALT and DEL at the same time. The computer should reboot.

Now that drive C is completed, if you have a large disk, type FORMAT D. The same warning will be displayed and ask if you want to proceed. Type Y and format D.

Congratulations! You can now copy all of your DOS files to C and all of your other programs to C or D. You can now replace the cover and enjoy the pleasures of a new hard disk.

Some Hard Disk Basics

Just as it is not necessary to be an engineer to be able to drive a car, you don't have to know too much about a hard disk in order to use one. But for those who might be interested, here are some details.

Basically, the hard disk is similar to the floppy. It is a spinning disk that has a coating that can be magnetized. The hard disks are also formatted similarly to the floppy. However, the 360K floppy disk has only 40 tracks per inch (TPI); the hard disks may have from 300 up to 2400 TPI. The 360K floppy has 9 sectors per track; the standard hard disk has 17 sectors per track, and some may have up to 34.

Another major difference is the speed of rotation. A floppy disk spins at about 300 RPM. A hard disk spins at 3600 RPM. As the disk spins beneath the head, a pulse of voltage through the head will cause the area of the track that is beneath the head at that time to become magnetized. If this pulse of voltage is turned on for a certain amount of time, then turned off for some amount of time, it can represent the writing or recording of 1s and 0s. The hard disk spins much faster than a floppy so the duration of the magnetizing pulses can be much shorter at a higher frequency. This allows much more data to be recorded in the same amount of space.

Everything that a computer does depends on precise timing. Crystals and oscillators are set up so that certain circuits perform a task at a specific time. These oscillating circuits are usually called *clock circuits*. The clock frequency for the standard Modified Frequency Modulation (MFM) method of reading and writing to a hard disk is 10 MHz per second. To write on the disk during one second, the voltage might turn on for a fraction of a second, then turn off for the next period of time, then back on for a certain length of time. The head sits over a track that is moving at a constant speed. Blocks of data are written or read during the precise timing of the system clock. Because the voltage must go plus or zero, that is two states, in order to write 1s and 0s, the maximum data transfer rate is only 5 megabits per second, just half of the clock frequency. The RLL systems transfers data at a rate of 7.5 megabits per second. The SCSI and ESDI systems have a transfer rate as high as 10 megabits or more.

You have probably seen representations of magnetic lines of force around a magnet. The magnetized spot on a disk track has similar lines of force. To read the data on the disk, the head is positioned over the track. Lines of force from each magnetized area cause a pulse of voltage to be induced in the head. During a precise block of time, an induced pulse of voltage can represent a 1, and the lack of a pulse, a 0.

The amount of magnetism that is induced on a disk when it is recorded is very small. It must be small so that it will not affect other recorded bits or tracks near it. Magnetic lines of force decrease as you move away from a magnet by the square of the distance. So it is desirable to have the heads as close to the disk as possible.

On a floppy disk drive, the heads actually contact the disk. This causes some wear, but not very much because the rotation is fairly slow and the plastic disks have a special lubricant and are fairly slippery. But heads of the hard disk systems never touch the disk. The fragile heads and the disk would be severely damaged if they make contact at the fast speed of 3600 RPMs. The heads "fly" over the spinning disk, just micro-inches above it. The air must be pure because the smallest speck of dust or dirt can cause the head to "crash" so most hard disks are sealed. You should never open one.

The surface of the hard disk platters must be very smooth. Because the heads are only a few millionths of an inch, or microinches, away from the surface, any unevenness could cause a head crash. The hard disk platters are usually made from aluminum, which is nonmagnetic, and lapped to a mirror finish. They are then coated or plated with a magnetic material. Some companies are now using glass as a substrate for the platters.

The platters must also be very rigid so that the close distance between the head and the platter surface is maintained. You should avoid any sudden movement of the computer or any jarring while the disk is spinning because it could cause the head to crash onto the disk and damage it. Most of the newer hard disk systems automatically move the heads away from the read/write surface to a parking area when the power is turned off.

Another difference in the hard disk and the floppy is that the floppy comes on only when it is needed. Because of its mass the hard disk takes quite a while to get up to speed and to stabilize. So it comes on whenever the computer is turned on and spins as long as the computer is on. This means that it is drawing power from the power supply all the time. This could possibly cause some problems if your system is fully loaded with boards and has a small power supply.

Clusters

When a disk has been used for some time and files have been recorded, updated, erased, and recorded over again, parts of some files might be located in several areas of the disk. A file will be recorded in the first empty space it finds. A sector is only 512 bytes, but most files are much longer than that. Many systems lump two or more sectors together and call it a cluster. If there is an empty cluster on track 5, it will record as much of the file as it can there, then move to the next empty cluster, which may be on track 20. The location of each part of the file is recorded in the FAT, so the computer has no trouble finding it.

Cylinders

If you could strip away all of the tracks except tracks number one, top and bottom, on all of the platters, it would look somewhat like a cylinder. Cylinder refers to each of those tracks with the same number on a stack of platters or on a double-sided disk.

Multiple Platters

So that more recording surfaces can be crammed into a hard disk, it can have from 2 platters up to as many as 10 or more. All the platters are stacked on a single shaft with just enough spacing between them for the heads. Each disk has a head for the top surface and one for the bottom. If the system has four disks, then it will have eight heads. All heads are controlled by the same positioner, and they will all move as one. If head number one is over track one, sector one, then all the other heads will be over track one, sector one on each disk surface.

Head Positioners

There are several different types of head positioners, or actuators. Some use stepper motors to move the heads in discrete steps to a certain track. Some use a worm gear or screw-type shaft that moves the heads in and out. Others use voice coil technology.

The voice coil of a loud speaker is made up of a coil of wire that is wound on a hollow tube which is attached to the material of the speaker cone. Permanent magnets are then placed inside the coil and around the outside. Whenever a voltage is passed through the coil of wire, it will cause magnetic lines of force to be built up around the coil. Depending on the polarity of the input voltage, these lines of magnetic flux will be either the same or opposite of the lines of force of the permanent magnets. If the polarity of the voltage, for instance a plus voltage, causes the lines of force to be the same as the permanent magnet, then they will repel each other and the voice coil might move forward. If they are opposite, they will attract each other and the coil will move backwards.

Some of the better and faster hard disks use voice coil technology with a closed loop servo control. They usually use one surface of one of the disks to store data and track locations. Most specification sheets give the number of heads on a drive. If you see one that has an odd number of heads such as 5, 7, or 9, it probably uses the other head for servo information. The voice coil moves the heads quickly and smoothly to the track area. Feedback information from the closed loop positions the head to the exact track very accurately.

The voice coil drives can cost 30 to 40 percent more than the stepper motor types with an equivalent capacity.

The 32Mb Hard Disk Limit

DOS 3.2 and earlier versions have a limit of 32Mb that can be addressed on a hard disk. You could have a 500Mb hard disk but you would only be able to use 32Mb of it without special software.

The 32Mb limit is due to the fact that DOS numbers each 512-byte sector sequentially and stores it as a 16-bit integer. Two taken to the 16th power (2^{16}) is 65,536, or 64K, of different 16-bit numbers. So DOS can only handle 65,536 sectors. If you multiply this number by the 512 bytes in each sector, it gives a total of 33,554,432 bytes or 32Mb.

If you buy a hard disk that is greater than 30Mb, you will need DOS 3.3 or a later version. DOS 3.3 and later versions allow you to make several partitions. If you have not done so, I would strongly recommend that you upgrade to DOS 3.3, or a later version.

Setup Routine

When you install a hard disk, your BIOS must be told what kind it is. The BIOS also must know the time, the number and type of floppies you have, and other information. The newer systems have the routines so that you can input this information from the keyboard. The older ATs and 286s require that you use a diagnostic disk. This disk will have the routines for checking out your machine and setting it up. It is also needed to set, or reset, the clock on the motherboard. The diagnostic routine asks several questions, then configures the BIOS for that configuration. This part of the BIOS configuration is in low-power CMOS semiconductors and is on all the time, even when the computer is turned off. On the older motherboards, they are powered by a battery pack on the back panel of the computer. Many of the newer motherboards have a small battery on board so that the battery pack is not needed. If the batteries go too low to power the BIOS, a large capacitor can power it for about 15 minutes, or the time it would take to replace the batteries.

One question that the routine asks is what type of hard disk do you have. There were only 15 different types when the AT was introduced in 1984. Now, hundreds exist. Most new BIOS ROMs list 46 types. If yours is not among the 46 listed, the BIOS usually allows you to input the parameters of any that is not listed. You must tell it what type you have installed. You should have some information from your vendor that tells you the number of heads, cylinders, and other specifications.

Worms and Optical Drives

The Write-Once Read-Many (WORM) type of laser disks are similar to the CD-ROM except that CD-ROM is read-only. The WORM lets you write data with a laser onto a disk. One gigabyte or more can be written on a single disk. The data can be arranged into the desired form with a computer, stored on a hard disk, then transferred to the WORM laser system. Some people have complained that the problem with WORMs is that they cannot be erased and changed like a magnetic hard disk. But as stated above, certain records should never be changed. Besides, there is enough space on these disks that an update can be written alongside the original. When a disk is filled, just start another.

Optical drives can also store data in the gigabyte range. However, both WORMs and optical drives are still fairly expensive. They would be primarily needed and used by large businesses.

8

Backup

Of course you know the importance of backing up the original floppy disks when you get a new program. Most software programs advise you to use DISKCOPY to make copies of the originals. But before you do anything, you should cover the write-protect notch with a piece of opaque tape. It is very easy to become distracted and wipe out a three- or four-hundred-dollar program. It only takes a minute to cover the write-protect notch, it might take weeks to get a replacement for the original disk that has been inadvertently erased.

Once the originals are backed up, they should be stored away and only the copies should be used. If you damage one of them, you can always make another copy.

I am sure you have heard the expression, "To err is human, forgive divine" (Alexander Pope, 1711). There is no doubt that I am human. I have been working with computers for several years, but I still make mistakes. One thing that I have learned is that computers do not forgive. Just recently, I copied some files from a floppy disk to my hard disk. I then decided to erase the files on the floppy disk so I could use it for something else. I typed DEL *.* and the message came up, Are you sure? (Y/N). I thought that I was on the A drive so I pressed the Y key. I sat there horrified as a whole directory on my hard drive was wiped out.

Luckily, I had backed the directory up recently, but there were a couple of recent files that had not been backed up. Before doing anything else, I got out my copy of Norton Utilities and used the Unerase program to restore the files. (When a file is erased, DOS goes to the FAT table and deletes the first letter of each file name. All of the data remains on the disk unless a new file is written over it. Norton Utilities, (213) 319-2000, allows one to restore the files by replacing the missing first letter of the file name. Mace Gold Utilities at (503) 488-0224, PC Tools at (503) 690-8090, DOSUTILS at (612) 937-1107, and several others have data recovery utilities.)

The early versions of DOS made it very easy to format your hard disk in error. If you happened to be on your hard disk and typed FORMAT, it would immediately begin to format your hard disk and wipe out everything. Later versions will not format unless you specify a drive letter. Later versions also allow you to include a volume label, or name, on the drive when you format it by including the /v, or you can add the name later by using the command LABEL. If the drive has a volume label, it cannot be formatted unless the drive letter and correct volume name is specified. (You can display the name of a volume by running CHKDSK on a disk.)

Many people have erased files in error in the past. They are only human, so they will do it again. Some of them will not have backups or unerase software. In a fraction of a second, some of them will wipe out data that might be worth thousands of dollars. It might have taken hundreds of hours to accumulate it and might be impossible to duplicate. Yet many of these unfortunate people have not backed up their precious data. Most of these people are those who have been fortunate enough not to have had a major catastrophe. Just as sure as California has earthquakes, if you use a computer long enough, you can look forward to at least one unfortunate disaster. There are thousands of ways to make mistakes, and there is no way that you can prevent them. But if your data is backed up, it doesn't have to be a disaster. It is a lot better to be backed up than sorry.

Why They Don't and Why They Should Do Backup

1. Don't have the time. It would probably take about a half hour to back up a 40Mb hard disk. But of course, once the first backup is made, all subsequent backups need only to be made of any data that has been changed or updated. Most backup programs can recognize whether a file has been changed since the last backup. Most of them can also look at the date that is stamped on each file and back up only those within a specified date range. So it may take only a few minutes to copy only those that have been changed. And of course, it is usually not necessary to back up your program software. You do have the original software safely tucked away, don't you?

2. Too much trouble. Unless you have an expensive tape backup system, it requires a lot of disk swapping, labeling, and storing. But with a bit of organizing, it can be done easily. If you keep them all together, you don't have to label each disk. Stack them in order, put a rubber band around them and use one label for the lot.

3. Don't have the necessary disks, software, or tools. Depending on the amount of data to be backed up, it can require 50 to 100 360K disks. Of course, it would require a lot fewer if the high-density disks are used.

Again, it takes only a few minutes and a few disks to make a backup of only the data that has been changed or altered. In most cases, the same disks can be reused the next day to update the files. Several discount mail order houses sell 360K disks for as little as 25 cents apiece, 49 cents each for 1.2Mb. (See Chapter 6 for addresses.)

As for backup software, there are several excellent packages that I will discuss later. But if you have a copy of DOS, then you have a fairly good backup and restore program.

4. Failures and disasters are something that happens to other people. People who believe this way are those who have never experienced a disaster. There is nothing you can say to convince them. They just have to learn the hard way.

A Few Other Reasons
Why You Should Do Backup

The Head Crash. The technology of the hard disk systems has improved tremendously over the last couple of years. But they are still mechanical devices, and as such, you can be sure that eventually they will wear out, fail, or crash.

Most hard disks are now relatively bug-free. Manufacturers quote figures of several thousand hours *mean time before failure* (MTBF). But these figures are only an average. There is no guarantee that a disk won't fail in the next few minutes. A hard disk is made up of several mechanical parts. If it is used long enough, it will wear out or fail.

A failure can be frustrating, time-consuming, and make you feel utterly helpless. In the unhappy event of a crash, depending on its severity, it is possible that some of your data can be recovered, one way or another. Several disk repair service companies specialize in recovering and repairing failed disks. Here are a couple who have helped me:

California Disk Drive Repair
3350 Scott Blvd., Bldg. 59
Santa Clara, CA 95054
(408) 727-2475

Rotating Memory Service
473 Sapena Court, #26
Santa Clara, CA 95054
(408) 988-2334

General Failure. Outside of ordinary care, there is little one can do to prevent a general failure. It could be a component on the hard disk electronics or in the controller system. Or any one of a thousand other things. Even things such as a power failure during a read/write operation can cause data corruption.

Theft and Burglary. Computers are easy to sell so they are favorite targets for burglars. It would be bad enough to lose a computer, but many computers have hard disks that are filled with data that is even more valuable than the computer.

It might even be a good idea to store your backup files in an area away from your computer so that there would be less chance of losing them in a burglary, theft, or fire.

Archival. Another reason to back up is for archival purposes. No matter how large the hard disk is, it will eventually fill up with data. Quite often, there will be files that are no longer used or they might only be used once in a great while. I keep copies of all the letters that I write on disk, and I have hundreds of them. Rather than erase the old files or old letters, I put them on a disk and store them away.

Fragmentation. After a hard disk has been used for some time, files begin to be fragmented. The data is recorded on concentric tracks in separate sectors. If part of a file is erased or changed, some of the data may be in a sector on track 20 and another part on track 40. There may be open sectors on several tracks because portions of data have been erased. Hunting all over the disk can slow the disk down. If the disk is backed up completely, then erased, the files can be restored so that they will again be recorded in contiguous sectors. The utility programs mentioned above can unfragment a hard disk by copying portions of the disk to memory and rearranging the data in contiguous files.

Data Transfer. Often it is necessary to transfer a large amount of data from one hard disk on a computer to another. It is quite easy and fast to use a good backup program to accomplish this. It is easy to make several copies which can be distributed to others in the company. This method could be used to distribute data, company policies and procedures, sales figures, and other information to several people in a large office or company. The data could also be easily shipped or mailed to branch offices, customers, or to others almost anywhere.

Methods of Backup

One of the least expensive methods of backup is to use the BACKUP .COM and RESTORE.COM that comes with MS-DOS. These are slow, time-consuming, and rather difficult to use, but they will do the job if nothing else is available. Some alternatives are explored in the following pages.

Tape

There are several tape backup systems on the market. Tape backup is easy, but it can be relatively expensive, $600 to over $1500 for a drive unit and $10 to $30 for the tape cartridges. Most of them require the use of a controller that is similar to the disk controller. So they will use one of your precious slots. Unless they are used externally, they will also require the use of one of the disk mounting areas. Because it is only used for backup, it will be idle most of the time.

If you have several computers in an office that must be backed up every day, you could possibly install a controller in each machine with an external connector. Then one external tape drive could be used to back up each of the computers at the end of the day. With this system, you would need a controller in each machine, but you would only have to buy one tape drive.

One of the biggest problems with tape is that no standards have been established for tape size, cartridges, reels, or format. Quite often a tape that is recorded on one tape machine, even from the same vendor, will not restore on another.

The most common type drives use a quarter-inch tape that is similar to that used in audio cassettes. Because the data from a hard disk is much more critical than the cacophony of a rock band, the tapes are manufactured to very strict standards. Even so, this tape could stretch and cause the loss of data.

There are also $1/2$ drive systems for high-end use. They will cost from $3000 to as much as $10,000 or more.

Videotape

Another tape system uses video tape and a standard home videotape recorder to make backups. This system requires that an interface board be installed in the computer. From 60 to 120Mb of data can be stored on a standard videotape that costs from 3 to 5 dollars.

This type of system is ideal for the home user. Two leads from the interface easily connect to the VCR. After the backup is completed, the machine can be moved back to the living room for home entertainment.

But this low-cost system is also sophisticated enough to be used in large businesses and offices. The Alpha Micro VIDEOTRAX system has an option that will even do an automatic backup. See Fig. 8-1.

Besides being used for backup, these videotapes can be used to distribute large amounts of data. For instance, the contents of a hard disk could be copied and sent to another computer across the room or across the country.

Alpha Micro has also demonstrated that it is possible to broadcast software over the TV channels. A VCR can record the software as easily as it does an old movie. The software can then be installed on any computer system that is equipped with an interface board.

Two companies are foremost in this type of backup, the AUTOFAX and the Alpha Micro VIDEOTRAX. Their boards cost about $300 to $500. Here are the addresses of these two companies:

AUTOFAX Corporation
4113-A Scotts Valley Dr.
Scotts Valley, CA 95066
(408) 438-6861

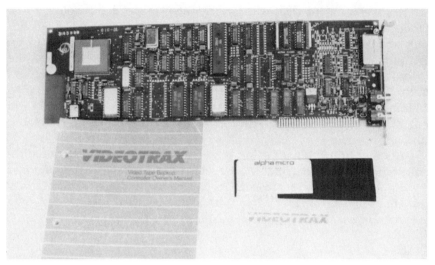

Fig. 8-1. A plug-in board that allows the use of a standard video tape recorder to be used to back up hard disks.

Alpha Micro Corporation
VIDEOTRAX
3501 Sunflower
Santa Ana, CA 92704-6944
(714) 641-6381

High-Density Disk Drive

Several companies are now making high-density floppy-disk drives. The Bernoulli drive can now put 44Mb on a 5^1/$_4$ inch floppy disk. Kodak has been marketing 10Mb high-density drives for some time. By the time you read this, Brier Technology will have a 3^1/$_2$ inch floppy on the market that can store 20Mb or more.

Even if they cost a bit more, a high-density floppy drive can be more advantageous than a tape. The tape drives would only be used for backup. But a high-density floppy would have much more utility, possibly even obviating the need for a hard disk.

Second Hard Disk

The easiest and the fastest of all methods of backup is to have a second hard disk. It is very easy to install a second hard disk because most controllers have the capability of controlling a second hard disk. You would have to make sure that the second hard disk would work with your first disk, but that should be easy to determine. It would not have to be a large one, a 20 or 30Mb would do fine. With a second hard disk as a backup, you would not need a backup software package. A good backup software package might cost $200 or more. You could probably buy a second hard disk for this amount.

An average hard disk will have an access speed of about 40 Ms. Floppy disks operate at about 300 Ms speed which can seem like an eternity compared to the speed of even the slowest hard disk. Depending on the number of files, how fragmented the data is on the disk and the access speed, a second hard disk can back up 20Mb in a matter of seconds. To back up 20Mb using even the fastest software will require 15 to 20 minutes. It will also require that you do a lot of disk swapping in and out. It can require 50 to 60 360K, about 17 1.2Mb, or about 14 1.44Mb disks.

Another problem with using software backup is that it is often difficult to find a particular file. Most backup software stores the data in a system that is not the same as DOS files. Usually there is no directory like that provided by DOS. Even the DOS BACKUP files show only a control number when you check the directory.

Hard Cards

It is now possible to buy a hard disk on a card for $300 to $600, depending on capacity and company. At this low price, it would be worthwhile to install a card in an empty slot and dedicate it to backup.

If there are no empty slots, you might even consider just plugging in the card once a week or so to make a backup, then removing the card until needed again. This would entail removing the cover from the machine each time. But I remove the cover to my computer so often that I only use one screw on it to provide grounding. I can remove and replace my cover in a very short time.

Software

Several very good software programs on the market let you use a $5^1/4$ inch or $3^1/2$ inch disk drive to back up your data. Again, you should have backups of all your master software, so you don't have to worry about backing up that software every day. Because DOS stamps each file with the date and time it was created, it is easy to back up only those files that were created after a certain date and time.

DOS also stores backup information about the file in the directory entry. One of the bits of information is the archive flag, either a 1 or 0. When the DOS BACKUP command has been used to back up the file, the flag is changed. Several commercial software packages make use of this flag so that only files that have not been backed up can be copied.

One popular backup software program is FASTBACK. It has lots of utilities, pull-down menus, and a well-written manual. The 120-page manual explains just about everything you need to know about backups, such as the difference in an image backup and a file-oriented backup. An image backup is an exact bit for bit copy of the hard disk copied as a continuous stream of data. This type of backup is rather inflexible and does not allow for a separate file backup or restoration. The file-oriented type of backup identifies and indexes each file separately. A separate file or directory can be backed up and restored easily. It can be very time consuming to have to back up an entire 20Mb or more each day. With a file-oriented system, once a full backup has been made, it is necessary only to make incremental backups of those files that have been changed or altered. The manual is written in plain language that should be easy for anyone to understand.

The program itself has lots of pull-down menus with on-screen help. The menus are layered and each selection will bring up another menu so that just about every option possible is offered.

Once the files to be backed up and the options are selected, the program can estimate how many disks will be needed and how long it will take to make the backup. FASTBACK PLUS uses a form of compression so that up to 70 percent more data can be stored on a given type of floppy disk. Several different types of floppy drives can be used such as the 360K, the 1.2Mb, the 720K, and the 1.44Mb. Their address is:

FASTBACK PLUS
Fifth Generation Systems
11200 Industriplex Blvd.
Baton Rouge, LA 70809

The discount price for FASTBACK PLUS is $98.

Another very good backup program is BACK-IT from Gazelle Systems, the people who developed the excellent disk management QDOS program. BACK-IT is very easy to use. A directory tree is presented and files can be tagged to be included or excluded. Wildcards can be used. Their address is:

Gazelle Systems
42 North University Ave., Suite 10
Provo, Utah 84601
(800) 233-0383

The list price for BACK-IT is $79.95.

Several other very good backup software packages are available. Check through the computer magazines for their ads and for reviews.

No matter what type of system or method is used, you should be using something to back up your data. You might be one of the lucky ones and never need it. But it is much better to have backups than to be sorry.

9

Memory

Memory is one of the most critical elements of the computer. If you open a file from a hard disk, the files and data are read from the disk and placed in RAM. RAM is an acronym for *Random Access Memory*, but it only tells part of the story. Besides being able to randomly access the memory, it also allows us to read and write to it. It is somewhat like an electronic blackboard. Here you can manipulate the data, do calculations, enter more data, edit, search databases, or do any of the thousands of things that software programs allow you to do. Because it is in RAM, you can access and change the data very quickly.

Need for More Memory

Depending on what kind of computer you have and what you use it for, you might need to buy more RAM. For some applications, you might need to buy several megabytes more. In the old days, people got by fine with just 64K of memory. Today it is almost impossible to get by with less than 640K. Many of the new software programs require even more than that. If you don't have at least 640K of RAM on your computer's motherboard, you might not be able to run some of the spreadsheets, databases, or accounting programs. The new Lotus 1-2-3 Release 3 requires about 2Mb of RAM in order to run.

If you have just bought a new motherboard, or a memory board, it probably came with 0K memory. (As I mentioned earlier, 0K does not mean okay, it means zero K memory.) The cost of memory is so high, and the price fluctuates so much, most vendors will not advertise a firm price. If they listed the price of the memory, it might frighten you away. They usually invite you to call them for the latest price. But the prices do seem to be coming down slowly.

Things To Consider Before You Buy Memory

There are several different types, sizes, speed, and other factors to consider before buying memory. You should buy the type that is best for your computer.

Dynamic RAM or DRAM

This is the most common type of memory used today. These chips are similar to capacitors or small rechargeable batteries. Units can be charged up with a voltage to represent 1s or left uncharged to represent 0s. But those that are charged up immediately start to lose their charge. So they must be constantly "refreshed" with a new charge. A computer can spend 7 percent or more of its time just refreshing the DRAM chips. When new data is entered, some of the units that were charged as 1s might be drained so that they become 0s and some of the 0s might be charged up to become 1s.

RAM is easily erased. If there is the slightest power interruption, even for a fraction of a second, all of the charges on the DRAMs, and therefore any data in memory, is lost. If the computer is turned off, the data in RAM is gone forever. You should get in the habit of saving your files to disk frequently, especially if you live in an area where there are power failures due to storms or other reasons. (Some programs, like WordStar 5, automatically save open files to disk at frequent intervals.)

Static RAM or SRAM

Static RAM is made up of actual transistors. They can be turned on to represent 1s or left off to represent 0s and will stay in that way until changed. They do not need to be refreshed. They are very fast, but are much more expensive than DRAMs. Most laptops use SRAM because it can be kept alive with a small amount of current from a battery. Because DRAM needs to be constantly refreshed, it takes a lot of circuitry and power to keep them alive.

Size or Chip Capacity

The most common sizes today are 64K, 256K, and 1Mb. But it takes eight chips of each size listed to make the stated size. For instance, it takes eight chips to make 64K, eight to make 256K, and eight to make 1Mb.

Almost all of the computers will use an extra ninth chip for parity checking. This chip checks and verifies the integrity of the memory at all times. It is usually the same type of chip as the eight that are used to make up the bank. The chips are usually arranged in banks or rows of nine.

RAM memory is usually located in the front left corner of the motherboard. To make 640K, most boards fill the first two banks, bank 0 and 1, with 256K chips which would equal 512K. The next two banks, 3 and 4, are then filled with 64K chips to make 128K for a maximum 640K. Many of the 286 and 386 systems fill all four banks with 256K chips for a total of 1Mb. The extra 384K can be used for a RAM disk, print spooling or for other extended memory needs with the proper software.

Single Inline Memory Module (SIMM)

SIMMs are assemblies of either 256K or 1Mb miniature DRAM chips. Usually nine chips are on a small board that is either soldered or plugged slantwise into a special connector. These chips require a very small amount of board real estate. Figure 9-1 shows a baby 386 motherboard with 2Mb of SIMM RAM installed in the upper left corner.

Fig. 9-1. A baby 386 motherboard with 2Mb of SIMM memory installed in the upper left corner.

Speed

It takes a finite amount of time for the computer to refresh and access the DRAMs. Access speed of the chips is rated in nanoseconds (ns) or billionths of a second. Chips are manufactured with access speeds from a slow 200 ns to a fast 70 ns. Of course, the faster the speed, the higher the cost. The size and speed of the chip is usually printed on the top of the chip. For instance, a 256K chip at 150 ns might have the manufacturer's logo or name and some other data. But somewhere among all this would be "256 – 15." The – 15 indicates 150 ns (the zero is always left off). A one megabyte 100 ns chip might have "1024 – 10." See Fig. 9-2.

Fig. 9-2. A closeup of a portion of a memory board that has both 16- and 18-pin sockets. Note the difference in the 256K and the 1024K or 1Mb chip. Note also the −15 on the 256 that indicates 150 ns and the −10 on the 1024 that indicates 100 ns.

Computers operate at very precise clock rates. The Central Processing Unit (CPU) is controlled by timing circuits and crystals. The original PCs and XTs operated at 4.77 MHz. Some of the newer 286s operate as high as 20 MHz. Many 386s are operating at 33 MHz, and it is only a matter of time before they operate at 50 MHz.

Many systems are just too fast for some of the other components. So in some cases, a *wait state* is inserted to cause the CPU to sit and wait for something to happen. Some computers are designed with built-in wait states so that they can use slower memory. Some of the newer BIOS chips will allow you to insert wait states. Wait states can cause a computer to operate 25 to 50 percent slower than one without wait states. For ordinary applications, this would probably only amount to a few billionths of a second. But for some applications, it could add up and seem like an eternity.

The following information will give you a rough idea of what speed chips you should buy for your system:

CPU speed	Wait state	DRAM speed
4.77 MHz	0	200
6-8 MHz	1	120-150
6-8 MHz	0	100-120
8-10 MHz	1	100-120
8-10 MHz	0	80-100
10-12 MHz	1	100
12-20 MHz	1	80
16-20 MHz	0	70

Again these are only rough figures. Your system may be designed to operate a bit differently. Check your system specifications or check with your vendor.

Buying chips that are faster than what your system can use only costs you extra money. It doesn't hurt to use faster chips, or even to inter-mix faster ones with slower ones.

Make sure that you buy only the type that will fit in your system. For instance, the 64K and 256K chips have 16 pins, the 1Mb chips have 18. Refer to Fig. 9-2. Notice that the 1Mb chip is larger than the 256K. This particular board has both 256K and 1Mb sockets interlaced so that you can use either size chip. You could not use 1Mb in the 256K sockets or vice versa. Also, you could not use a SIMM module unless your mother-board was designed for it.

Note that 1Mb chips are becoming readily available. There are a few 4Mb chips available, but there should be plenty of them on the market soon.

Prices

Here are some advertised prices from a discount house in the latter quarter of 1989:

Type	150	120	100	80	70
64K × 1	2.50	2.75	3.15		
256K × 1	4.25	4.50	5.00	5.75	
1000K × 1			14.00	15.00	16.00
SIMM 256K × 9		40.00	50.00	59.00	
SIMM 1000K × 9			165.00	190.00	220.00

Memory prices are coming down, so they should be a bit lower than the prices quoted above. Also note that the above price list is from a discount house. The prices at the average store might be higher. But this should give you some idea as to the differences in the cost of the various types.

Note that the prices are ×1 or ×9 in the SIMMs. Remember that it takes 9 chips to make a bank, so it would take four banks of 256K chips to make 1Mb. If you wanted to install 1Mb with 100 ns 256K chips, it would take 36 of them at $5 each for a total of $180. It would only take 9 chips of the 1000K × 1 to make 1Mb. So if your system has the proper sockets, you could buy 9 1000K × 1 100 ns chips at $14 each for a total of $126.

Installing the Chips

Now that you have bought your chips, you need to install them in the sockets on the motherboard. Or you might be installing them on a plug-in memory board.

One of the first things that you should do is to discharge any static charge that you may have on you. This is especially important if you are working in an area where there is carpet. If you have ever walked across a carpet and gotten a shock when you touched the door knob, then you know that you can build up static electricity. It is quite possible to build up 3000 to 5000 volts of static electricity in our bodies. So if you touch a fragile piece of electronics that normally operates at 5 to 12 volts, you can severely damage it. You can discharge this static electricity from your body by touching any metal that goes to ground. The metal case of the power supply in your computer is a good ground if it is still plugged into the wall socket. The power does not have to be on for it to connect to ground. You should always discharge yourself before you touch any plug-in board or other equipment where there are exposed electronic semiconductors.

Now that you have discharged yourself, you can plug in the chips. If you have 64K or 256K chips, they will have 16 legs. The 1Mb chips have 18 legs. Some memory boards have both types of sockets side by side. (See Fig. 9-2.) You must determine what type of chips you should use and which banks to fill.

You can mix chips of different speeds in the same bank, such as 100 ns and 120 ns, but you would be limited to the 120 ns speed. You should not use a chip slower than the speed of your CPU. You cannot mix chips of different capacities in the same bank, such as 64K and 256K in the same row of nine chips.

The chips might have a small notch at one end or a round dot in one corner. The notch or dot indicates the end that has pin one. The socket will have a matching notch or outline on the board to indicate how the chip should be plugged in. Ordinarily, all of the chips on a board are installed or oriented in the same direction.

To install a chip, set the leads in one side of the socket, then with a bit of pressure against that side, line up the leads on the other side and press the chip in. Be careful that you do not bend the leads. Check to make sure that all of the leads are inserted in the sockets. It is very easy to have one slip out and not be noticed. If this happens you will have memory errors when you try to run the system.

If you are installing the memory on a PC or XT, you might have to reset the dip switch on the motherboard to reflect the amount of memory. Some of the older ATs had a jumper that has to be set.

Cache Memory

Some systems use a small cache, about 32K or so, of static RAM (SRAM) for very fast memory access. Some programs might require a very large amount of memory. The computer would be slowed down considerably if it has to search the entire memory each time it has to fetch some data. The data that is used most frequently can be stored in the fast cache memory and speed may be increased by several magnitudes. Again, the system would have to be designed to accept static RAM.

Read-Only Memory

Read-Only Memory (ROM) is another kind of memory. You can write to or read RAM memory. But ROM is firmware that can only be read, usually only by the computer. It usually contains instructions and rules, such as those contained in the BIOS ROM, that controls the operation of the computer. Ordinarily, you don't have to worry about ROM except to update the BIOS chips.

The 640K DOS Barrier

At one time it was believed that 1Mb of RAM would be more than sufficient for any eventuality, so DOS was designed for that limit. How little they knew.

The 8088 CPUs found in all PCs and XTs can access 1Mb of RAM. But only 640K is available for applications, the other 384K is reserved for internal use of the BIOS, the display, and other functions.

The PC and XT Bus and the AT Bus

The PCs and XTs use an 8-bit bus. The AT systems, which include the 80286s and 80386s, use a 16- and 32-bit bus.

The 8088 accepts two parallel 8-bit chunks of data, then internally adds 4 bits and sends them out over a 20-line bus. With the 20 lines, it is possible to address any individual byte in 1Mb, that is $2^{20} = 1,048,576$ bytes. Most motherboards will have from five to eight 62-pin connectors for 8-bit hardware.

The 80286 accepts 16-bit chunks of data, then internally adds 8 bits and sends them out over 24 lines which allows them to address 16Mb or $2^{24} = 16,777,216$ bytes.

The 80286 motherboard has all of the standard 8-bit slots plus four or more 16-bit slots with 36-pin connectors directly in front of the 8-bit slots.

The 80386 accepts data 32 bits at a time and sends it out over 32 lines. It can address 4 gigabytes or $2^{32} = 4,294,967,296$ bytes. A *gigabyte* is also the same as a billion bytes.

In its virtual mode, the 80386 can address 64 terabytes, or 64 trillion bytes, that is 64,000,000,000,000 bytes. This is the amount of data that could be stored on 3,200,000 20Mb hard disks.

Most of the 80386 motherboards have all of the 8-bit slots. Most of them will have three or four of the extra 36-pin 16-bit slots directly in front of the 8-bit slots. They might also have connectors for one or two 32-bit boards. Some developers have designed a board without 32-bit slots. Instead, they make provisions for up to 2 or more megabytes to be installed on the motherboard. Extra memory can be installed in 16-bit slots.

Types of Memory

The four main types of memory are *real* or *conventional, extended, native 386,* and *expanded.* Real or conventional memory is the 1Mb of memory that the 8088 and 8086 systems are able to directly address. Each one of those million bytes has a unique address, much like the individual addresses of streets and houses in a city. The CPU can go to any one of those addresses in the lower 640K and read the data that might be there or write data to that address.

Extended Memory

Extended memory is memory that can be installed above 1Mb. If it weren't for the DOS 640K limitation, it would be a seamless continuation of memory. OS/2, Xenix, and Unix regard it as such and will let you address it. But because the 8088 and 8086 have only 20 address lines, they are not physically able to address more than 1Mb.

Native 386

The 80386 can address up to 4 gigabytes of RAM or ROM. It can address up to 64 terabytes of virtual memory. In the virtual 86 mode it can behave as if it were several independent 8086 machines, each with 1Mb of address space and up to 640K of real or conventional memory.

Chances are that you will probably not ever install the maximum amount of memory possible in your 386, especially if you are using it at home.

Expanded Memory

Some large spreadsheets require an enormous amount of memory. A few years ago in a rare instance of cooperation among corporations, Lotus, Intel, Microsoft, and some other large corporations got together and devised a system and standard specification called *LIM EMS 4.0.* It allows a computer, even a PC or XT, to address up to 32Mb of memory. See Fig. 9-3 for a diagram showing how memory is allocated.

The memory is installed on boards and plugged into the computer's expansion slots. Memory on the boards is divided into pages of 16K each. Expanded memory finds a 64K window above 784K of the 1Mb memory. Hardware circuits on the boards and software programs can switch the pages in and out of the expanded memory into this window.

Several of the OS/2 functions can be run with DOS and LIM EMS 4. It is now possible to load *terminate-and-stay-resident* (TSR) programs such as SideKick, in memory outside of our precious 640K. It also includes functions to allow multitasking so that several programs can be run simultaneously.

Many of the 80386 systems are being shipped with up to 2Mb of memory installed on the motherboard. Of course, DOS will not let you

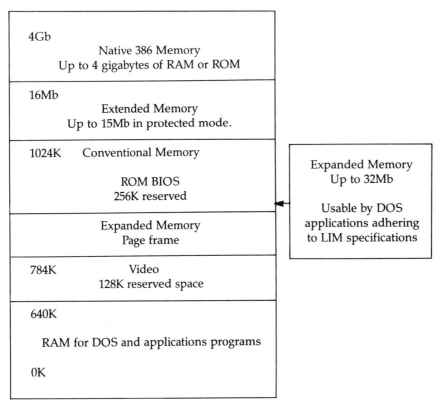

Fig. 9-3. How memory is allocated.

use more than 640K of that extended memory except for RAM disks or print spoolers. But LIM EMS 4.0 will allow the extended memory be used as expanded memory with the proper software and drivers.

OS/2 vs. DOS Plus Expanded Memory

At the present time, DOS 3.3 is selling for about $50, and DOS 4.01 costs about $90. If you are trying to get by with anything less than DOS 3.3, you really should upgrade.

OS/2 costs $325 and Presentation Manager portion costs over $700. (Incidentally, OS/2 1.0 requires about 2.5 to 3Mb of hard disk space. Presentation Manager adds considerably more to that amount of required disk space. DOS 3.3 requires about 500K.)

To use OS/2, you will need a 286 or better yet, a 386, computer. You probably know DOS fairly well already. You might not need all of the multitasking and other exotic functions of OS/2. Depending on what you need to do with your computer, you might be able to get by with an *Expanded Memory Specification* (EMS) board and the DESQview software package.

Memory Boards

Several companies in the United States and overseas who are manufacturing boards with large amounts of memory on them. Memory boards are still expensive from $500 to over $5000.

Some boards might advertise a 2Mb board for a fairly low price. But if you look closely at the ad, this may be with 0K memory, or no memory installed for the price advertised.

Intel Above Board

I am using an Intel Above Board (see Fig. 9-4) to write this chapter. It has 2Mb of memory. I am using it as expanded memory, although I could use it as extended memory on my 386. Using the software that came with the board, I have set up a RAM disk in memory and loaded my WordStar files onto it. I have also set up a portion of memory as a print buffer. The software and excellent manual made it very easy to install and set up the board.

Fig. 9-4. The Intel Above Board Plus 8 memory board.

Using the board for word processing is not the ideal use for a board of this type. However, it can be used for almost any purpose where large amounts of memory are needed.

The Above Board can be used in a 16-bit or an 8-bit system. It has a 16-bit connector, but a small shorting plug can be used to configure the board when it is used in an 8-bit system.

Intel offers two versions: the Above Board Plus 8 and the Above Board Plus 8 I/O. The I/O version provides a serial and parallel port on the memory board so that a printer or modem can be operated from this board. If you are running out of slots, this board can do two functions and save a slot.

Memory Board Vendors

The following is a partial list of vendors who manufacture memory boards. Contact them for your particular needs.

AST Research	(714) 863-1333
Advantage Premium (PC/XT)	
Rampage 286	
Boca Research	(305) 997-6227
Bocaram/AT	
IDEAssociates	(800) 257-5027
Intel Corp.	(503) 629-7354
Above Board Plus 8 (PC/XT/AT)	
Above Board Plus 8 I/O (PC/XT/AT)	
Micron Technology	(800) 642-7664
Newer Technology	(316) 685-4904
Concentration	
Orchid Technology	(415) 490-8586
Quadram Corp.	(404) 564-5566
STB Systems	(214) 234-8750
Tecmar Inc.	(800) 624-8560

Call the companies for their latest price lists and specifications. Though not listed above, many of them also make memory boards for the PCs and XTs.

10

ROM BIOS

ROM is an acronym for *Read-Only Memory*. BIOS is an acronym for *Basic Input Output System*. The ROM BIOS is a program that has been burned onto EPROM chips. EPROM is an acronym for *Erasable Programmable Read-Only Memory*. EPROM chips are available in 64K, 128K, 256K, and 512K sizes as shown in Fig. 10-1. The EPROM chips are made up of special transistors. A clear glass window over the transistor circuits on the chip allows these circuits to be sensitive to ultraviolet light (UV). The transistor circuits can be electronically programmed in an EPROM programmer or burner. A program can be read from a floppy or hard disk and fed to the burner. The individual transistors on the chip will be set to either on or off to reflect the 1s and 0s of the software program. So the program is copied to the chip, just as if it were being copied to another floppy or to a hard disk. Once it is programmed, the glass window is covered with opaque tape.

Fig. 10-1. EPROM chips. From left to right, a 512K, 256K, 128K, and 64K.

If the program is not exactly right, it is possible to remove the tape over the glass window, expose the chip to ultraviolet light to erase the chip. It can then be rewritten or reburned.

Just as it is possible to copy software from one disk to another, it is possible to copy the contents of one EPROM chip to another with the EPROM burner. Of course, you know that it is illegal to make and distribute copies of software that is copyrighted (but that has not stopped a lot of people from doing it). The same is true for illegal copying of ROM chips. Illegal copying has cost vendors millions of dollars.

The Function of ROM BIOS

"BIOS" sounds a bit like "boss." Actually, the function of the BIOS is quite similar to that of a boss in a small factory. He gets there early, checks all the equipment to make sure it is in working order, then he opens the doors for business. This is similar to the startup procedures that happen when you first turn your computer on. It first does a *power-on self-test* or POST. It checks the RAM memory chips for any defects. (The IBM memory check takes a considerable amount of time to make the memory check. Almost always the memory checks okay. The clone makers noted this so they designed a BIOS that did a much faster check. Most of the newer BIOS chips give you the option to bypass the RAM memory test if you want to.) The BIOS then checks the keyboard, the floppy and hard disks, the printer, and other peripherals. If everything is okay, it then sends a signal to the drive A to run the boot program. If there is no disk in drive A, it then tries to find a boot program on the hard disk. This boot program initializes the peripheral equipment, runs the CONFIG.SYS and AUTOEXEC.BAT programs and allows you to start doing business.

During the day the BIOS, or boss, will receive several interruptions or requests for services. These interrupts might be minor or major. Depending on the type of request, the BIOS might shut down everything and put everybody to work to satisfy that one request. If it is a minor request, it might have to wait until the present task is finished.

Depending on the software and type of computer, the BIOS might have the facilities to accomplish several tasks at the same time, or do multi-tasking. With the proper hardware and software, the BIOS might even be able to do multi-using functions and allow several computers to access this one.

The BIOS must be savvy enough to work with many different types of requests and orders. There are thousands of different software programs and hardware. The BIOS must be able to take the orders, route them to the proper hardware device such as the screen, keyboard, disks, printers, modems, or whatever. Sometimes the BIOS might be asked to do something that it doesn't have the equipment or the ability to do.

Because the BIOS is very conscientious, it will get hung up and keep trying to accomplish the impossible task. It might ignore any requests from the keyboard to stop. Depending on the type of problem, you might have to do a "warm boot," Ctrl – Alt – Del, to restart the computer. You might even have to turn the power off and do a "cold boot" to completely clear the computer in order to restart it.

The BIOS also provides you with the date and time when you ask for it. It also appends the date and time to any file or program that you create.

As you might imagine, the BIOS is quite an important part of our computers.

Compatibility

Many of the chips that are used to make a computer such as the CPU, the DMA, the RAM chips, and others are made by various companies. But IBM designed and developed their own BIOS program for the PCs. In those days, almost everyone used the BASIC language for developing their own programs and for running programs that were developed elsewhere. Most of the floppy drives were single-sided and could only store 160K. The early PC BIOS had never even heard of a fixed or hard disk. Because everybody used BASIC and storage was at a premium, IBM put the BASIC language on ROM chips and plugged them in right alongside the ROM BIOS chip. It was a great idea, quite convenient and useful.

Because IBM was the biggest, the industry leader and standard setter, a whole lot of software was written for the IBM PC.

As I said earlier, it is very easy to copy a ROM BIOS. In order to be compatible with IBM, several of the clones did just that. Naturally, IBM was not too happy about this and threatened to sue.

Phoenix Technologies and Award software were two of the several companies that began developing a compatible BIOS for the clone makers. Because they could not copy the IBM BIOS, their BIOS chips could never be 100 percent compatible. But they did almost everything that the IBM did. And in some cases, they did things better than IBM did, such as the reduced time for checking RAM memory.

It wasn't long before there were more compatible clones in existence than IBM PCs. Newer double-sided floppy disk drives were developed that could hold a whopping 360K bytes. With two drives, you could have GWBASIC on a disk and still do a lot of productive work. You really didn't need BASIC in ROM.

A few early software programs written specifically for IBM still could not be run on the clones. Before long, the software developers took note of the many clones in existence, so they began writing programs that could be run on any machine. Very few, if any, programs sold today will not work in the clones.

IBM set the standard with the first PC, but many more clones have been sold with the Phoenix and Award BIOS programs than with IBM's, so who is to say what the standard should be?

The early BIOS programs were relatively simple. PCs and XTs used a single 64K chip for the BIOS; the ATs used two 128K chips. The ever-changing technological advances have forced changes. Most of the 286 and 386 machines today use two 256K chips for a total of 512K of memory. To give you an idea of how much memory that is, this entire book can be stored in about 400K of memory.

The clone BIOS companies, like Phoenix, Award, AMI, Quadtel, and others, have been the leaders and innovators in new BIOS development. They have recognized the needs and requirements and have been quick to respond.

For instance, when IBM introduced the AT in 1984, their BIOS recognized only 15 types of hard drives. If your drive wasn't on the list, you were in trouble. IBM also had a Diagnostic or setup disk that was used to tell the computer such things as the type of floppy drives and hard drives, and the type of monitor that was installed. You also needed the floppy disk to set the time and date.

The compatible BIOS developers soon came out with BIOS chips that allowed these functions to be set from the keyboard. You didn't need the floppy disk. They upgraded the list from 15 to 46 different types of hard disks that you could choose from. A forty-seventh type was included that let the user input any characteristics or types not included in the 46 types listed. Many of the clone ROM BIOS programs also included other goodies such as letting you switch from standard speed to turbo from the keyboard. They all now include the ability to recognize the $3^1/_2$ inch 1.44Mb floppy. In all fairness, IBM has upgraded their BIOS also. But most of their changes have been made some time after the clones had made a change.

The American Megatrends Inc. (AMI) has an excellent set of very comprehensive diagnostics built into their 286 and 386 BIOSes. These diagnostics can be used to do a low-level format on a hard disk. They can test and determine the optimum interleave factor. They can do a surface analysis of the disk and mark the bad sectors. They can check the performance of the hard and floppy disk drives, measure their access speed, the data transfer rate, and measure the rotational speed of the drives. They can run tests on the keyboard, the monitor and adapter, serial and parallel ports, and do several other very useful diagnostic tests. At computer shows in the last couple of years, I have seen more installed AMI BIOS chips than any others.

BIOS Differences

I have a clone 286 motherboard that was designed and built in late 1984. The vendor that I bought it from tried both the Phoenix and the Award BIOS in it. They both worked, and I ended up with the Award

Fig. 10-2. ROM BIOS chip sets from Quadtel, Award, Phoenix, and DTK.

BIOS. A while back, I tried to install a 1.44Mb floppy disk drive in it. Of course, the 1984 BIOS had never heard of such a thing. I was able to buy a DRIVER.SYS that let me run it. I also wanted to install a new hard drive that didn't fit any of the 15 types listed. I also had a few other minor problems, so I decided that it was time to upgrade to new BIOS.

I went to a nearby dealer who used the Phoenix BIOS in his systems. He cautioned me that it might not work in my system, but he sold me a set. I figured that if it worked with Phoenix in the beginning, it should work now; but it did not. It would not boot up at all. I went to another dealer who used the Phoenix BIOS, but he had a version that was just a bit newer. It worked perfectly.

It seemed strange that the early Phoenix BIOS would work, but the much later version would not. In the early days, things were a lot simpler with fewer options and choices available, so there was more compatibility. But now many of the motherboard manufacturers are designing their boards so that they might be a little bit different than others. Many are using a customized BIOS for their motherboards, so one that has been customized for one board might not work on another.

I was curious to find out how much compatibility there is between BIOS chips nowadays. I was able to get several BIOS chips made by several different manufacturers for both my 286 and 386, and I found some that would not run on either machine. A Quadtel 286 set would not work with my Vutek video adapter installed; it worked perfectly with other video adapters. The AMI 286 would not work with the Perstor hard disk controller, but it worked great with other controllers.

If you have an older computer, no doubt you need a new BIOS. Try to contact a dealer or vendor who sells the same type machine that you have. Of course, if it is a no-name clone and is a bit old, you might not be able to find the original vendor. However, some BIOS chips are available that will work with almost all of the clones. Work out an understanding with the dealer to let you return the chips if they do not work.

There usually isn't too much trouble in upgrading an older XT BIOS. Most of the new ones are very compatible. It is very worthwhile, especially if you are installing high-density disk drives. Most of the new XT BIOSes now recognize the 1.2Mb or the $3^1/2$ drives; the old ones do not.

If you have an older true-blue IBM you may have some trouble getting a new BIOS. IBM will not sell a BIOS to an individual. You will have to take your computer to the dealer and let him install it. In many cases, he might have to send it out to have the factory do it. As you might imagine, it will take quite a bit of time to get your computer back, and it will be quite expensive.

You might be better off installing a clone BIOS in the IBM. You should be able to find one that will work, and it will cost you a lot less money and time. A good clone BIOS such as the AMI, Phoenix, Award, or Quadtel will provide more utility and capability for your computer than you had before. Putting a clone BIOS in an IBM won't cause it to lose any of its perceived value as long as you keep that IBM logo on the front panel.

Sources

Most of the BIOS developers do not supply chips to end users. They usually have a license agreement with a motherboard developer or system vendor. The vendor then uses the supplied software to burn as many BIOS chips as needed. Not many advertise the fact, but most of the vendors will gladly sell you a BIOS. Check with your local dealers or with any of those who sell systems by mail.

Several companies sell BIOSes by mail. As mentioned above, not all of them are compatible. Secure an understanding with the vendor that you can return it in good order if it does not work. There shouldn't be much trouble with the XT BIOS; most are still compatible. Here are a couple mail order vendors. Wholesale Direct Company, (206) 883-0227, advertises the Phoenix BIOS for the 286 for $49.95 and $59.95 for the 386. The USA Electronics Company, (214) 631-1574, advertises new BIOS chips for the XT from $19.95 to $24.95 and $49.95 for the 286.

How to Install a BIOS

The first thing of course is to turn off the power and remove the cover of the computer.

Step 1. After the cover is removed, look for the location of the BIOS chips. Depending on the designer of your motherboard, they could be almost anywhere. They will probably be near the memory banks. You might have to remove one or more plug-in boards to get at them. But before you remove any boards or cables, make a diagram of how they are connected and installed. Be especially careful to note where the BIOS chips are located and how they are oriented. Note the small notch or other marking on the chips which indicates which end has pin one. One of the chips will be marked either HI or ODD. The other will be marked LO or EVEN. Most boards are stamped with a chip number. The integrated circuit numbers usually begin with a U. Look for the U number of each of the BIOS chips and write it down on your diagram.

Step 2. After you have made your diagram, remove the chips. A small screwdriver can be used to lift the chips from each end. There are metal covers on the back panel to cover the openings for unused slots. One of these blank covers makes a great tool for lifting out chips. Be careful that you do not get your screwdriver or lifter under the socket itself. There is space under some of the sockets. If you pry up on them it could damage the board or socket. Make sure that your lifter is under the chip only; then lift one end, then the other.

Step 3. Carefully plug in the new BIOS chips. Make sure that you replace the HI or ODD chip and the LO or EVEN chip in its proper socket.

CAUTION! *Make sure that they are oriented properly so that pin one goes into pin one on the board. If you plug it in backwards, it will be destroyed!* If necessary, use a flashlight to check that all of the legs or pins are inserted into the sockets. If one of the pins or legs get bent, remove the chip and use a pair of long-nose pliers to straighten it out.

Step 4. Replace any boards and cables that were removed. Plug in the power cable and turn on the system. If it boots properly, then replace the cover and give yourself a pat on the back for doing a good job.

11

Monitors

No matter what you use your computer for, if you are still sitting in front of a small monochrome monitor, or even a CGA, you definitely need to upgrade. The time spent working on a computer will be primarily spent looking at the monitor, and life is too short not to have a good color monitor to enjoy. (It also helps if you have a good loving person of the opposite sex beside you.) Even if you do nothing but word processing, color makes the job a lot easier and more pleasant.

Of course, what you plan to use your computer for should determine what kind of monitor to buy. Lots of competition among the monitor manufacturers means prices are quite reasonable and they keep coming down.

Because there are so many types of monitors and options, you will have some difficult decisions to make when you buy your system. You will have a very wide choice as to price, resolution, color, size, and shape. If you are buying a starter system for the kids, I have seen fairly good monochrome monitors for as little as $65. I have seen good EGA monitors for less than $300 and super high resolution 19 inch color monitors for $2000 and up to $10,000.

Monitor Basics

I will explain a few of the monitor specifications, terms, and acronyms so that you can make a more informed decision as to which monitor to buy.

In IBM language, a *monitor* is a display device. This is probably a better term, since the word "monitor" is from the Latin which means "to warn." But despite IBM, most people still call it a monitor.

Basically, a monitor is similar to a television set. The face of a TV set or a monitor is the end of a *cathode ray tube* (CRT). They are vacuum tubes and have many of the same elements that made up the old vacuum tubes that were used before the advent of the semiconductor age. The CRTs have a filament that boils off a stream of electrons. These electrons have a potential of about 25,000 volts. They are "shot" from an electron gun toward the front of the CRT where they slam into the phosphor on the back side of the face and cause it to light up. Depending on the type of phosphor used, once the dot is lit up, it continues to glow for a period of time. The electron beam moves rapidly across the screen, but since the phosphor continues to glow for awhile, you see the images that are created.

When you watch a movie, you are seeing a series of still photos, flashed one after the other. Due to the persistence of vision, it appears to be continuous motion. It is because of this same persistence of vision phenomenon that allows you to see motion and images on your television and video screens.

In a magnetic field, a beam of electrons acts very much like a piece of iron. Just like iron, a stream of electrons can be attracted or repelled by the polarity of a magnet. In a CRT, a beam of electrons must pass between a system of electromagnets before it reaches the back side of the CRT face. In a basic system, one electromagnet is on the left, one on the right, one at the top, and one at the bottom. Voltage through the electromagnets can be varied so that the beam of electrons is repulsed by one side and attracted by the other, or pulled to the top or forced to the bottom.

Scan Rates

When you look at the screen of a TV set or a monitor, you see a full screen only because of the persistence of vision and the type of phosphor used on the back of the screen. Actually, the beam of electrons starts at the top left corner of the screen, then under the influence of the electromagnets, it is pulled across to the right-hand top corner. It is then returned to the left-hand side, dropped down one line and swept across again. On a TV set, this is repeated so that 512 lines are written on the screen in about $1/60$ of a second.

The time that it takes to fill a screen with lines from top to bottom is the *vertical scan rate*. Some of the newer multiscan, or multifrequency, monitors can have variable vertical scan rates from $1/40$ up to $1/100$ of a second to paint the screen from top to bottom.

The horizontal scanning frequency of a standard TV set is 15.75 kHz. This is also the frequency used by the CGA systems. The EGA is about 22 kHz, the VGA is 31.5 kHz and up. The higher resolutions require higher frequencies. The multiscan monitors can vary from 15.5 kHz up to 64 kHz or more.

Controlling the Beam

The CRT also has control grids, much like the old vacuum tubes, for controlling the signal. The control grid, along with the electromagnetic system, controls the electron stream somewhat as if it were a pencil. The grid causes the stream to copy the input signal and write it on the screen. As the beam sweeps across the screen, if the input signal is tracing the outline of a figure, the control grid will turn the beam on to light up a dot of phosphor for the light areas. If the input signal is of a dark area, the beam is shut off so that a portion of the screen will be dark for that area of the image.

Resolution

If you look closely at a black-and-white photo in a newspaper, you can see that the photo is made up of small dots, with a lot of dots in the darker areas and fewer in the light areas. The text or image on a monitor or a television screen is also made up of dots very similar to the newspaper photo. You can easily see these dots with a magnifying glass. If you look closely you can see spaces between the dots. This is much like the dots of a dot matrix printer. The more dots and the closer together they are, the better the resolution. A good high-resolution monitor will have solid, sharply defined characters and images.

An ideal resolution would look very much like a high-quality photograph. Because that is not possible at this time, you have to make do with something less than ideal. But with modern technology, you have some very good monitors. But of course, like everything else in life, the better the monitor, the higher the resolution, the higher the quality, the higher the cost.

Pixels

Resolution is also determined by the number of picture elements (*pixels*) that can be displayed. The following figures relate primarily to text, but the graphics resolution will be similar to the text. A standard color graphics monitor (CGA) can display 640 × 200 pixels. It can display 80 characters in one line with 25 lines from top to bottom. If you divide 640 by 80, you find that one character will be 8 pixels wide. There can be 25 lines of characters, so 200/25 = 8 pixels high. The entire screen will have 640 × 200 = 128,000 pixels.

Most monitor adapters have text character generators built onto the board. When you send an A to the screen, the adapter goes to its library and sends the signal for the preformed A to the screen. Each character occupies a cell made up of the number of pixels depending on the resolution of the screen and the adapter. In the case of the CGA, if all the dots within a cell were lit up, there would be a solid block of dots 8 pixels or dots wide and 8 pixels high. When the A is placed in a cell, only the dots necessary to form an outline of an A will be lit up. It is very similar to the dots formed by the dot matrix printers when it prints a character.

A graphics adapter, along with the proper software, allows you to place lines, images, photos, normal and various text fonts, and almost anything you can imagine on the screen.

An enhanced graphics system (EGA) can display 640 × 350, or 640/80 = 8 pixels wide and 350/25 = 14 pixels high. The screen can display 640 × 350 = 224,000 total pixels. Enhanced EGA or VGA can display 640 × 480 = 307,200 total pixels; each character will be 8 pixels wide and 19 pixels high.

The Video Electronics Standards Association, (VESA) has chosen 800 × 600 to be the Super VGA standard which is 800/80 = 10 wide and 600/25 = 24 high.

Resolution on a monitor is quite similar to the resolution of a dot matrix printer. The dots that make up the characters printed by a 9-pin printer in the draft mode will have lots of space between them and will not be very well formed. But a 24-pin printer can squeeze 24 dots into the same amount of space. It can print good solid characters that are near letter quality. It is the same with a monitor; the more dots that can be lit up within a cell, the better the resolution.

Some very high resolution monitors might have 1024 × 768. Monitors used for CAD and other high resolution needs may have 1024 × 1024 or more.

Landscape vs. Portrait

Most monitors are wider than they are tall. These are called landscape styles. Others that are taller than they are wide are called portrait styles. You will find many of this style used for desktop publishing and other special applications.

Monochrome

A monochrome monitor has a single electron beam gun and a single color phosphor. It writes directly on the phosphor and can provide very high resolution for text and graphics. It is even possible to get monochrome analog VGA which can display in as many as 64 different shades. Large monochrome monitors can be ideal for some desktop publishing systems (DTP) and even some computer-aided design (CAD) systems.

Colorgraphics

Color TVs and color monitors are much more complicated than monochrome systems. During the manufacture of the color monitors, three different phosphors, red, green, and blue, are deposited on the back of the screen. Usually a very small dot of each color is placed in a triangular shape. They have three electron beam guns, one for each color. By lighting up the three different colored phosphors selectively, all the colors of the rainbow can be generated.

The guns are called red, blue, and green (RGB), but the electrons they emit are all the same. They are called RGB because each gun is aimed so that it hits a red, a green, or blue color. They are very accurately aimed so that they will converge or impinge only on their assigned color.

Dot Pitch

To make sure that the guns hit their own color only, a metal shadow mask with very tiny holes is laid over the deposited phosphors. The more holes in the shadow mask, and the closer together the color dots of phosphor, the higher the possible resolution of a monitor.

The distance between the holes or perforations in the shadow mask is called the *dot pitch*. The dots per inch determines the resolution. A high-resolution monitor might have a dot pitch of .31 millimeter (1 mm = .0394 inches; .31 mm = .0122 inches, or about the thickness of an average business card). A typical medium-resolution monitor might have a dot pitch of .39 mm. One with very high resolution might have a dot pitch of .26 mm or even less.

Adapter Basics

It won't do you much good to buy a high-resolution monitor unless you buy a good adapter to drive it. You can't just plug a monitor into your computer and expect it to function. Just as a hard disk needs a controller, a monitor needs an adapter to interface with the computer. Also like the hard disk manufacturers, most of the monitor manufacturers do not make adapter boards. Just as a hard disk can operate with several different types of controllers, most monitors can operate with several different types of adapters.

The original IBM PC came with a green monochrome monitor with a *monochrome display adapter* (MDA) that could display text only. If you are still using one of these cards, then you are severely limited. The Hercules Company immediately saw the folly of this limitation so they developed the *Hercules monographic adapter* (HMGA) and set a new standard. It wasn't long before a lot of companies were selling similar MGA cards. This adapter provides a high resolution of 720 × 350 on monochrome monitors.

IBM then introduced their color monitor and color graphics adapter (CGA). It provides only 640 × 200 resolution. The CGA allows a mix of the red, green, and blue to make 8 colors. It then allows two different intensities, bright or dim, for each of those colors so that the CGA has a limit of 16 colors. The CGA monitors have very large spaces between the pixels so that the resolution and color is terrible. It is similar to the 9-pin dot matrix printer.

An enhanced graphics adapter (EGA) can drive a high-resolution monitor to display 640 × 350 resolution. The EGA allows each of the primary colors to be mixed together in any of 4 different intensities. So there are 4^3 or 64 different colors that they can display.

The EGA boards are downward compatible so that they will also display older programs that were developed for the CGA or MGA. A couple of years ago, EGA boards cost from $400 to $600. I have seen no-name EGA boards today for less than $100.

Low-Cost EGA

Just a couple of years ago, EGA monitors cost from $600 up to $800. Adapters cost from $300 to $500. I have recently seen some fairly good monitors selling today for as little as $250 and EGA boards for less than $100. You can buy a system that might have cost $1000 a couple of years ago for about $350 today.

Analog vs. Digital

IBM introduced a new analog video graphics array (VGA) display system with its PS/2 systems. It has become the new standard.

Up until the introduction of the PS/2, most displays used a digital system, but the digital system has some limitations. A CGA system can only display 4 colors at any one time out of a palette of 16; the EGA can display up to 16 out of a palette of 64; the VGA can display up to 256 colors out of a palette of 262,144. The EGA has a resolution of 640 × 350; the VGA has a resolution of 640 × 480.

Both the EGA and VGA are downward compatible and can run any of the older software programs. However most of the older programs will not be able to take full advantage of the higher resolution unless special software drivers are supplied by the vendors.

The digital signals are discrete, either fully on or completely off. The signals for color and intensity require separate lines in the cables. The analog signals that drive the color guns are voltages that are continuously variable. It takes only a few wires in the cable to carry a very large number of colors, hues, and intensities as a variable voltage.

Enhanced EGA, or Super EGA, boards have been developed that can produce resolutions of 640 × 480 on an appropriate digital monitor, the same as the analog systems. But even with the higher resolution, the digital systems are still limited to 16 colors out of a palette of 64. At this time these boards are selling for $395 and up to $600 each.

Several manufacturers have developed compatible VGA monitors and boards that are equivalent to the IBM system. Many of the multiscan monitors can accept both digital TTL (transistor-to-transistor logic), RGB (red, green, and blue), or analog signals. Of course, they must have an appropriate adapter to drive them. Some adapters can output both types of signals.

Boards have been developed for both 8-bit and 16-bit systems. See Figs. 11-1 and 11-2. This means that even the 8-bit PC and XT systems can take advantage of the latest in the wonderful world of color.

The VGA introduced by IBM was not a multiscan monitor. Many VGAs operate at a fixed frequency. They might not be quite as versatile or flexible as the multiscan in some instances, but the resolution can be every bit as good as the multiscan.

Most of the multiscan monitors can handle both analog and digital signals. The multiscan monitors may sell for as little as $300 and up to as

Fig. 11-1. An 8-bit adapter card. (Courtesy Genoa Corp.)

Fig. 11-2. A 16-bit adapter card. (Courtesy Genoa Corp.)

much as $3199 for the NEC 19 inch MultiSync XL. The VGA boards are selling for about the same price as the Enhanced or Super EGAs, $395 up to $700.

An analog VGA monitor requires less circuitry and can be manufactured for less cost. And because the VGA boards offer so much more for the same cost as the Enhanced or Super EGAs, I expect that this market will dry up. It is sad news for the developers, but good news for us consumers. Eventually, you will be able to buy the Super EGAs for about what the EGAs are selling for now, less than $100.

The new standard is the VGA at 800 × 600. Most of the new boards are downward compatible and can run software written for MGA, CGA, or EGA. The MGA, CGA, and EGA will be around for quite a while on low-end inexpensive type systems. Depending on what you want to do with your computer and how much you want to spend, they might be all you need.

What You Should Buy

The primary determining factor for choosing a monitor should be what it is going to be used for and the amount of money you have to spend. If money is no object, buy a large 19-inch analog monitor with super-high resolution and a good VGA board to drive it for about $3000.

But for many applications, a low-cost EGA board and a 13-inch EGA monitor, both for about $350, will be more than sufficient.

If you expect to do any kind of graphics or CAD/CAM design work, you will definitely need a good large screen color monitor with very high resolution. A large screen is almost essential for some types of design drawings so that as much of the drawing as possible can be viewed on the screen. You will also need a high-resolution monitor for close tolerance designs.

For desktop publishing, some very high-resolution monochrome monitors have been developed. Many of these monitors are the portrait type and are higher than they are wide. Many of them have a display area of $8^1/2$ by 11 inches. Instead of 25 lines, they will have 66 lines, which is the standard for an 11-inch sheet of paper. They also have a phosphor that will let you have black text on a white background so that the screen looks very much like the finished text. Many of these monitors are WYSIWYG, or "What You See Is What You Get." Many of the newer color monitors have a mode that will let you switch to pure white with black type.

For accounting and spreadsheets or for word processing, a monochrome monitor would probably be sufficient, but not nearly as pleasant as with color.

What To Look For

If at all possible, go to a computer show and look at the various types of monitors available. At a large show, you can usually find several vendors who are demonstrating the monitors in booths, sometimes side-by-side.

My first choice would be to look for an analog monitor, or a good multiscan that could accept both digital and analog signals.

If possible, go to several stores and compare various models. Turn the brightness up and check the center of the screen and the outer edges. Is the intensity the same in the center and the outer edges? Check the focus, brightness, and contrast with text and graphics. There can be vast differences even in the same models from the same manufacturer. I have seen monitors that displayed demonstration graphics programs beautifully, but were not worth anything when displaying text in various colors.

Ask the vendor for a copy of the specs. Check the dot pitch. For good high resolution it should be .31 mm or less.

Check the horizontal and vertical frequency specs. Here is a brief chart:

Adapter	Resolution	Horiz. freq.	Vert. freq.
MGA/CGA	640 × 200	15.75 kHz	60 Hz
EGA	640 × 350	21.9 kHz	60 Hz
VGA	640 × 480	31.5 kHz	60 Hz
SUPER VGA	800 × 600	35 kHz	60 Hz

Bandwidth

The *bandwidth* of a monitor is the range of frequencies that its circuits can handle. A multiscan monitor can accept horizontal frequencies from 15.75 kHz up to about 40 kHz and vertical frequencies from 40 Hz up to about 75 Hz. To get a rough estimate of the bandwidth required, multiply the resolution pixels times the vertical scan or frame rate. For instance, a VGA monitor should have $640 × 350 × 60 = 13.44$ MHz. But the systems require a certain amount of overhead, such as *retrace*, the time needed to move back to the left side of the screen, drop it down one line and start a new line. So the bandwidth should be about 15 MHz for a VGA. For a Super VGA of $800 × 600 × 60$, the bandwidth should be at least 30 MHz.

Drivers

Most of the new software being developed today has built-in hooks that will allow it to take advantage of the new EGA and VGA goodies.

Because the older software programs were written before EGA and VGA was developed, many of them cannot take advantage of the higher resolution and extended graphics without special software drivers to the older programs to utilize the advantages of the new adapters.

Vendors have written drivers for older programs such as Windows, Lotus, AutoCAD, GEM, Ventura, WordStar and others. Some vendors supply as many as two or three disks full of drivers. Some vendors, such as IBM and Compaq, don't supply any at all with their VGA boards.

Depending on what software you intend to use, the drivers supplied with the adapter you purchase should be an important consideration.

Screen Size

The stated screen size is very misleading and almost fraudulent. The size is supposed to be a diagonal measurement. But on my NEC 14-inch Multisync, it only measures about 13 inches. I suppose it would measure

14 inches if I took it out of the case and measured the face of the bottle. There is also a border on all four sides of the screen. The usable area that I have is about 10 inches wide and about $7^1/2$ inches high on this 14-inch monitor. This is plenty big enough for most of the things that I do. But for some types of CAD work or desktop publishing, it would be helpful to have a bigger screen.

Again the size monitor that you should buy depends on what you want to do with your computer and how much money you want to spend.

Controls

You might also check for available controls to adjust the brightness, contrast, and vertical/horizontal lines. Some manufacturers place them on the back or some other difficult area to get at. It is much better if they are accessible from the front so that you can see what the effect is as you adjust them.

Glare

If a monitor reflects too much light, it can be like a mirror and be very distracting. Some manufacturers have coated the screen with a silicon formulation to cut down on the reflectance. Some have etched the screen for the same purpose. Some screens are tinted to help cut down on glare. If possible, you should try the monitor under various lighting conditions.

If you have a glare problem, several supply companies and mail order houses offer glare shields that cost from $20 up to $100.

Zenith has developed a flat screen monitor that has very good resolution and little glare, but it is rather expensive at near $1000.

Cleaning the Screens

Because about 25,000 volts of electricity hit the back side of the monitor face, it creates a static attraction for dust. This can distort and make the screen difficult to read.

Most manufacturers should have an instruction booklet that suggests how the screen should be cleaned. You should not use any harsh cleansers on it, especially if you have a screen that has been coated with silicon to reduce glare. In most cases, plain water and a soft paper towel will do fine.

VDT Radiation

The National Institute of Occupational Safety and Health contends that there is no scientific evidence that radiation from a video terminal or monitor is dangerous. Scientists say that the radiation is so low that it is difficult to measure it.

However, many people are still concerned. Several supply and mail order houses are playing on the fears of those people and are offering shields that fit on the screens of monitors. The vendors claim that these screens block 99 percent of the radiation. Because there is almost none there to begin with, it is difficult to prove them wrong. Most of these screens also reduce any glare, which is about the only reason a person should buy one. They cost from $150 up to $200.

A health problem that is probably more important than VDT radiation is eyestrain, headache, and backache. Most of these problems could be due to not having the proper furniture. Problems can also be caused by poor posture or poor work habits.

Computer Furniture

If you have just bought a new computer you might not have a room for it, and you might not have any computer furniture for it. So sooner or later, your spouse is going to insist that you take it off the dining room table and move it to some other place.

If you spend a lot of time at your computer, it could be well worth the money to invest in a good desk, chair, and lighting.

If you don't have a lot of money and are not too proud, you might do what I did. I went to a used office furniture store and bought a very good used desk, chair, and filing cabinet for $125.

Tilt and Swivel Base

Most people set their monitor on top of the computer. If you are short or tall, have a low or high chair, or a nonstandard desk, the monitor might not be at eye level. A tilt and swivel base can allow you to position the monitor to best suit you. Many monitors now come with this base. If yours does not have one, many specialty stores and mail order houses sell them for $15 to $40.

Several supply and mail order houses also offer an adjustable arm that clamps to the desk. Most have a small platform for the monitor to sit on. The arm can swing up and down and from side to side; It can free up a lot of desk space. They can cost from $50 up to $150.

Monitor and Adapter Sources

NOTE: I have only bought a half dozen monitors in my lifetime, so I have not personally had a chance to evaluate the following products. However, I subscribe to *Computer Shopper, PC Magazine, PC Week, Byte, Personal Computing, InfoWorld, PC World,* and several others. Most of these magazines have test labs and do extensive reviews of products. Because I can't personally test all of these products, I rely heavily on their reviews.

I can't possibly list all of the vendors. I suggest that you subscribe to the magazines listed on the following page and in Chapter 17. Check the reviews and advertisements for other vendors.

Note that the prices below are list prices. In many cases, the products can actually be purchased for less. Besides, in this volatile market, the prices change almost daily. Call first, even if ordering from a magazine ad.

Multiscan Monitors (13 inch, unless noted)

CTX Model 1435 (14 inch) $435
CTX International
260 Paseo Tesoro
Walnut, CA 91789
(714) 595-6146

Conrac Model 7250 (19 inch) $2995
Conrac Corp.
1724 South Mountain Ave.
Duarte, CA 91010
(818) 303-0095

Intecolor MegaTrend/2 (19 inch) $1995
Intecolor
225 Scientific Dr.
Norcross, GA 30092
(404) 449-5961

Logitech Autosync TE5155 $699
Logitech Inc.
6505 Kaiser Dr.
Fremont, CA 94555
(425) 795-8500

Magnavox Multimode Model 8CM873 $899
Magnavox
P.O. Box 14810
Knoxville, TN 37914
(615) 521-4316

Microvitec Model 1019 (19 inch) $2195
Microvitec Inc.
1943 Providence Ct.
Airport Perimeter Business Center
College Park, GA 30337
(404) 991-2246

Nanao Flexscan 8060S $919
Nanao USA Corp.
23510 Telo Ave., Suite 5
Torrance, CA 90505
(213) 325-5202

NEC MultiSync Plus (14 inch) $1395
NEC MultiSync XL (19 inch) $3195
NEC Home Electronics
1255 Michael Dr.
Wood Dale, IL 60191
(312) 860-9500

Princeton Ultrasync $795
Princeton Graphics Systems
601 Ewing St., Bldg. A
Princeton, NJ 08540
(609) 683-1660

Taxan Multivision 770 Plus $915
Taxan USA Corp.
18005 Cortney Ct.
City of Industry, CA 91748
(818) 810-1291

Thompson Ultrascan 4375M (14 inch) $895
Thompson Consumer Products
5731 West Slauson Ave. Suite 111
Culver City, CA 90230
(800) 325-0464

Zenith ZCM-1490 (14 inch) $999
Zenith Data Systems
100 Milwaukee Ave.
Glenview, IL 60025
(312) 699-4839

Enhanced EGA Adapter Boards

American Mitac SEGA $199
American Mitac Corp.
410 East Plumeria Dr.
San Jose, CA 95134
(408) 432-1160

Boca Research MultiEGA $299
Boca Research
6401 Congress Ave.
Boca Raton, FL 22487
(305) 997-6227

Genoa Systems SuperEGA $489
Genoa Systems
73 East Trimble Rd.
San Jose, CA 95131
(408) 432-9090

IGC EGAcard $450
Intelligent Graphics Corp.
4800 Great America Pkwy. Suite 200
Santa Clara, CA 95054
(408) 986-8373

NSI Smart EGA $499
NSI Logic
Cedar Hill Business Park
257B Cedar Hill Rd.
Marlborough, MA 01752
(617) 460-0717

Paradise Autoswitch $349
Paradise Systems
99 South Hill Dr.
Brisbane, CA 94005
(415) 468-7300

Quadram ProSync! $395
Quadram
One Quad Way
Norcross, GA 30093
(404) 923-6666

SMT Pro-EGA $249
SMT Corp.
1145 Linda Vista Dr.
San Marcos, CA 92069
(619) 744-3590

Tecmar EGA Master $595
Tecmar Corp.
6225 Cochran Rd.
Cleveland, OH 44139
(216) 349-0600

Tseng EVA 480 $595
Tseng Labs
10 Pheasant Run
Newtown, PA 18940
(215) 968-0502

VGA Adapter Boards
NOTE: Most VGA adapters have 256K of DRAM memory on board. Many have provisions for adding an additional 256K. Also note that prices listed are list prices. The "street price" or discount price will be considerably less.

ATI VIP VGA $449
ATI Technologies
3761 Victoria Park Ave.
Toronto, Ontario
Canada M1W 3S2
(416) 756-0711

SigmaVGA $499
Sigma Designs
46501 Landing Pkwy.
Fremont, CA 94538
(415) 770-0100

STB VGA Extra $395
STB Systems Inc.
1651 North Glenville
Richardson, TX 75081
(214) 234-8750

Tatung Platinum Card $445
Tatung Co. of America
2850 El Presidio Dr.
Long Beach, CA 90810
(213) 979-7055

VEGA VGA $499
Video Seven
46355 Landing Pkwy.
Fremont, CA 94538
(415) 656-7800

Vision Master VGA $499
Computer Peripherals
667 Rancho Conejo Blvd.
Newbury Park, CA 91320
(800) 854-7600

Zenith Z449 $499
Zenith Data Systems
100 Milwaukee Ave.
Glenview, IL 60025
(312) 699-4839

12

Input Devices

Before you can do anything with a computer, you must input data to it. You can input data from a disk, by modem, by a mouse, by scanner, by fax, or on-line from a mainframe or a network, but by far the most common way to get data into the computer is by way of the keyboard. For most common applications, it is impossible to operate the computer without a keyboard.

The Keyboard

The keyboard is a very important part of your system. If you do a lot of typing, it is very important that you get a keyboard that suits you. I have a very heavy hand. I bought a computer once that had a keyboard with very soft keys. If I just barely touched a key, it would take off. I finally gave up. I took the keyboard to a swap meet and sold it for about half of what it cost me. I then went around to all the booths at the show and tried several keyboards until I found one that had a good tactile feel.

Special Key Functions

Here is a brief summary of the functions of several of the symbol keys on the keyboard. Many of them have two or more functions.

* The asterisk is used as the multiplication symbol; it is also used as a wildcard in DOS. For instance, if you want a listing of all the programs that have a .COM extension such as COMMAND.COM you could type in DIR *.COM.

\ The backslash is used by DOS to denote a subdirectory. To change from one subdirectory to another you must type CD\ then the directory name. If no name is given, you will be returned to the root directory. The backslash should not be confused with the slash. If you use the slash where the backslash should be used, you will get an error message, or if it is part of a program, the program will not work.

/ The slash is also called the *virgule* and the *solidus*. In calculations it
is used as the division symbol.

   < Means less than.

   > Means greater than.

   ^ The caret is the symbol for exponents.

   + − = Plus, minus, and equal do those normal functions.

Function Keys

The 12 *function* keys are multi-purpose keys. What they do is usually
dependent on the software you are using at the time. Many software programs use the function keys to accomplish a goal with a minimum of
keystrokes. Often the function of the keys will be displayed somewhere
on the screen.

Certain functions are available from DOS:

F1—If you have entered a DOS command, pressing F1 will redisplay
the command a character by character each time the key is pressed.

F2—If you have entered a DOS command and you want to change
part of it, you can enter a letter of the command and all of the command up to that letter will be displayed. You can then change the
command from that point onward. This can save a few keystrokes.

F3—Will redisplay the entire command that was previously entered.
For instance, you can enter the command COPY A: B: and when it
has finished, if you want to make a second copy, just press F3 and
the command will come up again. All you have to do then is press
Enter.

F4—If a command has been entered and you want to reuse the last
portion of it, just press a letter of the command and the portion
from that letter to the end of the command will be displayed.

The arrow keys move the cursor one line up or down and one character right or left. The Page Down and Page Up will move a whole page up
or down. The Home key will send the cursor to the top left corner of the
screen. The End key will send it to the end of the current line.

With the Ins (Insert) key on, it will push the characters to the right
and insert anything typed. With Insert off, anything typed will overwrite
other characters that happen to be on the same line.

The 84-Key and the 101-Key Keyboards

Typewriter keyboards are fairly standard. With only 26 letters in the
alphabet and a few symbols, most QWERTY typewriters have about 50
keys. But the several computers I have had over the last few years have
each had a different keyboard. The main typewriter characters aren't
changed or moved very often, but some of the very important control
keys like the Esc, the Ctrl, the Prtsc, the \ , the function keys, and several others are moved all over the computer keyboard.

Very few of the early CP/M machines had identical keyboards. But IBM came along and established a layout that everyone thought would be a standard. It was an excellent keyboard, built like a Sherman tank and had a very good tactile feel. There were some minor gripes because it did not indicate whether you were in the Caps or Num Lock mode. It also had a small Return key. But the clone makers soon fixed that by adding LEDs to indicate when the Caps and Num Locks were on and a larger Return key.

About a year later, IBM came out with a keyboard that also had LED indicators and a large Return or Enter key, but for some unknown reason, they rearranged and moved several of the very important keys. The Esc, the \, Prtsc, and several others were moved. These are very important keys and are used constantly. I have not been able to find anyone who can give me any reason why they were moved.

Just when I thought for sure that the 84-key keyboard would be the standard, IBM released their new PS/2 line with a new keyboard layout with 101 keys.

The lower keyboard in Fig. 12-1 has 84 keys. The upper keyboard has 17 extra keys for a total of 101. Except for F11, F12, and Pause, the other 14 extra keys are duplicates of keys that were already on the keyboard. They separated the numeric key pad with four keys with the Up, Down, Right and Left arrow keys that perform the same function as those arrows on the numeric keypad. They also installed six separate keys above the arrow keys for Insert, Home, Page Up, Delete, End, and Page

Fig. 12-1. Comparison of an 84-key keyboard and a 101-key.

Down. Again, these keys perform the same function as those on the numeric key pad. They also added an extra Enter on the numeric key pad. And they now have Ctrl and Alt keys in line with, and on each end of, the shortened spacebar.

A lot of people and many large companies use their computers for spreadsheet and accounting programs that require intensive numeric input. The separate numeric keypad makes the entry of data and numbers much easier which can increase productivity.

The original IBM keyboard had the very important and often used Esc key just to the left of the 1 key in the numeric row. The 84-key keyboard moved the Esc key over to the top row of the key pad. The tilde (~) and grave (`) key was moved to the original Esc position to the left side of the 1. The new 101-key keyboard moves the Esc back to its original position.

Another very important and often used key is the Control or Ctrl key. The 101-key keyboard added an extra Ctrl key. I don't mind having an extra Ctrl key, but they moved it from its original position alongside the A down to where the Alt key was on the 84-key keyboard. They put the other Ctrl key in the position that the Caps Lock occupied on the 84-key keyboard and moved the Caps Lock over to where the Ctrl key had been for years. This is quite frustrating for WordStar users because the Ctrl key is one of those most often used.

Also, IBM decided to move the function keys to the top of the keyboard above the numeric keys. Many people have bought programs like Framework, WordStar, WordPerfect, and others that use the function keys intensively. Anyone who buys a copy of those programs gets a cutout plastic overlay that describes the uses of the function keys. These overlays are great for learning and even a novice can become productive in a short time. These overlays will not fit on the 101-key keyboards.

The 101-key keyboards are 20 inches long and take up about 30 percent more desk space than the 18-inch 84-key keyboards. If you have a large desk, that might not be important. One of my desks has a section in the middle that is lower than the rest of the desk. This makes the keyboard just the right height for comfortable typing. It is great with an 84-key keyboard, but there is just not enough room for a 101-key keyboard in this space.

Several companies have taken note of the complaints about wasted desk space and are producing a 101-key keyboard that is the same size as the 84 key. They have also recognized that some of the layout changes can mean relearning a keyboard, so many of them also offer an option to change the Ctrl key back to where it should be, by the A.

I would not buy a keyboard that did not have a good tactile feel and had an option to change the Ctrl key to where it should be. I would suggest that you go to a store, or better yet to a swap meet, and try out several keyboards before you buy one.

Model Switch

I should note that the PC, XT, AT, 80286, 80386, and the PS/2 keyboards all have the same connectors. Any keyboard will plug into any one of those machines, but the PC and XT keyboards have different electronics and scan frequencies. An older PC or XT keyboard can be plugged into an 80286 or 80386 machine, but they will not operate. Most of the clone makers now install a small switch beneath their keyboards that allows them to be switched so that they can be used on a PC or XT or on the 80286 or 80386. Some of the newer keyboards sense the type of computer and automatically switch.

Prices

The brand-name manufacturers will charge from $80 to $150 for their keyboards. But there are hundreds of clone makers who offer keyboards that I believe are just as good for $36 to $90. If at all possible, try them out and compare. If you are buying a system through the mails, ask about the keyboard options.

You might have an older system, or even a new system, with a keyboard that doesn't suit you. You might become frustrated and make errors that slow you down. If that is your case, you should explore the possibility of upgrading to one that suits you. It might not cost more than $40. If you are having problems, it can be worth much more than that in time saved.

Specialized Keyboards

Several companies have developed specialized keyboards. I have listed only a few of them below.

Quite often I have the need to do some minor calculations. One keyboard that is available from the Shamrock Company, (800) 722-2898, has a built-in solar powered calculator where the number pad is located. It has the option to switch the Ctrl and Caps Lock keys and has tactile keys.

The STI Company offers the Chicony 5581 keyboard with a trackball built into the right-hand area of the keyboard. (I discuss trackballs later.) This gives a person the mouse benefits and capabilities without using up any desk real estate. The trackball is compatible with the standard Microsoft and Mouse Systems. The advertised price for the keyboard/trackball system is $105 (a real bargain when you consider that a stand-alone trackball might cost about $100).

The CAD & Graphics Company of San Francisco at (800) 288-1611 offers a slightly different keyboard/trackball for $129.

Just as IBM set the standard for the PC, Key Tronic in Spokane at (509) 928-8000 has been the leader in keyboard design. Most of the clone keyboards are copied from the Key Tronic designs. Besides the standard keyboards, they have developed a large number of specialized ones. One has a bar code reader attached to it which could be extremely handy if you have a small business that uses bar codes.

Sources. There are so many manufacturers that I am not going to list the sources. Look in any of the computer magazines listed in Chapter 17. You will see many ads for all types of keyboards.

Mouse Systems

One of the biggest reasons for the success of the Macintosh is that it is easy to use. With a mouse and icons all you have to do is point and click. You don't have to learn a lot of commands and rules. A person who knows nothing about computers can become productive in a very short time.

The people in the DOS world finally took note of this, and began developing similar programs and applications for the IBM and compatibles. Dozens of companies now manufacture mouses (or is it mice?). Many software programs can be used without a mouse, but operate much faster and better with a mouse. Some of the programs are Windows, CAD programs, some paint and graphics programs, and many others.

One of the problems for mouse systems is that there are no standards for software or for mouse operating systems. You can't just plug in a mouse and start using it. The software, whether Windows, WordStar or a CAD program, must recognize and interface with the mouse.

Most mouse companies develop software drivers that allow the mouse to operate with various programs. The drivers are usually supplied on a disk. Ordinarily they are installed in the CONFIG.SYS file of a system. The Microsoft Mouse is the closest to a standard, so most other companies emulate the Microsoft driver.

Mechanical vs. Optical

There is also no standardization of the types of mouses. Some use optics with a LED that shines on a reflective grid. As the mouse is moved across the grid the reflected light is picked up by a detector and sent to the computer to move the cursor.

For a design that demands very close tolerances, the spacings of the grid for an optical mouse might not provide sufficient resolution. You might be better off in this case with a mouse that utilizes a ball that provides a smooth and continuous movement of the cursor. You don't need a grid for the ball-type mouses, but you do need about a square foot of clear desk space to move the mouse about. The ball picks up dirt so it should be cleaned often.

Some of the less expensive mouses have a resolution capability of only 100 to 200 dots per inch (DPI). Logitech has developed a HiREZ mouse that has a resolution of 320 DPI.

Number of Buttons

The Macintosh mouse has only one button; that doesn't give you much choice except to point and click. Almost all of the PC mouses have at least two buttons which gives the user three choices: click the left button, click the right button, or click both buttons at the same time. Some of the mouses have three control buttons. With three buttons the user has a possible seven choices: click left, click middle, click right, click left and middle, click middle and right, click left and right, or click all three. Despite all these choices, most software requires that only two of them be used, one at a time.

Interfaces

Most of the mouses require a voltage. Some come with a small plug-in transformer that should be plugged into your power strip.

Some of the mouses require the use of one of your serial ports for their input to the computer. This might cause a problem if you already have a serial printer using COM1 and a modem on COM2. Some of the motherboards have ports built into the board so that you don't have to use a slot and install a board for a port. But you will still need a cable from the on-board COM ports to the outside world.

Microsoft, Logitech, and several other mouse companies have developed a bus mouse. It interfaces directly with the bus and does not require the use of one of your COM ports. However, the systems come with a board that requires the use of one of your slots.

I have an IMSI mouse that plugs into the keyboard connector. It has a straight-through connector so that the keyboard is then plugged into the mouse connector. This means that you do not have to install a bus board in one of your slots or use one of your COM ports.

Cost

It is difficult to quote prices because most of them change frequently. Besides, the prices quoted in most instances are list prices. Except for products from the very large companies, you can usually get an item at much less than the list price.

Another difficulty with the cost of the mouses is that some companies include options of software packages and other goodies with their products.

Another problem is that not all mouses are created equal. Some have a resolution of only 100 dots. The better ones have a resolution of 200 and up to 350 dots. The higher resolution is necessary for some CAD and critical design work that requires close tolerances.

I have seen some mouse systems advertised for as little as $30. These would probably be perfectly all right for point and click type work with icons. Of course the higher-resolution systems are going to cost more, from $80 up to $300. It is best to call the companies for their latest price list and spec sheets.

Sources. These are only a very few of the companies that manufacture mouse systems. Again, check the ads in the computer magazines listed in Chapter 17.

IMSI Economouse	(415) 454-7101
Logitech Inc.	(415) 795-8500
Microsoft Mouse	(206) 882-8088
Mouse Systems Corp.	(408) 988-0211
Numonics Cordless Mouse	(800) 654-5449
Summagraphics Corp.	(203) 384-1344

Trackballs

Trackballs usually do not require as much desk space as the ordinary mouse. If your desk is as cluttered as mine, then you need a trackball.

The Honeywell Disc Instruments Company has developed a couple of trackball cursor devices that look much like the ball on some of the video games. The MicroLYNX trackball has a connector that plugs in series with your keyboard connector. This device derives its needed voltage from the same line that feeds your keyboard. The ComLYNX is an identical trackball except that it plugs into a serial port. They both have three buttons and come with a pop-up menu software program and several drivers. They are integral units $8^1/2 \times 3$ inches. Cost is $169 for either one.

Fulcrum Computers has also developed a trackball that has six buttons. The six buttons can be used for certain emulations and control. The Fulcrum is unlike the LYNX in that it uses an optical system; it is a serial device that must be plugged into a port. The cost is $95.

The MicroSpeed Fasttrap trackball is available in serial or bus versions. It is compatible with Microsoft Mouse programs and comes with several drivers. The serial version is $99, the bus $119.

Another device that is somewhat similar in operation to the trackballs is the Felix PC200. It is $5^1/2$ inches square with a single slide button. It is a serial device and must be plugged into a serial port. It also must have power from a small five volt plug in transformer. The cost is $199.

Sources. Here are the phone numbers of the companies I mentioned:

Felix PC200	(415) 653-8500
Fulcrum Computer	(707) 433-0202
Honeywell LYNX	(800) 224-3522
MicroSpeed PC-Trac	(415) 490-1403

Digitizers and Graphics Tablets

Graphics tablets and digitizers are similar to a flat drawing pad or drafting table. Most of them use some sort of pointing device that can translate movement into digitized output to the computer. Some are rather small, some may be as large as a standard drafting table. Some might cost as little as $150 up to over $1500.

Some of the tablets have programmable overlays and function keys. Some will work with mouse-like devices, a pen light or a pencil-like stylus. The tablets can be used for designing circuits, for CAD programs, for graphics designs, freehand drawing, and even for text and data input. The most common use is with CAD-type software.

Most of the tablets are serial devices, but some of them require their own interface board. Many of them are compatible with the Microsoft and Mouse systems.

Sources. Check the ads in the magazines listed in Chapter 17 for additional vendors.

CalComp	(714) 821-2142
Genius	(800) 288-1611
GTCO Corp.	(301) 381-6688
Koala Pad	(408) 438-0946
Kurta Corp.	(602) 276-5533
Pencept Inc.	(617) 893-6390
Summagraphics Corp.	(203) 384-1344

Scanners and Optical Character Readers

Most large companies have mountains of memos, manuals, documents and files that must be maintained, revised, and updated periodically. If a manual or document is in a loose-leaf form, then only those pages that have changed will need to be retyped. But quite often a whole manual or document will have to be retyped and reissued.

Several companies now manufacture optical character readers (OCR) that can scan a line of printed type, recognize each character and input that character into a computer just as if it were typed in from a keyboard. Once the data is in the computer, a word processor can be used to revise or change the data, then print it out again.

Or the data can be entered into a computer and stored on floppies or a hard disk. If it is a huge amount of data it could be stored on a Write-Once Read-Many (WORM) optical disk or on a CD-ROM so that it takes less space to store.

If copies of the printed matter are also stored in a computer they can be searched very quickly for any item. Many times I have spent hours going through printed manuals looking for certain items. If the data had been in a computer, I could have found the information in just minutes.

Optical character readers have been around for several years. When they first came out they cost from $6,000 to more than $15,000. They were very limited in the character fonts that they could recognize and were not able to handle graphics at all. Vast improvements have been made in the last few years. Many are now fairly inexpensive, starting at about $900. Some handheld ones that are very limited might be as low as $200, but some very sophisticated commercial models such as the Palantir and Kurzweil can cost as much as $40,000. The more expensive models usually have the ability to recognize a large number of fonts and graphics.

Sources. The Houston Instruments Company specializes in manufacturing plotters. They have developed a scanning head for one of their plotters that can scan a large drawing, digitize the lines and symbols, then input them to a computer. The drawing can then be changed and replotted very easily. Other companies are also listed below:

AST Research	(714) 863-1480	
Canon U.S.A.	(516) 488-6800	
CompuScan	(201) 575-0500	
Datacopy Corp.	(415) 965-7900	
DFI Handy Scanner	(800) 722-2898	(800) 538-5000
GeniScan GS-4000	(800) 344-2370	(800) 288-1611
Houston Instrument	(512) 835-0900	
Howtek	(603) 882-5200	
Microtek Lab	(213) 321-2121	
Saba	(800) 654-5274	
Scanman	(800) 288-1611	
Shape	(800) 247-1724	
Transimage 1000	(408) 733-4111	

Bar Codes

Bar codes are a system of black and white lines that are arranged in a system much like the Morse code of dots and dashes. By using combinations of wide and narrow bars and wide and narrow spaces, any numeral or letter of the alphabet can be represented.

Bar codes were first adopted by the grocery industry. They set up a central office that assigned a unique number, a Universal Product Code (UPC) for just about every manufactured and prepackaged product sold in a grocery store. Different sizes of the same product have a different and unique number assigned to them. The same type products from different manufacturers will also have different and unique assigned numbers. Most large grocery stores nowadays sell everything from automobile parts and accessories to books and medicines. Each item has its own unique bar code number.

When the clerk runs an item across the scanner, the dark bars absorb light and the white bars reflect the light. The scanner decodes this number and sends it to the main computer. The computer then matches the input number to the unique number stored on its hard disk which has the price of the item, the description, the amount in inventory, and several other pieces of information about the item. The computer sends back the price and the description of the part to the cash register where it is printed out. The computer then deducts that item from the overall inventory and adds the price to the overall cash received for the day.

At the end of the day, the manager can look at the computer output and know exactly such things like how much business was done, what inventories need to be replenished, and what items were the biggest sellers. With the push of a button on the computer, the manager can change any or all of the prices of the items in the store.

In the middle 1970s the Department of Defense (DOD) started looking for a better way of keeping track of its huge inventories of military items. They set up a committee and in 1982 they decreed that all military materials sold to the government would have a bar code label on it. Many of the suppliers screamed and cried because it added to their cost, but it was passed on to the government, so it wasn't too much of a burden.

It wasn't long before many of the people who had complained about having to use the bar codes found that they could make good use of them in many other ways to increase productivity, keep track of their inventory, and other benefits. Very few businesses, large or small, cannot benefit from the use of bar codes.

There are several different types of bar code readers or scanners. Some are actually small portable computers that can store data, then be downloaded into a PC, XT, 286, or 386. Some systems have their own interface card which must be plugged into one of your slots. Some companies have devised systems that can be inserted in series with the keyboard so that no slot or other interface is needed. Key Tronic has a keyboard with a bar code reader as an integral part of the keyboard.

Printers

Special printers have been designed for printing some types of bar codes. For many applications, they can be printed on dot matrix and laser printers. Several companies specialize in printing up labels to your specifications.

A Typical Application

A videotape rental store has put bar code labels on all of their tapes. When a customer rents a tape, they get the customer's name, address, phone number, and credit references. They type this information into their computer, then use it to make a small bar code label for that customer. The small label can be taped to a credit card and the next time the customer comes in, the bar code labels on the tapes that have been chosen are scanned, then the customer's label is scanned. The whole check out transaction takes only a few seconds. I have seen some stores with long lines of people waiting even though there have been two or three clerks writing down all of the information by hand.

Many hospitals, pharmacies, and blood banks are now using bar codes. This is an area where accuracy can mean life or death. Bar codes can be very accurate.

Several companies make Point of Sale (POS) systems that have a bar code reader, a computer, and a cash drawer all integrated into a single system. Some of these POS systems can be tied together in a local area network for a larger type store that might have several cash registers.

A bar code scanner can read data into a computer at about 1700 characters per minute—and do it with absolute accuracy. Do you know anyone who can type that fast?

Whole books have been written about the bar code and other means of identification. Hundreds of vendors and companies offer service in this area. If you are interested in the bar code and automatic identification technology, you should be subscribing to a free magazine called the *ID Systems*. Almost everyone who has any business connections can qualify. Write to them for a qualifying subscription form at:

ID Systems
174 Concord St.
Peterborough, NH 03458
(603) 924-9631

The ID Systems also publishes a very comprehensive directory of all the companies who offer bar code and automatic identification hardware, software, services, and supplies.

Another magazine is sent free to those who qualify. Write to them at:

Automatic I.D. News
P.O. Box 6158
Duluth, MN 55806-9858

Radio Frequency I.D.

Another system of identification is the use of small tags on materials that can be read by a RFID system. These systems can be used on production lines and many places that are difficult to access.

One RFID system is being used in California for toll bridge collection. A person buys a small tag that is good for a month of tolls. The tag is placed in the window of the auto and is automatically read as the driver passes through the toll gate. The driver doesn't even have to slow down for the tag to be read and fed to the computer.

Computer Vision

Many companies have set up cameras on their production lines to control them in many ways. One way would be to inspect the items as they came off the assembly line. For instance, an image of a "golden" circuit board that is perfect concerning component placement and appearance, is digitized and stored in the computer. Each time a circuit board comes off the assembly line, the camera focuses on it and the computer compares it to the stored image. If the two images match, the board is sent on to be further assembled or electronically tested. A computer can check a circuit board much, much faster than a human being, do it better, and more consistently.

Computerized Voice Output

Computer synthesized voice systems have been developed to do hundreds of tasks. Sensors can be set up so that when a beam is broken, it sends a signal to a computer to alert a person of danger. The Atlanta airport has an underground shuttle to move people to the various airline gates. It has several sensors that feed into a computer. If a person is standing in the doorway, it will ask the person to move, and the train will not move until it is safe to do so.

Many automated banking systems will allow you to dial a number over the telephone into a computer. A computerized voice asks questions, lets you pay your bills, move money from one account to another, and do almost all of your banking by telephone.

The telephone system has computerized voices for the time and for giving out numbers when you dial 411. Many more uses are being developed every day.

Voice Data Input

Another way to input data into a computer is to talk to it with a microphone. Of course you need electronics that can take the signal created by the microphone, detect the spoken words, and turn them into a form of digital information that the computer can use.

The early voice data input systems were very expensive and limited. One reason was that the voice technology required lots of memory. But the cost of memory has dropped considerably in the last few years, and the technology has improved in many other ways.

Voice technology involves "training" a computer to recognize a word spoken by a person. When you speak into a microphone, the sound waves cause a diaphragm, or some other device, to move back and forth in a magnetic field and create a voltage that is analogous to the sound wave. If this voltage is recorded and played through a good audio system, the loudspeaker will respond to the amplified voltages and reproduce a sound that is identical to the one input to the microphone.

A person can speak a word into a microphone which creates a unique voltage for that word and that particular person's voice. The voltage is fed into an electronic circuit, and the pattern is digitized and stored in the computer. If several words are spoken, the circuit will digitize each one of them and store them. Each one of them will have a distinct and unique pattern. Later when the computer hears a word, it will search through the patterns that it has stored to see if the input word matches any one of its stored words.

Of course, once the computer is able to recognize a word, you can have it perform some useful work. You could command it to load and run a program, or perform any of several other tasks.

Because every person's voice is different, the computer would not recognize the voice of anyone who had not trained it. Training the computer might involve saying the same word several times so that the computer can store several patterns of the person's voice.

Voice data input is very useful whenever you must use both hands for doing a job but still need a computer to perform certain tasks. One area where voice data is used extensively is in the new military fighter planes. They move so fast that the pilot does not have time to manipulate computer keys because both hands are usually busy. The pilot can have the computer do hundreds of jobs by just telling it what he wants done.

Voice data is also useful on production lines where the person does not have time to enter data manually. It can also be used in a laboratory where a scientist is looking through a microscope and cannot take his eyes off the subject to write down the findings or data. There might be times when the lighting must be kept too dim to input data to a computer manually. In other instances, the person might have to be several feet from the computer and still be able to input data through the microphone lines. The person might even be miles away and be able to input data over a telephone line.

In most of the systems in use today, the computer must be trained to recognize a specific word so the vocabulary is limited. But every word that can be spoken can be derived from just 42 phonemes. Several companies are working on systems that will take a small sample of a person's voice that contains these phonemes. Using the phonemes from this sample, the computer could then recognize any word that the person speaks.

Computers and Devices for the Disabled

Several computer devices have been developed that can help the disabled person live a better life. Devices allow the blind, the deaf, the quadriplegic, and other severely disabled persons to communicate. The use of these devices has allowed many people to lead productive lives as programmers, writers, and scientists. These communication devices have helped them express themselves.

Several organizations can help in locating special equipment and lend support. If you know someone who might benefit from the latest technology and devices for the handicapped, contact these organizations:

AbleData
Adaptive Equipment Department
Newington Children's Hospital
181 E. Cedar St.
Newington, CT 06111
(800) 344-5405

Accent on Information
P.O. Box 700
Bloomington, IL 61702
(309) 378-2961

Apple Computer
Office of Special Education & Rehabilitation
20525 Mariani Ave. MS 43F
Cupertino, CA 95014
(408) 996-1010

Closing The Gap, Inc.
P.O. Box 68
Henderson, MN 56044
(612) 248-3294

Direct Link for the Disabled
P.O. Box 1036
Solvang, CA 93463
(805) 688-1603

Easter Seals Systems Office
5120 S. Hyde Park Blvd.
Chicago, IL 60615
(312) 667-8626

IBM National Support Center
for People with Disabilities
P.O. Box 2150
Atlanta, GA 30055
(800) 426-2133

American Foundation for the Blind
15 W. 16th St.
New York, NY 10011
(212) 620-2000

Trace Research and Development Center
University of Wisconsin
Madison Room S-151, Waisman Center
1500 Highland Ave.
Madison, WI 53705
(608) 262-6966

National ALS Association
21021 Ventura Blvd. Suite 321
Woodland Hills, CA 91364
(818) 340-7500

13

Communications

The communications capability of the computer is one of its most important aspects. Thousands of software programs and hardware components can allow you to communicate with millions of other computers, bulletin boards, and on-line services. Much of this software and hardware can be used to link up and share the hard disks, data, and resources of other computers.

I briefly discuss some of the important communications methods, including both hardware and software that involves modems, electronic mail (E-Mail), and facsimile or fax systems.

Modems

A *modem* is an electronic device that allows a computer to use an ordinary telephone line to communicate with other computers that are equipped with a modem. Modem is a contraction of the words *modulate* and *demodulate*. The telephone system is analog, computer data is usually in a digital form. The modem modulates the digital data from a computer and turns it into analog voltages for transmission. At the receiving end, a similar modem will demodulate the analog voltage back into a digital form.

Baud rate. Telephone systems were originally designed for voice and have a very narrow bandwidth. They are subject to noise, static, and other electrical disturbances. The original modems could only operate at about 50 baud, or about 5 characters, per second. There have been some fantastic advances in the modem technologies. About one-third of the modems today operate at a 1200 baud rate, or at about 120 characters per second. Another one-third are operating at 2400 baud. Thousands of others are operating at 4800 and 9600 baud. The 9600 baud rate will no doubt become the standard.

As of this date, there is no standard for baud rates higher than 2400. There is still a lot of squabbling among the various manufacturers. Hayes has developed a 9600 baud machine, and because they are the leader, it will more than likely set the standard.

Some of the 9600 baud modems can cost up to $3000. Some of the 9600 baud modems can only communicate at this rate with a similar modem from the same manufacturer. Unless you perform extensive and heavy duty file transfers, you would probably be better off buying a 2400 baud machine. These modems may cost from $100 up to $700. Many of them come with bundled software.

Both the sending and receiving modem must operate at the same baud rate. Most of the faster modems are downward compatible and can operate at the slower speeds.

The faster the baud rate, the less time it will take to download or transmit a file. If the file is being sent over a long-distance line, the length of time can be critical. If the modem is used frequently, the telephone bills can be very substantial.

Besides the phone line charges, the major on-line service companies, such as CompuServe, Dataquest, and Dow Jones News/Retrieval, charge for connect time to their service. The connect time is much less with some of the high-speed modems. However, to keep their revenue up, some companies are charging more for the higher-speed modems.

Laptop Modems

Many people are now using laptop computers. Several companies have developed modems so that a person can plug in his laptop anywhere in the world and communicate with the office or wherever.

The Sunhill Company of Seattle has a small pocket-size modem they call Discovery 2400P shown in Fig. 13-1. It runs off a nine volt battery or an AC power adapter. It is Hayes compatible and can operate at 300, 1200, or 2400 baud. It has a speaker and five LEDs. It is $4^5/8''\times2^1/2''\times1^1/8''$ and weighs 5.3 ounces. It would seem to be ideal for portable or laptop computers. Because it takes up so little space, it would even be good as an external modem for a desktop computer. It lists for $289. For more information, contact:

Sunhill
1000 Andover Park East
Seattle, WA 98188
(800) 544-1361

Here is a short list of some of the other companies who make miniature modems:

Touchbase Worldport	(516) 261-0423
Aprotek Minimodem	(805) 482-3604
Novation Parrot	(714) 841-8791
QIC Research Mini Modem	(408) 432-8880

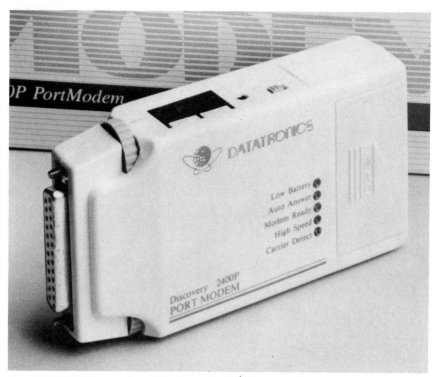

Fig. 13-1. Miniature modem. (Courtesy of Sunhill Company.)

Software

In order to use a modem, it must be driven and controlled by software. Dozens of communication programs can be used.

One of the better programs is Relay Silver from VM Personal Computing, at (203) 798-3800. Their Relay Gold is one of the most versatile of the communications software packages. It has features that allow remote communications, accessing main frames, and dozens of utilities not found on the usual communications programs.

Crosstalk, at (404) 998-3998, was one of the earlier modem programs. ProComm, at (314) 474-8461, is one of several low-cost shareware programs. Also, several public domain programs such as QModem will do almost everything that the high-cost commercial packages do.

Besides using a faster baud rate, another way to reduce phone charges is to use file compression. Bulletin Boards have been using a form of data compression for years. Several public domain programs squeeze and unsqueeze the data.

Firmware. Several new advances have recently been made in some of the newer modems. They use a system for the compression of data before it is transmitted, then decompression after it is received. The methods are similar to the algorithms used to compress data on some hard disk systems. Some schemes can compress a file and reduce it to 50 or down to 25 percent of the original file size. Again, the smaller the file, the less time on the telephone line. Squeezed or compressed files also take up less room when recorded on a hard disk or floppy.

Basic Types of Modems

The two basic types of modems are the external desktop and the internal. Each type has some advantages and disadvantages.

The external type requires some of your precious desk space and a voltage source. It also requires a COM port to drive it. The good news is that most external models have LEDs that light up and let you know what is happening during your call.

Both the external and the internal models have speakers that let you hear the phone ringing or if you get a busy signal. Some of the external models have a volume control for the built-in speaker.

The internal modem is built entirely on a board, usually a half or short board. The good news is that it doesn't use up any of your desk real estate, but the bad news is that it uses one of your precious slots. And it does not have the LEDs to let you know the progress of your call.

Hayes Compatibility

One of the most popular early modems was made by Hayes Microcomputer Products. They have become the "IBM of the modem world" and have established a *de facto* standard. Of hundreds of modem manufacturers, except for some of the very inexpensive ones, almost all of them emulate the Hayes standard.

Installing an Internal Modem

Internal modems are built on a plug-in board. So the first thing you have to do is to remove the computer cover. (Refer to Chapter 2 for the procedure to remove the cover and install a board.)

The modem will have to be set to access either serial port COM1 or COM2. These two ports are accessible on any of the 8-bit plug-in slots. If you have a mouse, a serial printer, or some other serial device, it will probably be set to access COM1. You cannot have two serial devices set to the same COM port. Check the documentation that came with your modem. It probably came from the factory set for COM1. Probably a switch or a jumper on the board can be set to change for COM2 if necessary.

Many of the later model 286 and 386 motherboards have these ports also built-in as rows of pins for plug-in cable connectors. The built-in ports save having to buy a board and using a slot. The motherboard should have a switch or a shorting bar to configure the system for either the motherboard built-in ports or for the bus ports. It is possible to use one of the built-in ports for one COM, and the bus for the other COM.

If your internal modem is your only serial device, then set it to COM1. If there is a built-in COM1 on the motherboard, make sure that it is disabled, or switched to the bus.

Plug in the board and hook it up to the telephone line. Unless you expect to do a lot of communicating, you probably will not need a separate dedicated line. The modem might have an automatic answer mode. In this mode, it will always answer the telephone. Unless you have a dedicated line, this mode should be disabled. Check your documentation; there should be a switch or some means to disable it. Having the modem and telephone on the same line should cause no problems unless someone tries to use the telephone while the modem is using it.

There should be two connectors at the back end of the board. One might be labeled for the line in, and the other for the telephone. Unless you have a dedicated telephone line, you should unplug your telephone, plug in the extension to the modem and line, then plug the telephone into the modem. If your computer is not near your telephone line, you might have to go to a hardware store and buy a long telephone extension line.

After you have connected all of the lines, turn on your computer and try the modem before you put the cover back on. Make sure you have software. Call a local bulletin board. Even if you can't get through, or have a wrong number, you should hear the dial tone, then hear it dial the number.

Installing an External Modem

The external modem will have to sit on your desk and be connected to one of the COM ports with a cable. If you did not get a cable with your unit, you will have to buy one. If you have built-in COM ports, it will cost about $5. If you have to use the bus to access the ports, you will need a cable and a board with serial ports, but check your system first. You might have an Input/Output multifunction board already installed. These boards usually have a built-in battery powered clock, serial and parallel ports, and several other functions. It might cost $30 to $75 if you have to buy one. If you don't need the other functions, you should be able to buy a short board with just the ports for about $20. If you go to a computer swap, someone should be selling them there. Otherwise, most computer stores carry them, or there are several mail order houses that specialize in communications boards and cables. Look in any of the computer magazines.

Modem and Fax Detector

Several companies have developed devices for people who have a fax or modem on a single telephone line. The device can detect whether an incoming call is from a modem or a fax. It can then switch the call to the appropriate unit.

I bought one from Technology Concepts, at (415) 349-0900, shown in Fig. 13-2. It has connections for a modem, a fax, a main phone and an extension. The Concepts switch must be connected to the main line and

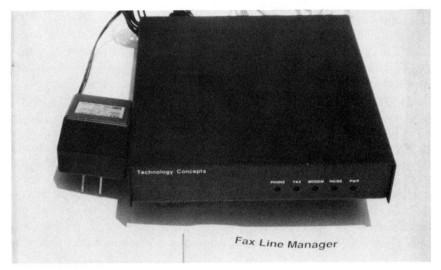

Fig. 13-2. *A device that recognizes and routes incoming fax and modem calls.*

any extensions must be plugged into the switch box. This might be a problem if you have several extensions in your house, located in separate rooms.

Bulletin Boards

If you have a modem, you have access to several thousand computer bulletin boards. There are over 100 in the San Francisco Bay area, and about twice that many in the Los Angeles area. Most of them are free of any charge. You only have to pay the phone bill if they are out of your calling area. Some of them charge a nominal fee to join, some just ask for a tax-deductible donation.

Some of the bulletin boards are set up by private individuals, and some by companies and vendors as a service to their customers. Some are set up by users groups and other special interest organizations. Over 100 boards nationwide have been set up for doctors and lawyers. There is even a gay bulletin board in the San Francisco area. Also, there are X-rated boards, and several for dating.

Most of the bulletin boards are set up to help individuals. They usually have lots of public domain software and a space where you can leave messages for help, advertise something for sale, or just chit-chat.

If you are just getting started, you probably need some software. There are public domain software packages that are equivalent to almost all of the major commercial programs, and the best part is that they are free.

Viruses

There have been several reports that some individuals have hidden "viruses" in some public domain and even in some commercial software. The software appears to be something functional, and it might perform for some time, then a hidden command in the software might erase an entire hard disk. Or it might gradually erase portions of the disk each time the machine is turned on, or in some other way damage your data. Any time a copy is made of this program, it will attach itself to the copy and spread. One form of virus attaches itself to the boot-up portion of the COMMAND.COM and slightly increases the number of bytes in this vital command each time the computer is booted up. One way to detect this virus is to do a check on your version of COMMAND.COM every so often to be sure that it remains the same. Just type DIR COMMAND.COM, and it will display the amount of bytes in the file.

You can automatically check your COMMAND.COM each time it is booted up by using the DOS COMPARE command. Just make a copy of COMMAND.COM and rename it something else. For instance I said, COPY COMMAND.COM KOMKOM. I then copied my AUTOEXEC.BAT file to WordStar and using the nondocument mode, I added the line Comp Command.Com KOMKOM. I then copied my AUTOEXEC.BAT back to the root directory. The file will then compare the files and report whether they are okay.

Among the many utilities in Mace Gold is one that automatically checks for viruses. Mace Gold is available at most larger software dealers, or contact Paul Mace Software at (503) 488-0224.

Now several public domain and commercial software "vaccine" programs will check for viruses. Here are a few:

Asky Inc.	(408) 943-1940
Data Physician	(800) 221-8091
Flu-Shot	(212) 889-6438
Sophco	(303) 444-1542

Most bulletin board operators are now screening their programs, but it is almost impossible to find some of the viruses. It is advisable to download programs on a floppy disk and run them for a while before putting them on a hard disk. If a floppy is ruined, you won't be hurt too much.

Other Illegal Activities

Some of the bulletin boards have been used for other illegal or criminal activities. For example, stolen credit card numbers and telephone charge numbers have been left on the bulletin boards. Also, some people have put bootleg copies of programs and applications on bulletin boards.

Because of these problems, many of the *SYSOPs*, bulletin board system operators, are now carefully checking any software that is uploaded onto their systems. Many of them are now restricting access to their boards. Some of them have had to start charging a fee because of the extra time it takes to monitor the boards.

Where to Find the Bulletin Boards

Several local computer magazines devote a lot of space to bulletin boards and user groups. In California, the *MicroTimes* and *Computer Currents* magazines have several pages of bulletin boards and user groups each month. The *Computer Shopper* has the most comprehensive listing of bulletin boards and user groups of any national magazine. See Chapter 17 for the addresses of these and other magazines.

The Bulletin Board listings in the *Computer Shopper* are compiled by:

Gale Rhoades
P.O. Box 3474
Daly City, CA 94015
(415) 755-2000

She works with an international nonprofit computer user group called FOG. If you know of a bulletin board or user group that should be listed, contact her. She can also supply you with a listing of boards.

On-Line Services

Several large national bulletin boards with information and reference services are Compuserve, Dataquest, Dow Jones, and Dialog. These companies have huge databases of information. As a caller, you can search the databases and download information as easily as pulling the data off your own hard disk. The companies charge a fee for the connect time.

Prodigy is unlike the other on-line services. Prodigy does not charge for connect time. They charge only a very nominal monthly rate. They have phone service to most areas in the larger cities so that there is not even a toll charge. They have an impressive list of services including home shopping, home banking, airline schedules and reservations, stock market quotations, and many others. In San Francisco, you can even order your groceries over the line through Prodigy and have them delivered to your door. One of its faults is that it is relatively slow. But because it is so inexpensive (a real bargain), I can live with it. You can contact Prodigy at (800) 759-8000. Figure 13-3 shows some of the software for Prodigy.

E-Mail

Many of the national bulletin boards offer electronic mail or *E-Mail* along with their other services. These services can be of great value to some individuals and businesses.

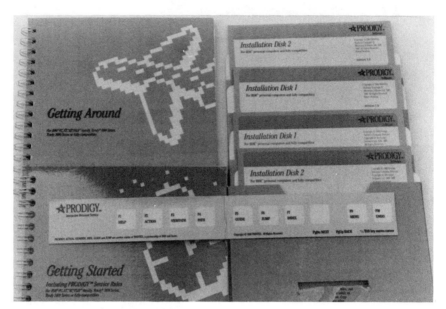

Fig. 13-3. Some of the Prodigy software.

E-Mail subscribers are usually given a "post office box" at these companies. This is usually a file on one of their large hard disk systems. When a message is received, it is recorded in this file. The next time the subscriber logs on to this service, he or she will be alerted that there is "mail" in their in-box.

E-Mail is becoming more popular every day and there are now several hundred thousand subscribers. The cost for an average message is about one dollar. (The cost for overnight mail from the U.S. Post Office, Federal Express, and UPS is $11 to $13.)

Some of the companies who provide E-Mail at the present time:

AT&T Mail	(800) 367-7225
CompuServe	(800) 848-8990
DASnet	(408) 559-7434
MCI Mail	(800) 444-6245
Western Union	(800) 527-5184

LAN E-Mail. Most of the larger local area network (LAN) programs also provide an E-Mail utility in their software. For those packages that do not provide this utility, there are programs available that work with installed LANs:

Action Technologies	(800) 624-2162
Lotus Express	(800) 345-1043
PCC Systems	(415) 321-0430

Banking by Modem

Many banks offer systems that will let you do all your banking with your computer and a modem from the comforts of your home. You would never again have to drive downtown, hunt for a parking space, then stand in line for a half hour to do your banking.

Other Services

If you don't own a modem, many cable tv services offer hookups to personal computers that provide news, stock quotations, airline schedules, and many other services for a small monthly fee.

If you don't have a modem yet, or if the local bulletin boards don't have the software you need, several companies will ship you public domain software on a floppy disk. These companies have thousands of programs and usually charge from $3 up to $24 for a disk full of programs. One company, PC-Sig, at (800) 245-6717, has their entire library of over 20,000 files on a CD-ROM disk. The cost of the disk is $295. PC-Sig also provides CD-ROM players that will interface with a PC so that the programs can be downloaded onto a floppy or a hard disk. They can also provide periodic updates on new CD-ROMs.

The Alde Publishing Company, at (612) 835-5240, also sells a CD-ROM disk that has over 3000 public domain and shareware programs. The cost of their disk is $99.

There are several other public domain software companies. Most of them advertise in the computer magazines listed in Chapter 17. Most of them can provide a catalog listing of their software. Some of them charge a small fee for their catalog. Call them for details and latest prices.

Facsimile Boards and Machines

Facsimile (fax) machines have been around for quite a while. Newspapers and businesses have used them for years. They were the forerunners of the scanning machines; a page of text or a photo was fed into the facsimile machine, the photo was scanned, digitized and transmitted out over the telephone lines.

The early machines were similar to the early acoustic modems. Both used foam rubber cups that fit over the telephone receiver-mouthpiece for coupling. They were very slow and subject to noise and interference. Fax machines and modems have come a long way since those early days.

Modems and facsimile machines are quite similar and related in many respects. A modem sends and receives bits of data. A fax machine or board usually sends and receives scanned whole page letters, images, signatures, etc. A computer program can be sent over a modem, but not over a fax.

Sometimes one or the other is needed. However, both units would not be in use at the same time for the same data so the same phone line can be used for both of them.

More than one million facsimile machines are in use today. There are very few businesses that cannot benefit from the use of a fax. It can be used to send documents, that includes handwriting, signatures, seals, letterheads, graphs, blueprints, photos and other types of data around the world, across the country or across the room to another fax machine.

An overnight letter costs $11 to $13 to send, but E-Mail only costs about $1. A fax machine can deliver the same letter for about 40 cents and do it in less than three minutes. Depending on the type of business, and the amount of critical mail that must be sent out, a fax system can pay for itself in a very short time.

Stand-Alone Units

Some facsimile machines are stand-alone devices that attach to a telephone. They have been vastly improved in the last few years, but they still accept and produce paper images only, so the stand-alone units cannot compare to the versatility and convenience of a computer equipped with a fax board.

Some overseas companies are making stand-alone units that are fairly inexpensive, some for as little as $400. Several large American companies are building more sophisticated ones that cost up to $2000 or more.

Fax Computer Boards

Several companies have developed fax machines on circuit boards that can be plugged into computers. Many of the newer models have provisions for a modem on the same board. Follow the same procedure to install a fax board as outlined above for an internal modem.

Special software allows the computer to control the fax boards. Using the computer's word processor, letters and memos can be written and sent out over the phone lines. Several letters or other information can be stored or retrieved from the computer hard disk and transmitted. The computer can even be programmed to send the letters out at night when the rates are lower.

But the computer fax boards have one disadvantage. They cannot scan information unless there is a scanner attached to computer. Without a scanner, the information that can be sent is usually limited to that which can be entered from a keyboard or disk. As I pointed out before, stand-alone units scan pages of information, including such things as handwriting, signatures, images, blueprints, and photos.

However, the computer can receive and store any fax that is sent. The digitized data and images can be stored on a hard disk, then printed out on a printer.

The fax boards cost from $395 up to $1500 depending on the extras and goodies installed.

I have an Intel Connection CoProcessor installed in my 386. But it can be used in a PC, XT, or 286. Figure 13-4 shows the sophisticated fax board with its own 10 MHz 80188 processor. It has provisions for a small daughter card that contains a 2400 baud modem. Because it has its own processor, it can send and receive fax messages in the background while the computer is busy on other projects.

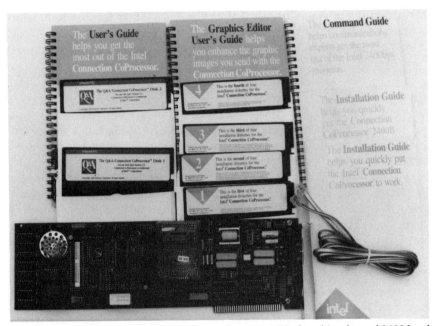

Fig. 13-4. The Intel Connection Coprocessor and software. The board is a fax and 2400 baud modem.

The Connection CoProcessor lists for $995, and the modem lists for $295. A discount house lists the CoProcessor for $769, and the modem for $229. For more information, contact:

Intel Corp.
PCEO Mail Stop CO307
5200 N.E. Elam Young Parkway
Hillsboro, OR 97124-6497
(800) 538-3373

Scanners

Scanners are not absolutely essential to operate a PC-based fax. But sometimes it might be necessary to transmit photographs, blueprints, documents, handwritten signatures on contracts, or a host of other needs, so a scanner is needed to get the most utility from a fax.

Several available scanners will operate with fax machines. The scanners may range in price from $700 up to $7000. Of course, the higher the cost, the more sophisticated and versatile the machine will be. These machines can scan a sheet of text, a graph, or a blueprint into a computer, then allow it to be changed, manipulated, updated, edited, or rearranged as necessary. Some of the low-cost scanners do not allow any manipulation of the data after it has been input.

Most of the scanners listed in the previous chapter will work with fax boards.

Advantages of a Fax System

Depending on the type of business, it would be possible to get by with a low-cost fax board, a PC, and a dot matrix printer. Such a system could cost less than $2000. But a scanner, a modem, a laser printer, and several other options could drive the price up to $6000 or more. But still, in any business that does a lot of communicating, a good fax system would pay for itself in a very short time.

A few businesses that can benefit from the use of a Fax system include any corporate office or branch office, financial institutions, insurance companies, law offices, accounting firms, retail/wholesale merchants, import/export businesses, hospitals, laboratories, publishers, and any place or person who needs electronic mail in real time.

Most fax boards are very easy to install and easy to operate. A person can be up and doing simple communications within a few minutes. Of course, for the more sophisticated type of communicating, it will take some time and study of the manuals to learn all the intricacies involved.

Here are the phone numbers of just a few fax board manufacturers. Call them for spec sheets and prices:

ADTech SMARTFAX	(818) 578-1339
Advanced Vision MegaFax	(408) 434-1115
Asher JT Fax	(800) 334-9339
Brooktrout Fax-Mail	(617) 235-3026
Carterfone DATAFAX	(214) 634-2424
Datacopy MicroFax	(800) 821-2898
GammaLink GAMMAFAX	(415) 856-7421
GMS Corporation EZ FAX	(800) 443-0500
KoFax Image Products	(714) 474-1933
Microtek Lab MFAX96	(213) 321-2121
OAZ Communications XAFAX	(714) 259-0909
Panasonic Fax Partner	(201) 348-7000
Pitney-Bowes PATH II & III	(203) 356-5000
Ricoh FB-1	(201) 882-2000
Spectrafax FAXCARD	(813) 775-2737

Telecommuting

Anyone who lives near a large city knows how bad the traffic is.

Millions of people have to risk their lives and fight the traffic every day. But some of them could avoid the traffic and still do their jobs by telecommuting.

Many people have jobs that would allow them to stay home, work on a computer, then send the data to the office over a modem or a fax. Even if the person had to buy their own computer, modem, and fax, it still might be worth it. You could save the cost of gasoline, auto maintenance, and lower insurance.

Being able to work at home would be ideal for working parents who want to stay home with small children, or anyone who hates traffic.

14

Printers

A bit of history. Johann Gutenberg started the printer revolution way back in 1436 when he developed movable type and started printing the first Bible. Though he started printing the first Bible, he did not complete it. He had borrowed money from a man named Johann Fust. When Gutenberg could not repay the loan, Fust took over the press and types and completed the work started by Gutenberg. So Fust was the first to print the Bible.

We have come a long way in the last 554 years.

Printer Types

For the vast majority of applications, a computer system is not complete without a printer. Choosing a printer for your system can be a difficult task because there are so many options with several types of printers and hundreds of manufacturers.

The type of printer needed will depend primarily on the computer's use. The following are some factors that should be considered when shopping for a printer.

If at all possible, before you buy a printer, visit a computer store or a computer show and try it out. Get several spec sheets of printers in your price range and compare them. You should also look for reviews of printers in the computer magazines.

Dot Matrix

Most of the printers sold today are 24-pin dot matrix. The dot matrix is very reasonable in price and is fast, sturdy and reliable. As its name implies, it forms characters from a matrix of pins in the print head. Small electric solenoids surround each of the wire pins in the head. As the head moves across the paper, the solenoids press the pins needed to form a character against the ribbon onto the paper.

The early dot matrix printers had only 7 or 9 pins. The print quality was very poor and difficult to read. But with 24 pins and better ribbons, a good dot matrix can deliver print almost as good as a laser at less than one-third of the cost.

Some things can be done with a dot matrix that can't be done with a laser. For instance, a dot matrix can have a wide carriage; the lasers are limited to $8^1/_2''$ by 11''. The dot matrix can use continuous sheets or forms; the laser uses cut sheets, fed one at a time. A dot matrix can also print carbons and multiple forms.

Lasers

Laser printers have excellent print quality. They are a combination of the reproduction type copy machine, computer, and laser technology. On the down side, they have lots of moving mechanical parts and are rather expensive. I discuss laser printers in more detail later.

Daisy Wheel

The daisy wheel has excellent letter quality. It has a wheel with all the letters of the alphabet on flexible "petals." As the wheel spins, a hammer hits a character and presses it against a ribbon onto the paper. It is very slow and cannot print graphics. It is practically obsolete.

Ink Jet

The Hewlett-Packard Ink Jet is a small printer with quality almost equal to that of the laser. It uses a matrix of small ink jets. As the head moves across the paper the ink is sprayed from the jets to form the letters.

Choosing a Printer

If the printer is to be used for business correspondence, a daisy wheel or laser can provide the best letter-quality type. A good 24-pin dot matrix can provide near-letter-quality (NLQ) type. For most purposes, a NLQ printer will be sufficient. It is possible to buy a very low cost 9-pin dot matrix. But if you do any serious printing at all, you will be unhappy with it. Some have 18 pins in the head, but the print is not as good as a 24-pin dot matrix.

The following terms will help you decide which features you should look for in a printer.

Dots per inch (dpi). The number of dots that a printer can place in one square inch determines its resolution. Most lasers today have a resolution of 300 × 300. Most dot matrix printers have a resolution of about 180 × 360 dpi.

Fonts. Font designs can be copyrighted. Many large corporations, such as IBM, have their own copyrighted fonts. Several major types of fonts include Roman, Times, Courier, Helvetica, and others. Even though they all have the same name, each of these types from different companies will be slightly different in shape.

If there is going to be several printers in a company or office, it might be worthwhile to consider buying all the same brand of printers because of the font differences. For instance, if several people worked on a report and each used a different printer, the differences in the fonts might detract from the importance of the report.

Lasers usually come with several fonts. Almost all of the lasers emulate the HP LaserJet and several other printers. The better dot matrix printers also have several font options. Many printers are now sold with a couple of little doors that will accept cartridges for different font styles. If you do any fancy printing, they can be valuable.

There are several software programs that can be used with dot matrix printers to print out large type, such as headlines, signs, banners, and all sorts of graphics.

Pitch. The number of characters that can be printed in one inch is the character pitch. The better printers are usually capable of responding to at least three different pitches. Ten characters per inch is called *pica* (most typewriters use this spacing which is 80 characters per line); 12 characters per inch is called *elite*. It is also possible to have *semi-condensed* type at 15 characters per inch and *expanded* type at 5 characters per inch. Many of the printers can be switched from one pitch to another with application software such as a word processor or with a simple BASIC program.

Proportional spacing. Typewriters and most printers give each character the same amount of space no matter how wide it is (*monospacing*). Pica pitch gives an "M" and an "i" each $1/10$ of an inch even though the "M" might be two or three times wider than the "i." Proportional spacing can be a critical consideration if the printer is going to be used for desktop publishing. Proportional spacing is possible with the better dot matrix printers and lasers.

Subscripts and superscripts. If you are going to be doing any kind of scientific writing, you will probably need this capability. The printer should also be capable of variable line spacing.

Boldface and underline. These capabilities are very important to stress or emphasize a point or to set a group of words apart.

Speed. The characters per second (CPS) is a factor to be considered when deciding on a printer. Considering cost and within reason, you want one that is as fast as possible. It can be awfully frustrating having to wait for a long document to print out. Depending on the type of printer and software, a computer may be tied up for as long as it takes to print out a document. In a business office, this could be expensive if the employee has to sit and do nothing until the printing is finished.

The fastest speed is *draft* quality which is often sufficient for such things as informal notes, memos, and preliminary reports. A quick draft hard copy makes proofreading and editing much easier than trying to do it on the computer. Most monitors have only 25 lines, and many word processors use 10 to 15 of those lines for menus and help. Only a small portion of the page can be seen at any one time, so a correction or amendment could be made on the portion of the page that is showing on the screen, but it could be overlooked when the other half of the page comes up.

Some manufacturers advertise draft speeds as high as 400 CPS in draft mode, but few claim more than 160 in NLQ mode. You should be aware that many vendors tend to exaggerate a bit on their CPS claims. One reason is that there is no standard speed test, and it takes less time to print some characters than others. So a printer might achieve 400 CPS in a burst of speed during the middle of a line, but the time required to print every character of the alphabet and for the carriage returns and line feeds would reduce the figure somewhat.

A full page might have about 4000 characters. In draft mode at 400 CPS a page could be printed in 10 seconds, or about 6 pages per minute. A laser can print 6 to 10 pages per minute of good letter quality print. So in draft mode a good dot matrix can print about as fast as some lasers. For NLQ print the dot matrix slows down to 100 to 150 CPS. So to print a sheet of 4000 NLQ characters would take from 27 to 40 seconds.

The daisy wheel printers are rated from 15 CPS up to 60 CPS. At 15 CPS, it would take about 4.5 minutes to print 4000 characters. At 60 CPS it would take a little over one minute.

Speed, or CPS, is important. But it should be placed in the proper perspective. Many of the magazines I subscribe to perform speed tests on just about everything in or near a computer. Some items might be just a fraction of a second faster than another, but cost hundreds of dollars more.

Compatibility. There are absolutely no standards for printers. Drivers are usually needed to take advantage of the capabilities offered. Software packages such as word processors, spreadsheets, databases, and graphics programs have to supply hundreds of different drivers with their software packages to try to make them compatible with whatever printer you happen to have. The closest thing to a standard is the character and graphics set first used by Epson. IBM bought the small Epson graphics dot matrix printers and put their own IBM logo on them. This helped to establish somewhat of a standard. Most of the printer makers are still installing their own operating systems, but many of them are including emulation firmware for the IBM and Epson standard.

Graphics capability. The printer should be able to emulate the IBM and Epson standard. If possible get a demonstration of it printing out a simple graphics pie chart or something similar. Note the speed and the fineness of lines, the shape of curves and circles and uniform density of filled in areas.

Parallel or serial. A parallel printer should be no more than 10 feet away from the computer. If the cable is much longer the signals can be degraded and possibly lose some data. A serial cable can be up to 50 feet long without causing any degradation of the signal.

IBM chose the parallel system, and it has become the closest thing to a standard available. Many printers will only accept parallel signals. Some of the better printers will accept either parallel or serial. This capability could be very important if the printer is located more than 10 feet from the computer.

Wide carriage. Most printers come in at least two different widths. I prefer the wide carriage. Quite often I have to address a large manila envelope which requires a wide carriage. If you are in a business office, you might want to do graphics or need the wide paper for a spreadsheet printout.

The wide carriage models may cost $100 to $200 more than the standard size. Otherwise, they usually have the same specifications as to speed and letter quality.

Tractors. The tractors are the sprockets that engage the holes in the margins of continuous feed paper. Most printers have standard friction feed for printing individual cut sheet. Several of them have built-in tractors. But some offer the tractor only as an added cost option, which might cost $75 to $100 extra. Tractors are essential, especially if you are going to be making labels or other types of work where the paper must be controlled. Most friction feeds will not hold the paper straight, or provide accurate and consistent line feed spacing—especially after the platen gets a bit old and hardened. I would recommend that you get a printer with a tractor.

Paper advance. Most of the printers have a couple of buttons that advance the paper. One may be marked "top of form" and the other one marked "paper feed." The "top of form" will move a sheet of paper forward to the top of the next sheet. The "paper feed" will advance the paper one line at a time as long as the button is held down.

Most printers also have a large knob attached to the platen which can be turned to position the paper. You should not use this knob whenever the power is on because it works against the electric clutches that advance the paper. This could damage and wear out the clutches. If you want to use the knob to position the paper, switch off the power, then switch it back on.

Buffers. Even a very high-speed printer is very slow compared to how fast a computer can feed data to it. If the printer has a large memory buffer, the computer can dump its data into the buffer, then be free for other work. Some printers may have a buffer as small as 1K, but the better ones have 8K or more. Many of them have an option to add more memory to the buffer. If the printer is in a large office, it might even be worth the cost to install a large stand-alone buffer between the printer and computer.

Print spoolers. Print spoolers are similar to buffers, except that they use a portion of your computer's RAM memory to store the data that is to be printed. Some programs will even store the data on your hard disk and spool it out to the printer as needed. The computer will then be free for doing more important things than just sitting idle most of the time while the printer is doing its thing.

Several of the LIM EMS boards come with software for using expanded memory for print spooling. Incidentally, SPOOL is an acronym for *Simultaneous Peripheral Operations On Line.*

Multiple bins. Some printers will allow you to attach several different paper bins to them. A standard-size cut sheet paper could be in one bin, the long legal size in another, and perhaps an envelope feeder also. In a busy office, it can save a lot of time. But some of the bins are rather expensive, especially those designed for laser printers.

Ribbons. Most dot matrix printers use a nylon cloth ribbon. They are relatively inexpensive and can last for quite a long time. Most ribbons cost between $4 and $10 each.

Many of the letter quality printers use a carbon film type of ribbon. This gives good crisp letters that are truly print quality. It is possible to use the cloth type ribbons, but cloth ribbons cannot produce the same quality print, no matter how good the printer is.

The carbon film ribbons are good for a single pass only. Some printers use a wide ribbon in a cartridge. The ribbon carriage moves the ribbon up and down so that three characters can be struck across the width of the ribbon. One of these ribbons will allow several thousand characters to be printed in a single pass.

Color. Both cloth and carbon film ribbons are available in various colors for most printers. Most ribbons are on cartridges that are very easy to change. It is quite simple in most word processors to insert a print pause, change ribbons, then resume printing. A little color can be a great way to call attention to a certain portion of a letter or an important report to the CEO.

Some printers can use a wide ribbon that has three or more colors on it. The printer can shift the ribbon to the desired color and actually blend the colors to achieve all the colors of the rainbow. Hewlett-Packard has an ink-jet type of printer that can print 7-color graphics.

Paper. Paper is a very important element. But there is a sea of confusion as to paper specifications such as weight, brightness and thickness. Different printers and different applications need various kinds of paper. Some specialty printers, such as thermal printers, requires a special paper. Here are a few definitions:

> *bond*—Early government bonds were printed on high-quality paper with a watermark. Nowadays almost anything can be called bond paper. But the better bond will have a watermark and at least 25 percent rag content. The better quality papers might also use terms like linen, wove, and laid. Linen has a regular weave pattern and a sheen. Laid paper has a sculpted feeling.

brightness—There are many shades of white. The better paper is rated as to the brightness. For best results from laser printers, the paper should have a uniform surface, anti-curl, anti-static, and a brightness rating above 85.

continuous sheet—The continuous sheets have perforations to separate each sheet. They also have a removable strip along each side for the pin feed sprocket holes of the printer tractor. Most of the continuous sheet paper is now laser cut so that the pages and pin strips tear off evenly.

cut sheets—This would be single sheets that would require the use of friction feed by the printer's platen. Cut sheets are also used for the laser printers.

weight—The weight is determined by weighing 500 sheets (1 ream) of 17 × 22 inch paper. The most common weight is 20 pounds. But the 17 × 22 inch sheets are cut in half to give $8^{1}/_{2}$ × 11 after they are weighed. Some very thin low-priced computer paper may weigh as little as 12, 15, or 18 pounds. This thin paper might be suitable for draft type printing or interoffice memos; it would not be very good for correspondence or for important data.

Soundproofing. Printers can be very noisy. In a large office, it can be disruptive. Several companies manufacture soundproofing enclosures. These are usually made from plywood and then lined with foam rubber. They usually have a clear plastic door so that you can see what is going on inside. These enclosures can be rather expensive though, costing from $150 to over $200. If you don't have that kind of money, you might even take a large cardboard box and put it over the printer. You can eliminate a lot of the printer noise by simply placing a foam rubber pad beneath the printer.

Most printers have covers that protect the head and other internal parts of the printer. The cover helps to cut down on the noise. Most of the printers have microswitches that will not allow the printer to operate without the cover.

Stands. You can buy several stands to raise the printer up off the table so that a stack of fanfold computer paper can be placed beneath it. They will cost from $20 up to $75. I have mine sitting on a couple of bricks. I put foam rubber on top of the bricks to eliminate some of the noise.

Cost. The cost of a dot matrix printer can range from $200 up to over $2000 depending on the speed, special features, and other extras.

The cost of the daisy wheels ranges from $400 up to $3000 depending on speed, buffers, and other accessories.

Sources. Listed below are the names and telephone numbers of some of the dot matrix printers. Many of them also manufacture daisy wheel and laser printers. Most companies have several models. Call them for information and their latest prices.

Advanced Matrix Technology	(805) 499-8741
Alps America	(800) 828-2557
Brother International	(201) 981-0300
C. Itoh Digital Products	(213) 327-2110
Canon U.S.A.	(516) 488-6700
Citizen America	(213) 453-0614
Dataproducts Corp.	(603) 673-9100
Datasouth Computer Corp.	(800) 222-4528
Epson America	(213) 539-9140
Fujitsu America	(408) 946-8777
Genicom Corp.	(703) 949-1000
IBM Corp.	(800) 426-2468
Infoscribe	(800) 233-4442
JDL Inc.	(805) 495-3451
Mannesmann Tally	(206) 251-5500
NEC Information Systems	(800) 343-4418
Newbury Data Inc.	(213) 372-3775
Nissho Information Systems	(714) 952-8700
Okidata	(800) 654-3282
Olympia	(201) 722-7000
Output Technology Corp.	(800) 422-4850
Panasonic Industrial Co.	(201) 348-7000
Printronix	(714) 863-1900
Seikosha America	(201) 529-4655
Star Micronics	(212) 986-6770
Tandy/Radio Shack	(817) 390-3011
Texas Instruments	(800) 527-3500
Toshiba America	(714) 730-5000

Laser Printers

Laser printers combine laser technologies and copy machine technologies. A laser uses synchronized, multifaceted mirrors, and sophisticated optics to write the characters or images on a photosensitive rotating drum. The drum is similar to the ones used in repro machines. This drum can then print a whole sheet of paper in one rotation.

The drum and its associated mechanical attachments is called an *engine*. Canon, a Japanese company, is one of the foremost makers of engines. They manufacture them for their own laser printers and reproduction machines, and for dozens of other companies such as the Hewlett-Packard Laserjet and the Apple LaserWriter.

The Hewlett-Packard LaserJet was one of the first low-cost lasers. It was a fantastic success and became the *de facto* standard. Hundreds of laser printers are now on the market, and most of them emulate the

LaserJet standard. Most software adheres to this standard. If you are buying a laser, check for this feature.

The competition has been a great benefit to us consumers. It has forced many new improvements and the discount price for some models is now down to less than $1500. The prices will drop even more as the competition increases and the economies of scale in the manufacturing process becomes greater.

Color

There are a few color printers available, but at a cost of $10,000 up to $25,000. Several companies are working to lower the cost. QMS has a new ColorScript 100 that sells for $9,995. NEC has a color printer for $11,000.

Several others will be on the market soon. There is lots of competition so the prices should come down.

Extras for Lasers

Don't be surprised if you go into a store to buy a $1500 laser printer and end up paying about twice that much. The laser printer business is much like the automobile, the computer, and most other businesses. The $1500 advertised price might be for a barebones model without several of the essential items needed to do any productive work. Such items as cartridge plug-in fonts, memory, controller boards, and software might all cost extra. Some sheet-bin paper feeders might cost as much as a basic printer.

Memory. If you plan to do any graphics or desktop publishing (DTP), you will need to have at least 1Mb of memory in the machine. Of course, the more memory, the better. It will cost about $400 extra for 1.5Mb of memory and about $1500 for an extra 4.5Mb.

Before you buy extra memory, check the computer magazines for prices of memory. You might be able to buy memory and install it yourself for much less than what a dealer charges.

Page description languages. If you plan to do any desktop publishing you will need a page-description language (PDL) controller board. Text characters and graphics images are two different species of animals. Monitor controller boards usually have all of the alphabetical and numerical characters stored in ROM. When you press the letter A from the keyboard, it dives into the ROM chip, drags out the A and displays it in the block on the screen wherever the cursor happens to be. It has another set of chips where it stores the symbols it uses to create graphics displays. Some of the early monitor drivers were capable of producing text only. Printers have the same limitations. They have a library of stored characters. When told to do so, they go to the library and print that character.

A dot matrix printer is concerned with a single character at a time. The laser printers compose, then print a whole page at a time. With a PDL, many different fonts, sizes of type and graphics can be printed. But the laser must determine where every dot that makes up a character, or image is to be placed on the paper before it is printed. This composition is done in memory before the page is printed. The more complex the page, the more memory it will require and the more time needed to compose the page.

Adobe is the best known PDL. Several companies have developed their own PDLs. Of course, none of them are compatible with the others. This has caused a major problem for software developers because they must try to include drivers for each one of these PDLs. Several companies are attempting to clone the Adobe PDL. But it is doubtful that they can achieve 100 percent compatibility. But just like the IBM clones, you might not need 100 percent compatibility.

Adobe PostScript upgrade. If you have a HP LaserJet, or a compatible, you can add a PostScript controller board to your PC/XT/286/386. The board can be installed in any of the slots. (See Chapter 2 for instructions for installing almost any board.) The controller board is made by the QMS Corporation, at (205) 633-4300. You should be aware that the controller board will probably cost more than your printer did. One distributor is advertising it at this time for $1,695 with 3Mb of RAM.

Speed. Laser printers can print from six to over ten pages per minute depending on the model and what they are printing. Some complex graphics may require more than one minute to print a single page.

Color. Several companies are working to develop a color laser printer. But there are some large problems, and it is not expected that they will be easily overcome. If and when color is available, the cost will probably be from $15,000 to $25,000.

Resolution. Almost all of the lasers have a 300 × 300 dots per inch resolution (DPI), which is very good, but not nearly as good as 1200 × 1200 dots per inch typeset used for standard publications. Several companies are working to develop 600 × 600 DPI machines.

Maintenance. Most of the lasers use a toner cartridge that is good for 3000 to 5000 pages. The original cost of the cartridge is about $100. Several small companies are now refilling the spent cartridges for about $50 each.

Of course there are other maintenance costs. Because these machines are very similar to the repro copy machines, they have a lot of moving parts that can wear out and jam up. Most of the larger companies give a mean time between failures (MTBF) of 30,000 up to 100,000 pages. But remember that these are only average figures and not a guarantee.

Sources. Here are the telephone numbers of a few laser printer companies. Call them for their product specifications and latest price list.

Apple Computer	(408) 973-2222
AST Research	(714) 863-1333
Brother International	(210) 981-0300
Canon USA	(516) 488-6700

C. Itoh	(213) 327-2110
Epson GQ-3500	(800) 421-5426
Hewlett-Packard LaserJet II	(800) 367-4772
IBM Corp.	(800) 426-2468
Kyocera Unison	(415) 848-6680
Mannesmann Tally Corp.	(206) 251-5500
Nec Information Systems	(800) 343-4418
Office Automation Systems (OASYS)	(619) 452-9400
Olympia USA	(201) 231-8300
Okidata	(800) 654-3282
Panasonic Office Automation	(201) 348-7000
Personal Computer Products	(619) 485-8411
Quadram Corp.	(404) 432-4144
QMS Inc.	(205) 633-4300
Ricoh PC Laser	(201) 892-2000
Sharp Electronics	(201) 529-9500
Star Micronics	(212) 986-6770
Texas Instruments	(800) 343-4418
Toshiba America	(714) 380-3000

Liquid Crystal Shutter Printers

At least two companies, Taxan and Data Technology, are manufacturing *liquid crystal shutter* (LCS) printers. They use an engine that is similar to that used by the lasers. But instead of using a laser beam to write on the photosensitive drum, they use high intensity lights that are turned on and off with a liquid crystal shutter with 2400 lights mounted in a line on a print bar.

The speed, resolution, and cost is about the same as the laser printers. But they have fewer moving parts than a laser, so should have fewer mechanical problems. They should cost less to manufacture so the price should come down to less than the lasers.

Sources. Call these companies for more information:

Taxan USA Corp.	(800) 772-7491
Data Technology	(408) 727-8899

Ink Jet Printers

Ink jet printers spray ink onto the paper to form characters. They are quiet since there is no impact. Hewlett-Packard is the major manufacturer of these printers. They are small, quiet, and capable of printing in various colors.

The Hewlett-Packard DeskJet is an ink jet printer that costs less than $1000. It can produce 300 DPI resolution that approaches that of a high-cost laser, but it does not use the laser type engine. Instead it has a head that is similar to that of the dot matrix printer. Ink is forced through a matrix of tiny ink holes to form characters on plain paper.

The DeskJet output looks very much like a laser. But it has many of the limitations of a dot matrix printer. It is limited in its graphics capabilities and fonts. A laser can print about 8 sheets per minute. The DeskJet can only print about 2 per minute. For more information, contact:

Hewlett-Packard
1820 Embarcadero
Palo Alto, CA 94303
(800) 367-4772

Other Types of Printers

Several other types of printers are available. One kind, thermal printers, are relatively inexpensive. They use heat to darken a specially treated paper. They are quieter than the impact type dot matrix printers, but the quality may be rather poor.

Plotters

Plotters are devices that can draw almost any shape or design under the control of a computer. A plotter may have from one up to eight or more different colored pens. There are several different types of pens for various applications such as writing on different types of paper or on film or transparencies. Some pens are quite similar to ballpoint pens, others have a fiber-type point. The points are usually made to a very close tolerance and can be very small so that the thickness of the lines can be controlled. The line thicknesses can be very critical in some design drawings.

The plotter arm can be directed to choose any one of the various pens. This arm is attached to a sliding rail and can be moved from one side of the paper to the other. A solenoid can lower the pen at any predetermined spot on the paper for it to write.

While the motor is moving the arm horizontally from side to side, a second motor moves the paper vertically up and down beneath the arm. This motor can move the paper to any predetermined spot and the pen can be lowered to write on that spot. The motors are controlled by predefined X-Y coordinates. They can move the pen and paper in very small increments so that almost any design can be traced out.

Values could be assigned of perhaps 1 to 1000 for the Y elements and the same values for the X or horizontal elements. The computer could then direct the plotter to move the pen to any point or coordinate on the sheet.

Plotters are ideal for such things as printing out circuit board designs, architectural drawings, making transparencies for overhead presentations, graphs, charts, and many CAD/CAM drawings. All of this can be done in as many as seven different colors.

There are several different sized plotters. Some desktop units are limited to only A and B sized plots. There are other large floor standing models that can accept paper as wide as four feet and several feet long.

A desk model might cost as little as $200 and up to $2000. A floor standing large model might cost from $4000 up to $10,000. If you are doing very precise work, for instance designing a transparency that will be photographed and used to make a circuit board, you will want one of the more accurate and more expensive machines.

Many very good graphics programs available can use plotters. But there are several manufacturers of plotters, and again, there are no standards. Just like the printers, each company has developed its own drivers. Again, this is very frustrating for software developers who must try to include drivers in their programs for all of the various brands. If you buy a software program that cannot drive your particular plotter, you will be *SOL* ("Sorry, Out of Luck").

Hewlett-Packard has been one of the major plotter manufacturers. Many of the other manufacturers now emulate the HP drivers. Almost all of the software that requires plotters includes a driver for HP. If you are in the market for a plotter, try to make sure that it can emulate the HP.

Houston Instruments is also a major manufacturer of plotters. Their plotters are somewhat less expensive than the Hewlett-Packard.

One of the disadvantages of plotters is that they are rather slow. There are now some software programs that will allow a laser printer to act as a plotter. Of course, the laser is limited to $8^1/2$ by 11 inch sheets of paper.

Sources. Here is a list of some of the plotter manufacturers. Call them for a product list and latest prices.

Alpha Merics	(818) 999-5580
Bruning Computer Graphics	(415) 372-7568
CalComp	(800) 225-2667
Hewlett-Packard	(800) 367-4772
Houston Instrument	(512) 835-0900
Ioline Corp.	(206) 775-7861
Roland DG	(213) 685-5141

Plotter Supplies

It is important that a good supply of plotter pens, special paper, film, and other supplies be kept on hand. Plotter supplies are not as widely available as printer supplies. A very high-priced plotter might have to sit idle for some time if the supplies are not on hand. Most of the plotter vendors provide supplies for their equipment. Here is the name of one company that specializes in plotter pens, plotter media, accessories, and supplies:

Plotpro
P.O. Box 800370
Houston, TX 77280
(800) 223-7568

Installing a Printer or Plotter

Most IBM compatible computers allow for four ports, two serial and two parallel. No matter whether it is a plotter, or dot matrix, daisy wheel, or laser printer, it will require one of these ports. If you have a 286 or 386 computer, these ports might be built into the motherboard. (See the previous chapter and the discussion for installing modems.)

If you have built-in ports, you will still need a short cable from the motherboard to the outside. You will then need a longer cable to your printer. If you don't have built-in ports, you will have to buy interface boards.

Almost all dot matrix printers use the parallel ports. Many of the daisy wheel, laser printers, and most of the plotters use serial ports. For the serial printers, you will need a board with a RS232C connector. The parallel printers use a Centronics-type connector. When you buy your printer, buy a cable from the vendor that is configured for your printer and your computer.

Interfaces

Printers can be very difficult to interface. In the serial system, the bits are transmitted serially, one bit at a time. The parallel system uses an 8-line bus and 8 bits are transmitted at a time, 1 bit on each line at a time. It takes 8 bits to make 1 character. So with the parallel system, a whole character can be transmitted on the 8 lines at one time.

The parallel system was developed by the Centronics Company. IBM adopted the parallel system as the default mode for their PC and PC-XT. Of course, the clones followed suit and so parallel inputs are the standard on most printers sold today. Many printers will accept either parallel or serial.

You can buy printer interface boards with a parallel or serial output port. Some multifunction boards provide both.

Serial Printers

If your computer is an IBM or a compatible clone, it automatically defaults to the parallel printer port. This means that when the computer is turned on it will use the parallel port unless told otherwise. To use the serial output port, use the DOS MODE command as follows:

```
MODE COM1:1200,N,8,P
```

Then

```
MODE LPT1:=COM1
```

The 1200 sets the baud rate to 1200, the N means No parity, the 8 means 8 bits, the P means to send the output to the Printer. The baud rate for some printers might be from 300 to 9600 or more. Check your documentation and set it to the appropriate rate. The parity can be none, one, or two, the bits are usually 8, but might be 7. The output could be directed to a modem or to some device other than the printer. The second MODE command means that LPT1 or LinePrinTer1 will be connected to the COM1 output port.

The computer will remain in this mode unless a subsequent MODE command is issued to change it, or the computer is turned off or rebooted. So that you don't have to go through the trouble of typing in this command every time you turn on your computer, you can put the MODE command in your AUTOEXEC.BAT file. This automatically loads the command each time the computer is turned on.

Printer Sharing

Ordinarily a printer will sit idle most of the time. Some days, I don't even turn my printer on. Usually most large offices and businesses have several computers. Almost all of them are connected to a printer in some fashion, but it would be a waste of money if each one had a separate printer that was only used occasionally. It is fairly simple to make arrangements so that a printer or plotter can be used by several computers.

If there are only two or three computers, and they are fairly close together, it is not much of a problem. There are manual switch boxes that cost from $25 to $150 that can allow any one of two or three computers to be switched on line to a printer.

But with a simple switch box, if the computers use the standard parallel ports, the cables from the computers to the printer should be no more than 10 feet long. Parallel signals will begin to degrade if the cable is longer than 10 feet and could cause some loss of data. A serial cable can be as long as 50 feet. But this means that the printer would have to be capable of accepting a serial input.

If the printer has a parallel-only input, it is possible to buy a serial-to-parallel converter. A fairly long serial cable can be used, then the signals can be converted to parallel just before the cable is connected to the printer.

If the office or business is fairly complex, then several electronic switching devices are available. Some of them are very sophisticated and can allow a large number of different types of computers to be attached to a single printer or plotter. Many of them have built-in buffers and can allow cable lengths up to 250 feet or more. The costs range from $160 up to $1400.

Of course, several networks are available to connect computers and printers together. Many of them can be very expensive to install.

One of the least expensive methods of sharing a printer is for the person to generate the text to be printed out on one computer, record it on a floppy disk, then walk over to a computer that is connected to a printer. If it is in a large office, a single low-cost XT clone could be dedicated to a high-priced printer.

Sources. Here are the names and phone numbers of some of these companies that provide switch systems. Call them for their product specs and current price list:

Logical Connection Fifth Generation Systems	(800) 225-2775
EasyPrint Server Technology	(800) 835-1515
Buffalo XL-256 Buffalo Products	(800) 345-2356
Auto Six Shooter Black Box Corp.	(412) 746-5530
Crosspoint 8 Crosspoint Systems	(800) 232-7729
PrintDirector MS-1 Digital Products	(800) 243-2333
ShareSpool ESI-2076 Extended Systems	(208) 322-7163
Caretaker Plus Rose Electronics	(713) 933-7673
Western Telematic PSU-81B Western Telematic	(800) 854-7226
Quadram Microfazer VI	(404) 564-5566

15

Other Ways to Get the Most From Your Computer

I hope that you already have a good use, excuse, or justification for your computer. Even if you do have a good use for your computer, you might not be utilizing it to its fullest. I am going to list a few things that might be helpful.

Desktop Publishing

Desktop publishing (DTP) can cover a lot of territory. A system could be just a PC with a word processor and a dot matrix printer. Or it could be a full-blown system that used laser printers with PostScript and lots of memory, scanners, 286 or 386 computers with many, many megabytes of hard disk space, sophisticated software, and other goodies.

As always, the type of system needed will depend on what you want it to do. (And of course, how much money you want to spend.)

DTP can be used for newsletters, ads, flyers, brochures, sales proposals, sophisticated manuals, and all sorts of printed documents. I have a friend who has written and published several books with a fairly simple and relatively inexpensive DTP system. (But I have to tell you, since the book business is very competitive, he hasn't made a lot of money.)

Software

If your project doesn't include graphics, then you only need a good printer and a good word processing program. WordStar 5.0, WordStar 2000, WordPerfect 5.0, and many others would more than suffice. Most of the more sophisticated word processors will even let you add a few graphics here and there.

If you need to do a lot of graphics and use different types and fonts, then you should look at higher-level software packages such as Ventura from Xerox for $895 or PageMaker from Aldus for $795. GEM Desktop Publisher from DRI at $299 and Inte Graphics from IMSI for $195 will do almost everything one would need to do for a lot less money. Many, many other software packages range from $89 up to $15,000. Here are just a few companies who supply page-layout software:

Company	Product	Price	Phone
Acorn Plus	Easy Laser	$ 99.95	(213) 876-5237
Aldus Corp.	PageMaker	$795.00	(206) 622-5500
Ashton-Tate	Byline	$295.00	(800) 437-4327
CSI Publishing	Pagebuilder	$299.00	(800) 842-2486
Data Transforms	Fontrix	$165.00	(303) 832-1501
Digital Research	GEM DTP	$299.00	(800) 443-4200
Haba/Arrays	Front Page	$199.00	(818) 994-1899
IMSI	Inte Graphics	$595.00	(415) 454-8901
LTI Softfonts	Laser-Set	$199.95	(714) 739-1453
Savtek	ETG Plus	$ 89.95	(800) 548-7173
Timeworks	Publish It	$199.95	(800) 535-9497
Xerox Corp.	Ventura	$895.00	(800) 832-6979

Clip Art

Several software packages have images that you can import and place in your page layout. The software will let you move them around, rotate, size, or revise them. The images are humans, animals, business, technical, industrial, borders, enhancements, etc. Most of the companies have the images set up in modules on floppies. Most have several modules with hundreds and even thousands of images. The cost of each of the modules ranges from $15 up to $200 so I will not list any of the prices. Contact the companies for more information.

Company	Product	Phone	Category
Antic	Cyber Design	(800) 234-7001	Architecture
Artware Systems	Artware	(800) 426-3858	Varied
CD Designs	Graphics	(800) 326-5326	Varied
EMS Shareware	DTP Library	(301) 924-3594	Varied
Kinetic Corp.	U.S. Maps	(502) 583-1679	Maps
Metro ImageBase	PicturePak	(800) 525-1552	Varied
Micrografx	Clip Art	(800) 272-3729	Varied
Micrograph	DrawArt	(206) 838-4677	Varied
PCsoftware	Exec. Picture	(619) 571-0981	Varied
Springboard	Clip Art	(800) 445-4780	Varied
Studio Ad Art	Click & Clip	(800) 453-1860	Varied

Printers

If you are going to be doing primarily text, then you can probably get by with a good 24-pin dot matrix printer. You will need a laser printer if you expect to be doing a lot of graphics and using different style types and fonts.

For a high-level DTP system, you will need a laser with a good page-description language (PDL). The Adobe PostScript is the original and most popular PDL. A PDL laser can be rather expensive if it is configured with sufficient memory, fonts, and type styles. If you have a laser printer that does not have PostScript, you can install a QMS PostScript controller board in your computer. Contact QMS below. Here are a few PostScript laser printers:

Company	Product	Memory	Phone	Price
Digital Equipment	ScriptPrinter	2Mb	(508) 493-1306	$5595
NewGen Systems	TurboPS/300	2Mb	(714) 641-8900	$5495
Phillips Info.	PS-8	2Mb	(800) 527-0204	$5591
QMS Inc.	QMS-PS 810	2Mb	(800) 631-2692	$4995
Ricoh Corp.	6000/PS	2Mb	(800) 447-4264	$4495
Texas Instruments	OmniLaser	2Mb	(800) 527-3500	$4595

If you are serious about DTP there are several books on the subject. Here are a few that Windcrest publishes:

Mastering PageMaker 3.0: IBM Version, G. Keith Gurganus, No. 3176, $16.95

Ventura Publisher: A Creative Approach, Elizabeth McClure, No. 3012, $17.95

The Print Shop Project Book, Deborah Homan and Philip Seyer Associates, No. 3218, $15.95

IBM Desktop Publishing, Gabriel Lanyi & Jon Barrett, No. 3109, $25.50 (Paper), $37.95 (Hard)

Desktop Publishing and Typesetting, Michael L. Kleper, No. 2700, $29.95

You can order these books from Windcrest Books, Blue Ridge Summit, PA 17294-0850 or telephone (717) 794-2191.

Apple Computer has developed a *Guide to Desktop Publishing* that is available at Apple dealerships for $8. This is a good primer, but of course it is a bit biased toward the Apple products.

There are also several magazines that are devoted to DTP. Here are three of them:

Publish!
P.O. Box 51966
Boulder, CO 80321-1966
$23.95

PC Publishing
P.O. Box 5050
Des Plaines, IL 60019
$36.00

EP&P
29 N. Wacker Dr.
Chicago, IL 60606-9980
$28.00

Most of the other magazines listed in Chapter 17 quite often have DTP articles.

Local Area Networks

If you have a small business with several computers, you could probably benefit from tying them all together into a local area network. A LAN can allow multi-tasking, multiusers, security, centralized backup, and shared resources such as printers, modems, fax machines, and other peripherals.

A LAN can be several dumb terminals tied to a large server or it can be two or more computers tied together so that they can share and process files. This would be called a *shared CPU* system since all the terminals share the same CPU. This can work well if there are only a few terminals on line. But if there are several vying for attention at the same time, there will usually be some delay.

A LAN can also consist of a combination of dumb terminals, low-cost PCs and 386s. Ordinarily, the PCs will have a floppy-disk drive. But there are some installations that have diskless PCs. Usually the reason for not having disks is for security purposes. For instance, a bank would not want to risk having an employee downloading information about their customers onto a floppy disk.

Most systems require a plug-in board and software to drive them. Some of the more sophisticated boards may cost from $300 up to $1000 each or more. This means that you would need one of these boards installed in each station terminal and a more expensive master in the server. If you have several nodes, it can become quite expensive.

Low-Cost Switches and LANs

You might just want to be able to have two computers share a printer, or perhaps have a computer be able to output to a laser printer or a dot matrix. This could be done very easily with mechanical switches. Some switch boxes can handle the switching needs for as many as four or five systems. These boxes may cost from $50 up to $500 or more. Here are some vendors of mechanical switchers:

Black Box Corporation	(412) 746-5530
Global Computer Supplies	(800) 845-6225
Inmac Supplies	(408) 727-1970
Lyben Computer Systems	(313) 589-3440
R + R Direct	(800) 654-7587

Some electronic switch boxes are a bit more sophisticated and have more capabilities and functions. Some might offer buffers and spooling. Here are a few vendors:

Bravo Communications	(408) 270-4500
Digital Products	(800) 243-2333
Fifth Generations	(800) 225-2775
Novotek Corp.	(415) 492-3393
Qubit Corp.	(408) 747-0740

Here are some companies who provide low cost LANs that use the RS232 serial port:

Applied Knowledge	(408) 739-3000
IDEAssociates	(617) 663-6878
Server Technology	(800) 835-1515
Software Link LANlink	(404) 448-5465

Servers

Quite often there will be one computer that will act as the server for one or more workstations. For instance, an 80386 computer could have an 80Mb or even up to 240Mb or larger, hard disk system. The disks could store a large database of the company's customers, their account numbers, their addresses, and other pertinent information. The database might also include a list of the company's products, part numbers, and inventory. It could also include the accounts payable, accounts receivable, employee payroll information, company assets and liabilities, computerized forecasts, budgets, and other financial information.

The server hard disk could have several software programs such as WordStar or WordPerfect for word processing, dBASE IV for database users, Quattro or SuperCalc5 for financial and spreadsheet needs, Windows, and several application specific programs. This software and the files on the hard disk could be available to anyone with a workstation tied to the system.

Printers sit idle much of the time. It would not be cost effective to have a printer at each workstation. The server could be attached to one or more printers such as a dot matrix or a laser. These printers would then be available to anyone on the network and be much better utilized.

All of the computer magazines carry articles on networking from time to time. The Novell Corporation is the leading manufacturer of network products. They publish a free magazine to qualified subscribers called *LAN Times*. If you need a network system, I would suggest that you contact Novell and ask for a subscription form. Here is the address:

LAN Times
151 East 1700 So., Suite 100
Provo, UT 84606

Also several books that have been published on networking. Here are a couple that Windcrest Books publishes:

TOPS: The IBM/Macintosh Connection, Stephen Cobb and Marty Jost, No. 3210, $24.95 (Paper), $34.95 (Hard)

Networking with the IBM Token-Ring, C. Townsend, No. 2829, $24.95 (Paper), $34.95 (Hard)

You can order them from Windcrest Books, Blue Ridge Summit, PA 17294-0850.

The Computer as a Tax Deduction

If you have a home office, you might be able to deduct part of the cost of your computer from your income taxes. You might even be able to deduct a portion of your rent, telephone bills, and other legitimate business expenses.

I can't give you all of the IRS rules for a home office, but I would recommend that you buy the latest tax books and consult with the IRS or a tax expert. There are many rules and regulations, and they change frequently. For more information, call the IRS and ask for publication #587, *Business Use of Your Home.*

Because I use my computer strictly for business, it is a legitimate business deduction. (It must be depreciated over a five-year period of time.) If you use your computer part-time for business, you might still be able to deduct some of its cost. You should check with a tax expert.

One Hour Photo

The new computerized photo developing machines take up very little space. Because they are computerized, they are fairly easy to learn and use.

Comparatively speaking, it takes very little money to rent or lease-to-buy the machinery in order to get started. Of course, you should have a computer to keep track of all of your business expenses and income. You might also install a laser printer for specialized print orders. And of course, a copy machine.

The photo industry often puts on large shows, much like the Computer Dealers EXposition (COMDEX). They display all of the equipment needed for a mini-lab. It is interesting and exciting to visit, even if you are not going to buy anything.

If you are interested, here are two magazines that you might subscribe to:

Photo Lab Management Magazine
PLM publishing
P.O. Box 1700
Santa Monica, CA 90406
(213) 451-1344

Photo Marketing
3000 Picture Place
Jackson, MI 49201
(517) 788-8100

This is the official publication of the Photo Marketing Association.

Other Home Businesses

The Small Business Administration of the U.S. Government prints a 48 page booklet called, *Starting and Managing a Business from Your Home*. It costs $1.75 and is available from the Superintendent of Documents, U.S. GPO, Washington, DC 20402.

Of course there are hundreds of types of businesses and professions that can be operated from the home. You might want to subscribe to a magazine called *Home Office Computing*, 730 Broadway, New York, NY 10003. Basic subscription price at this date is $19.97 per year.

Home Office Equipment

If you had the best computer in the world, but you couldn't work comfortably with it, you would not be getting the most out of your system. Adequate lighting, a comfortable work area, shelves (to keep manuals within reach), a good chair, and other amenities can make a difference.

If you don't have a lot of money to spend on filing cabinets, chairs, and desks, most large cities have used office furniture stores. If you are not too proud, you can usually save quite a lot of money. If you have more time than money, you can also buy shelving and install it yourself.

16

Essential Software

Software is never as easy to learn and use as they say it is. (Three of the greatest lies are the check is in the mail, of course I will respect you in the morning, and you can learn this software package in just a few minutes.)

More software is already written and immediately available than you can use in a lifetime. Off-the-shelf programs can do almost everything that you could ever want to do with a computer. Yet thousands and thousands of software developers are working overtime to design new programs. In some cases, the old version can do all you need to do.

For most general applications, there are certain basic programs that you will need. For instance BASIC is a common programming language. GW-BASIC from Microsoft is more or less the standard. Many applications still use BASIC. Even if you are not a programmer, it is simple enough that you can design a few special applications yourself with it.

The six categories of programs that you will need to do most types of ordinary productive work with your computer are disk operating system (DOS), word processors, databases, spreadsheets, utilities, disk management, and communications. Depending on what you intend to use your computer for, there might be other specialized needs.

Software can be more expensive than the hardware. The prices might also vary from vendor to vendor. Few people pay the *list* price. It will pay you to shop around; software that had a list price of $700 has been advertised from a discount house for as little as $350. Also remember that there are excellent public domain programs that are free that can do almost everything that the high-cost commercial programs can do. Check your local bulletin board, user group, or the listings for public domain software.

I can't possibly list all of the thousands of software packages available. Most computer magazines have detailed reviews of software in every issue. Briefly, here are some popular examples of the essential software packages that you will probably need.

Operating Systems Software

MS-DOS. DOS to a computer is like gasoline to an automobile. Without it, it won't operate. DOS is an acronym for *disk operating system*, but it does much more than just operate the disks. In recognition of this, the new OS/2 has dropped the D.

You can use any version of DOS on your computer. I would recommend version 3.3 or 4.01. Version 3.3 adds a few utilities that are not in 3.2 such as the ability to use hard disks larger than 32Mb. Of course the higher DOS versions can operate any software that was written for an earlier version.

OS/2. Unless you have some special need for multitasking or multiusing, you might not need OS/2. You can probably get by with DOS. Besides, there isn't that much software available yet to take advantage of OS/2. Cost can be another factor in staying with DOS, and it will also take some time to learn OS/2. Another factor is that there will be slight variations in versions released by different companies; IBM will have a version, Compaq has theirs, and several other companies will have their own versions.

But if you just have to have it, it will allow you to more fully utilize your fantastic 386. It will do almost everything that you always wanted DOS to do.

DESQview. This is an excellent alternative to OS/2. It allows multitasking and multiusers. You can have up to 50 programs running at the same time and have as many as 250 windows open. It runs all DOS software and is simple to learn and use.

Concurrent DOS 386. This is another excellent alternative to OS/2 that is also a multitasking and multiuser operating system. It takes advantage of the 80386 virtual 8086 mode and allows simultaneous processing of DOS applications. It is easy to install and operates with familiar DOS commands.

Word Processors

The most used and useful of all software is word processing. There are literally hundreds of word processor packages, each one slightly different than the others. I only list a few of the better known packages. Most of the word processor programs come with a spelling checker. Some of them come with a thesaurus which can be very handy. They often include several other utilities for such things as communications programs for your modem, outlines, desktop publishing, or print merging.

WordStar. There are probably more copies of WordStar (in various versions) in existence than any other word processor. Many magazine and book editors expect their writers to send manuscripts to them on a disk in WordStar.

WordStar 2000 Release 3 includes some desktop publishing features. Like WordStar 5.5 it has a spelling corrector, an excellent thesaurus, an outline program, communications program, and many improvements over earlier versions. The latest version of WordStar comes on 21 360K disks. My original WordStar for my little CP/M Morrow with 64K memory came on a single 180K disk.

WordPerfect. WordPerfect is presently the hottest selling word processor. They offer free unlimited toll-free support. WordPerfect has the ability to select fonts by a proper name, has simplified printer installation, the ability to do most desktop publishing functions, columns, and many other useful functions and utilities.

Microsoft Word. This package was developed by the same people who developed MS-DOS. It has lots of features and utilities. It is one of top ten bestsellers in the country.

PC-Write. This is a shareware word processor, and is free if copied from an existing user. They ask for a $16 donation. Full registration with manual and technical support is $89. It is easy to learn and is an excellent personal word processor.

If you want to learn more about word processors, subscribe to almost any computer magazine. Most of them will have a review of a package almost every month.

Database Programs

Database packages are very useful for managing large amounts of information. Most programs allow one to store information, search it, sort it, do calculations, make up reports, and several other very useful features.

At the present time there are almost as many database programs as there are word processors. Few of them are compatible with others, but a strong effort in the industry is to establish some standards under the *Structured Query Language* (SQL) standard. Several of the larger companies have announced their support for this standard.

The average price for the better known database packages is almost twice that of word processors.

dBASE IV. Ashton-Tate with their dBASE II was one of the first with a database program for the personal computer. dBASE IV, the latest version, is a very powerful program with hundreds of features. It is a highly structured program and can be a bit difficult to learn. dBASE IV is much faster than dBASE III, has a built-in compiler, SQL, and an upgraded user interface along with several other enhancements.

askSam 4.2. The name is an acronym for *Access Knowledge via Stored Access Method*. It is a free-form, text-oriented database management system, almost like a word processor. Data can be typed in randomly, then sorted and accessed. Data can also be entered in a structured format for greater organization. It is not quite as powerful as dBASE IV, but is much easier to use. It is also much less expensive. It is ideal for personal use and for the majority of business needs. They also have discount program for students.

Spreadsheets

Spreadsheets are primarily number crunchers. They have a matrix of cells in which data can be entered. Data in a particular cell can be acted on by formulas and mathematical equations. If the data in the cell acted on affects other cells, recalculations are done on them.

Spreadsheets are essential in business for inventory, for expenses, for accounting purposes, for forecasting, for making charts, and dozens of other business uses. A large number of spreadsheet programs are available, so I only list a few of them.

Microsoft Excel. For years, Lotus 1-2-3 has been the premier spreadsheet, but it appears that Excel is now taking the top spot and honors. Excel is a very powerful program with pull-down menus, windows, and dozens of features, including performance as a database.

Quattro. The Quattro spreadsheet looks very much like Lotus 1-2-3, but it has better graphics capabilities for charts, calculates faster, has pull-down menus, can print sideways, and has several other features not found in Lotus 1-2-3.

SuperCalc5. SuperCalc was one of the pioneer spreadsheets (it was introduced in 1981), but it has never enjoyed the popularity of Lotus, although it had features not found in Lotus. It is an excellent spreadsheet compatible with Lotus 1-2-3 files and can link to dBASE and several other files. Computer Associates has also developed several excellent account packages.

VP-Planner Plus. Adam Osborne started the Paperback Software Company after his Osborne Computer Company went bankrupt. He developed several low-cost software packages. VP-Planner has several features not found in Lotus 1-2-3 including pull-down menus, mouse support, and a macro library.

Lotus 1-2-3. Lotus finally released version 3.0, but it requires an enormous amount of memory, so they have also released 2.2 which can still be run on machines with 640K. Some of the changes in the releases are the ability to link between spreadsheets, a macro "learn" keystroke capture feature, a library of reusable macros, a single operation for undo, search and replace, and several new macro commands.

If you are a registered 2.01 user, you can upgrade for $150. Call (800) 872-3387 for upgrade information.

Utilities

Utilities are essential tools that can unerase a file, detect bad sectors on a hard disk, diagnose, unfragment, sort, or do many other things.

Norton's Utilities was the first and is still foremost in the utility department. Mace Utilities has several functions not found in Norton. Mace Gold is a new integrated package of utilities that includes most of those in the original Mace, plus POP (a power-out protection program), a backup utility, and TextFix and dbFix for data retrieval. PC Tools has even more utilities than Norton's or Mace's.

Ontrack, the people who have sold several million copies of Disk Manager for hard disks, also has a utility program called DOSUTILS. It provides tools to display and modify any physical sector of a hard disk, to scan for bad sectors, and to diagnose and analyze the disk.

Steve Gibson's SpinRite, Prime Solution's Disk Technician, and Gazelle's OPTune are excellent hard disk tools for low-level formatting, for defragmenting, and for detecting potential bad sectors on a hard disk.

CheckIt is a program that quickly checks and reports on your computer's configuration, the type of CPU it has, the amount of memory, and the installed drives and peripherals. It runs diagnostic tests of the installed items and can do performance benchmark tests.

Directory and Disk Management Programs

Dozens of disk management programs can help you keep track of your files and data on the hard disk, find it, rename it, view it, sort it, copy, delete it, and many other useful utilities. They can save an enormous amount of time and make life a lot simpler.

Executive Systems XTree was one of the first and still one of the best disk management programs. It has recently been revised to *XTree Pro*. It is now much faster and has several new features. Gazelle Systems Q-DOS II was introduced shortly after Xtree and does just about everything that XTree does.

Other Utilities

If you have a lot of files in several subdirectories, you can sometimes forget in which subdirectory you filed something. A couple of programs can go through all of your directories and look for a file by name, but since you are only allowed eight characters for a file name, it is difficult to remember what is in each file. Several programs can search through all the files and help you find what you want. You can even use wildcards and find matches.

Magellan from Lotus is a very sophisticated program that can navigate and do global searches through files and across directories.

Three other search programs, O'Neill Software's Text Collector, Microlytic's Gofer, and Access Softek's Dragnet, are very similar. They are not as sophisticated as Magellan and are somewhat limited. Text Collector is a bit faster than Gofer and has a few more features. Dragnet works under the Windows environment.

Windows

Windows gives the DOS world most of the best features of the Macintosh. If you have a 386 machine, it will run Windows 2.0, but only one program at a time. If you really want to take advantage of more of the fantastic features of the 386, then you need Windows/386.

Windows works best with a mouse. It brings Macintosh-type screens and ease of use to the DOS world. Several application and utility programs are built-in to Windows that are similar to the utilities in SideKick (discussed next).

Many third-party application programs have been developed to run in the Windows environment and take advantage of the windows and pull-down menus.

Windows Graph. Windows Graph is a presentation graphics program that uses Windows. Data from spreadsheets and other files can be ported to the program to make all sorts of graphs.

Omnis Quartz. Blythe Software has developed Omnis Quartz, a database program that works in the Windows environment with a mouse. It takes full advantage of the Windows capabilities in the screens and multiple windows.

ClickStart. The hDC Computer Corp. has developed ClickStart, an applications organizer for Windows. It allows you to customize Windows and your applications, design your own icons and help screens, password protect confidential files, and more.

HyperPAD. The Brightbill-Roberts Company has developed Hyper-PAD, which makes the PC look more and more like the Macintosh. HyperPAD is quite similar to HyperCard. HyperPAD can be used with or without a mouse. It can create, modify, and run personal applications from a *pad*. The pads are similar to a menu. It comes with several pads which can be modified and customized. You need only point and click, or use an arrow key to run an application.

SideKick Plus

SideKick is in a class by itself. SideKick loads into memory and pops up whenever you need it, no matter what program you happen to be running at the time. It was first released in 1984 and has been the most popular pop-up program ever since. It now has scientific, programmer, and business calculators; a note pad; a calendar; an automatic phone dialer; a sophisticated script language; and much more.

Menu Creation

VM Personal Computing, the creators of the relay series of communications programs, has developed Beyond Bat. It allows someone who has a bit of computer experience to create complex batch files and design menus to make using the computer much easier. It can also set up the function keys for easy data input and file manipulation.

I can't possibly mention all of the fantastic software that is available. Thousands and thousands of ready-made software programs will allow you to do almost anything with your computer. Look through any computer magazine for the reviews and ads. You should be able to find programs for almost any application.

17

Mail Order and Magazines

I tried to list a few vendors when I mentioned a product, but it is not possible to list all of the sellers and sources for the products that you may need. There are thousands of vendors and many more thousands of products.

One of the best ways to find what you need is through the magazine advertisements. The magazines also usually have informative articles scattered among the ads.

If you live near a city, you can also visit the computer stores in town. You can actually see and touch the merchandise, maybe even try it out before you buy it.

Again, if you live near a large city, there will probably be a few swap meets every now and then. In the San Francisco Bay area and in the Los Angeles area, there is one almost every weekend. Going to a swap meet is usually better than going to a computer store. You can look at lots of items and compare prices and features. Often several booths or vendors will sell the same thing. You can get each vendor's best price, then make your best deal. Some vendors will try to meet the price of their competition. When it gets near closing time, some vendors would rather sell at a reduced price rather than pack the goods up and take them back to their store.

Mail Order Guidelines

Shopping at a local computer store can be a hassle time-wise and traffic-wise. Or you can look through a magazine, find an ad for what you need, call, and have your order delivered to your door. And, an extra plus, it might cost you 40 percent less than what you would pay at the local store. On the down side, you might have to wait three or four weeks before you get your goodies unless you pay extra to have them shipped by an express service. Another big minus is that you are buying the components sight unseen.

Because of mail fraud, the publishers and the advertisers got together and formed the *Microcomputer Marketing Council* (MMC) of the Direct Marketing Association. They now police the advertisers fairly closely. But just to be on the safe side, here are a few rules that you should follow when ordering through the mail.

1. Make sure to get the advertiser's street address. In some ads, they give only a phone number. Also, if possible, look through past issues of the same magazine for previous ads. If the advertisement has been in several issues, then the vendor is probably okay.

2. Check through the magazines for other vendors' prices for this product. The prices should be fairly close. If it appears to be a bargain that is too good to be true, then . . . (you know the rest).

3. Buy from a vendor who is a member of the Microcomputer Marketing Council (MMC) of the Direct Marketing Association (DMA) or some other recognized association. Members who belong to marketing associations have agreed to abide by the ethical guidelines and rules of the associations. Except for friendly persuasion and the threat of expulsion, the associations have little power over the members, but most members put a great value on their membership. Most advertisers in the major computer magazines are members.

4. Do your homework. Know exactly what you want, state precisely the model, make, size, component, or any other pertinent information. Tell them which ad you are ordering from, ask them if the price is the same, if the item is in stock, and when you can expect delivery. If the item is not in stock, indicate whether you will accept a substitute or want your money refunded. Ask for an invoice or order number. Ask the person's name. Write down all of the information, the time, the date, the company's address and phone number, the description of item, and the promised delivery date. Save any and all correspondence.

5. Ask if the advertised item comes with all the necessary cables, parts, accessories, software, etc. Ask what the warranties are. Know the seller's return or refund policies and with whom should you correspond if there is a problem.

6. Don't send cash. You will have no record of it. If possible, use a credit card. A personal check can cause a delay of three to four weeks while the vendor waits for it to clear. A money order or credit card order should be filled and shipped immediately. Keep a copy of the money order.

7. If you have not received your order by the promised delivery date, notify the seller.

8. Try the item out when you receive it. If you have a problem, notify the seller immediately by phone, then in writing. Give all details. Don't return the merchandise unless the dealer gives you authoriza-

tion. Make sure to keep a copy of the shipper's receipt or packing slip or evidence that it was returned.

9. If you believe the product is defective or you have a problem, reread your warranties and guarantees. Reread the manual and any documentation. It is very easy to make an error or misunderstand how an item operates if you are unfamiliar with it. Before you go to a lot of trouble, try to get some help from someone else or have someone verify that you do have a problem. Many times a problem can disappear, and the vendor will not be able to duplicate it.

10. Try to work out your problem with the vendor. If you cannot, then write to the consumer complaint agency in the seller's state. You should also write to the magazine and to the DMA at 6 E. 43rd St., New York, NY 10017.

Magazines

Here are some good magazines that you might want to subscribe to if you want current information on hardware or software:

Byte Magazine
70 Main St.
Peterborough, NH 03458

Compute!
P.O. Box 3244
Harlan, IA 51593-2424

Computer Currents
5720 Hollis St.
Emeryville, CA 94608

Computer Shopper
407 S. Washington Ave.
Titusville, FL 32796

CompuMag
1747 E. Ave. Q #A-3
Palmdale, CA 93550

Home Office Computing
P.O. Box 51344
Boulder, CO 80321-1344

LAN
12 West 21 Street
New York, NY 10010

MicroTimes Magazine
5951 Canning St.
Oakland, CA 94609

PC Computing
P.O. Box 50253
Boulder, CO 80321-0253

PC World Magazine
501 Second St.
San Francisco, CA 94107

PC Magazine
One Park Ave.
New York, NY 10016

PC Resource
P.O. Box 950
Farmingdale, NY 11737-9650

Personal Computing
10 Mulholland Dr.
Hasbrouck Hts., NJ 07604

Publish!
P.O. Box 55400
Boulder, CO 80321-5400

Vulcan's Computer Buyer's Guide
#2 River Chase Plaza
Birmingham, AL 35244

Free Magazines to Qualified Subscribers

The magazines listed below as free are sent only to qualified subscribers. The subscription price of a magazine usually does not come anywhere near covering the costs of publication, mailing, distribution, etc. Most magazines depend almost entirely on advertisers for income. More subscribers means a magazine can charge more for its ads. Naturally, if the magazine is free, it can attract more subscribers.

PC Week and *InfoWorld* have a limited number of subscribers. They have set standards which have to be met in order to qualify. Even if you answer all of the questions on the application, you still might not qualify. To get a free subscription, you must write to the magazine for a qualifying application form. The form asks several questions such as how you are involved with computers, the company you work for, whether you have any influence in purchasing the computer products listed in the magazines, and several other questions that give them a profile of their readers.

PC Today is another good magazine which is fairly new and still growing. It is aimed at the novice user.

The list of magazines below is not nearly complete. Hundreds of trade magazines are sent free to qualified subscribers. Many of the trade magazines are highly technical and specialized.

PC Week
P.O. Box 5920
Cherry Hill, NJ 08034

InfoWorld
1060 Marsh Rd.
Menlo Park, CA 94025

PC Today
P.O. Box 85380
Lincoln, NE 68501-9815

Computer Design
Circulation Dept.
Box 3466
Tulsa, OK 74101-3466

Computer Systems News
600 Community Dr.
Manhasset, NY 11030

Communications Week
P.O. Box 2070
Manhasset, NY 11030

Computer + Software News
P.O. Box 3119
Grand Central Station
New York, NY 10164-0659

Computer Products
P.O. Box 14000
Dover, NJ 07801-9990

Computer Technology Review
924 Westwood Blvd. Suite 650
Los Angeles, CA 90024-2910

California Business
Subscription Dept.
P.O. Box 70735
Pasadena, CA 91117-9947

Designfax
P.O. Box 1151
Skokie, IL 60076-9917

Discount Merchandiser
215 Lexington Ave.
New York, NY 10157-003

EE Product News
P.O. Box 12982
Overland Park, KS 66212-9817

Electronics
Circulation Dept.
McGraw-Hill Bldg.
1221 Avenue of the Americas
New York, NY 10020

Electronic Manufacturing
Lake Publishing
P.O. Box 159
Libertyville, IL 60048-9989

Electronic Publishing & Printing
650 S. Clark St.
Chicago, IL 60605-9960

Federal Computer Week
P.O. Box 602
Winchester, MA 01890-9948

Identification Journal
2640 N. Halsted St.
Chicago, IL 60614-9962

ID Systems
174 Concord St.
Peterborough, NH 03458

LAN Times
122 East, 1700 South
Provo, UT 84606

Machine Design
Penton Publishing
1100 Superior Ave.
Cleveland, OH 44114

Manufacturing Systems
P.O. Box 3008
Wheaton, IL 60189-9972

Mini-Micro Systems
P.O. Box 5051
Denver, CO 80217-9872

Office Systems 90
P.O. Box 3116
Woburn, MA 01888-9878

Office Systems Dealer 90
P.O. Box 2281
Woburn, MA 01888-9873

Photo Business
1515 Broadway
New York, NY 10036

Quality
P.O. Box 3002
Wheaton, IL 60189-9929

Reseller Management
301 Gibraltar
Box 601
Morris Plains, NJ 07950-9811

Robotics World
P.O. Box 5111
Pittsfield, MA 01203-9830

Scientific Computing & Automation
301 Gibraltar Dr.
Morris, Plains, NJ 07950-0608

Surface Mount Technology
Lake Publishing Corp.
P.O. Box 159
Libertyville, IL 60048-9989

Mail Order Magazines

Some magazines are mail order catalogs for computers and computer-related products.

A magazine that is filled with ads from companies and individuals is *Nuts & Volts*. It is given away free at most computer swaps, but you can subscribe to it for $10 for one year, or $50 for a lifetime subscription. The address is:

Nuts & Volts
P.O. Box 1111
Placentia, CA 92670
(714) 632-7721

A weekly magazine that deals strictly with buy and sell ads is the *Computer Hotline Weekly*. Subscription is $29 for 52 issues. The address is:

Computer Hotline Weekly
Box 1373
Fort Dodge, IA 50501
(800) 247-2000

Many mail order firms list in their catalogs office supplies, paper, ribbons, disks, cartridges, toner, hardware, software, and electronic supplies.

Thumbing through the computer magazines is a great way to become aware of what is available, get some catalogs, and do some price comparisons without leaving home. You should be aware that some of the businesses are not discount houses. They might have slightly higher prices than those you may see advertised in some of the computer magazines.

Public Domain Software

Here is a short list of companies that provide public domain and low-cost software:

PC-Sig
1030D East Duane Ave.
Sunnyvale, CA 94086
(800) 245-6717

Selective Software
903 Pacific Ave. Suite 301
Santa Cruz, CA 95060
800-423-3556

MicroCom Systems
3673 Enochs St.
Santa Clara, CA 95051
(408) 737-9000

The Computer Room
P.O. Box 1596
Gordonsville, VA 22942
(703) 832-3341

Public Brand Software
Box 51315
Indianapolis, IN 46251
(800) 426-3475

Softwarehouse
3080 Olcott Dr., Suite 125A
Santa Clara, CA 95054
(408) 748-0461

Software Express/Direct
Box 2288
Merrifield, VA 22116
(800) 331-8192

PC Plus Consulting
14536 Roscoe Blvd. #201
Panorama City, CA 91402
(818) 891-7930

Micro Star
P.O. Box 4078
Leucadia, CA 92024-0996
(800) 443-6103

National PD Library
1533 Avohill
Vista, CA 92083
(619) 941-0925

International Software Library
511 Encinatas Blvd. Suite 104
Encinatas, CA 92024
(800) 992-1992

Most of the companies listed above can provide a catalog listing of their software. Some of them charge a small fee for their catalog. Write or call them for details and latest prices.

The above list is not complete. You might find several other companies advertised in some of the magazines listed earlier.

Books

One of the better ways to learn about computers is through books. Several companies publish computer books. Windcrest Books publishes several good computer books. For a catalog write to the address in the front of this book. You can find many books at your local bookstore or library. If they do not have exactly what you want, write the publisher (the address can often be found on the copyright page) for a catalog.

18

Troubleshooting

Not too many books have been written on the subject of troubleshooting. Some that you find might be obsolete and out of date. Even if you find one that is current and up to date, chances are rather slim that it will address your particular problem.

I don't want to discourage anyone, but thousands of things can go wrong. It is very easy to plug a cable in backwards or forget to set a switch. Sometimes it is difficult to determine if it is a hardware problem caused by software, or vice versa. Not every problem can be addressed. But several common-sense things can solve many of your problems.

One of the best ways to find answers is to ask someone who has had the same problem. One of the best places to find those people is at a user's group. If at all possible, join one.

You can also get help from local bulletin boards. Your computer is not complete without a modem so that you can contact them.

Several local computer magazines list user groups and bulletin boards as a service to their readers. The nationally published *Computer Shopper* prints a very comprehensive list each month.

Is It Worth It

If you find a problem on a board, a disk drive, or some component, you might try to find out what it would cost before having it repaired. With the low-cost clone hardware that is available, it is often less expensive to scrap a defective part and buy a new one.

Write It Down

The chances are if your computer is going to break down, it will do it at the most inopportune time. If it breaks down, try not to panic. Ranting, cussing, and crying might make you feel better, but it won't solve the problem. Under no circumstances should you beat on your computer with a chair or baseball bat.

Instead get out a pad and pencil and write down everything as it happens. It is very easy to forget. Write down all the particulars, how the cables were plugged in, the software that you were running, and anything that might be pertinent. If you have error messages on your screen, use the PrtSc (for Print Screen) key to print out the messages.

If you can't solve the problem, you might have to call a friend or your vendor for help. If you have all the written information before you, it will help. Try to call from your computer, if possible, as it is acting up.

Power-On Self-Test (POST)

Everytime you turn your computer on, it does a power-on self-test or POST. It checks the RAM, the floppy drives, the hard disk drives, the monitor, the printer, the keyboard, and other peripherals that you have installed.

If it does not find a unit, or if the unit is not functioning correctly, it will beep and display an error code. The codes start with 100 and may go up to 2500. Ordinarily, the codes are not displayed if there is no problem. If there is a problem, the last two digits of the code will be something other than 00s. Here are some of the codes that you might encounter:

101	Motherboard failure.
109	Direct Memory Access test error.
121	Unexpected hardware interrupt occurred.
163	Time and date not set.
199	User indicated configuration not correct.
201	Memory test failure.
301	Keyboard test failure or a stuck key.
401	Monochrome display and/or adapter test failure.
432	Parallel printer not turned on.
501	Color Graphics display and/or adapter test failure.
601	Diskette drives and/or adapter test failure.
701	Math coprocessor test error.
901	Parallel printer adapter test failure.
1101	Asynchronous Communications adapter test failure.
1301	Game control adapter test failure.
1302	Joystick test failure.
1401	Printer test failure.
1701	Fixed disk drive and/or adapter test failure.
2401	Enhanced Graphics display and/or adapter test failure.
2501	Enhanced Graphics display and/or adapter test failure.

DOS has several other error messages if you try to make the computer do something it can't do. Many of the messages are not very clear. The DOS manual explains some of them, but it doesn't give very much detail.

Electrostatic Discharge (ESD)

Before you touch any of the components or handle them, you should ground yourself and discharge any static voltage that you might have built up. You can discharge yourself by touching an unpainted metal part of the case of a computer or other device that is plugged in. A person can build up a charge of 4000 volts or more of electrostatic voltage. If you walk across some carpets and then touch a brass doorknob you can often get a shock and sometimes see a spark fly. Most electronic assembly lines have the workers wear a ground strap whenever they are working with any electrostatic discharge sensitive components.

When I am installing memory chips, or handling other ICs, I often use a clip lead to ground myself. I clip one end to my metal watchband and the other end to the computer case.

Power Supply

Most of the components in your computer are fairly low power and low voltage. The only high voltage in your system is in the power supply, and it is pretty well enclosed. So there is no danger of shock if you open your computer and put your hand inside it. But you should NEVER connect or disconnect a board or cable while the power is on. Fragile semiconductors can be destroyed if you do so.

Most of the power supplies have short-circuit protection. If too much of a load is placed on them, they will drop out and shut down, similar to what happens when a circuit breaker is overloaded.

The fan in the power supply should provide all the cooling that is normally needed. But if you have stuffed it into a corner and piled things around it to shut off all its circulation, it could possibly overheat. Heat is an enemy of semiconductors, so try to give it plenty of breathing room.

The semiconductors in your computer have no moving parts. If they were designed properly, they should last indefinitely. Heat is the enemy that can cause semiconductor failure. The fan in the power supply should provide adequate cooling. All of the openings on the back panel that correspond to the slots on the motherboard should have blank fillers. Even the holes on the bottom of the chassis should be covered with tape. This forces the fan to draw air in from the front of the computer, pull it over the boards and exhaust it through the opening in the power supply case. Nothing should be placed in front of or behind the computer that would restrict air flow.

Here are the pin connections and wire colors from the power supply:

Disk drive power supply connections

Pin	Color	Function
1	Yellow	+12 VDC
2	Black	Ground

Pin	Color	Function
3	Black	Ground
4	Red	+5 VDC

Power supply connections to the motherboard

	Pin	Color	Function
P8	1	White	Power Good
	2	No connection	
	3	Yellow	+ 12 VDC
	4	Brown	– 12 VDC
	5	Black	Ground
	6	Black	Ground
P9	1	Black	Ground
	2	Black	Ground
	3	Blue	–5 VDC
	4	Red	+5 VDC
	5	Red	+5 VDC
	6	Red	+5 VDC

The eight slotted connectors on the motherboard have 62 contacts, 31 on the A side and 31 on the B side. The black ground wires connect to B1 of each of the eight slots. B3 and B29 have +5 VDC, B5 –5 VDC, B7 –12VDC, and B9 has + 12 VDC. These voltages go to the listed pins on each of the eight plug-in slots.

Levels of Troubleshooting

There are many levels of troubleshooting. To do a thorough analysis of a system requires some rather sophisticated and expensive instruments. This advanced level of troubleshooting would require tools such as a good high-frequency oscilloscope, a digital analyzer, a logic probe, signal generators, a voltohmmeter, some clip leads, a pair of side cutter dikes, a pair of long-nose pliers, various screwdrivers, nut drivers, a soldering iron and solder, different-sized screws and bolts, and a test bench with a power supply, disk drives, and a computer with some empty slots so that you could plug in the suspect boards and test them. You would also need plenty of light over the bench and a flashlight or a small light to light up the dark places in the case.

And most importantly, you would need quite a lot of training and experience. You probably won't need all that equipment and training. Most problems that you encounter will be rather minor problems, where just a little common sense and some investigation will tell you what is wrong.

Recommended Tools

Here are some tools that you should have around the house for troubleshooting:

- You should have several sizes of screwdrivers. A couple of them should be magnetic for picking up and starting small screws. You can buy magnetic screwdrivers, or you can make one yourself. Just take a strong magnet and rub it on the blade of the screwdriver a few times. The magnets on cabinet doors will do, as will the voice coil magnet of a loudspeaker. Remember to be very careful with any magnet around your floppy disks, because it can erase them.

- You should also have a small screwdriver with a bent tip that can be used to pry up ICs. Some of the larger ICs are very difficult to remove. One of the blank fillers for the slots on the back panel also makes a good prying tool.

- You should have a couple pairs of pliers. You should have at least one pair of long-nose pliers.

- You will need a pair of side cutter dikes for clipping leads of components and cutting wire. You might buy a pair of cutters that also have wire strippers.

- You shouldn't have to do any soldering but you never know when you might need to. A soldering iron might come in handy. And, of course, some solder.

- No home should be without a voltohmmeter. A voltohmmeter can be used to check for the correct wiring in house wall sockets (the wide slot should be ground), and it can be used to check switches and wiring continuity in your computer, house, phone lines, etc. The only four voltages to check for are $+12$ volts, -12 volts, $+5$ volts and -5 volts. Voltohmmeters are relatively inexpensive.

- You might also want to have several clip leads. You can buy them at the local electronic store.

- You will need a flashlight for looking into the dark places inside the computer.

Fewer Bugs

In the early days, the clone computers had lots of bugs and errors. Some manufacturers didn't spend a lot of money on quality control and testing. Most of the computer manufacturers have been making the parts long enough now that the designs have been firmed up and most bugs have been eliminated.

The Number One Cause of Problems

If you assembled your computer properly, it should work perfectly. But there is always the possibility that something was not plugged in correctly or some minor error was made.

By far the greatest problem in assembling a unit, or adding something to a computer, is not following the instructions. Quite often it is not necessarily the fault of the person trying to follow the instructions. I have worked in the electronic industry for many years, but sometimes I have great difficulty in trying to decipher and follow certain manuals and instructions. Sometimes a very critical instruction or piece of information might be inconspicuously buried on page 300 of a 450-page manual.

If you have just assembled your computer or added something to it, turn it on and check it out before you put the cover on. If something is wrong, it is usually easier to find the problem.

Before you turn it on, though, recheck all the cables and any boards or chips. Make sure that they are seated properly and in the right place. Read the instructions again, then turn on the power. If it works, then put the cover on and button it up.

Common Problems

For most of the common problems, you won't need a lot of test gear. Most of my problems were due to my stupid errors. Many problems are caused by not taking the time to read the manual or instructions, or not being able to understand them.

If you look closely, you might see a cable that is not plugged in properly, a board that is not completely seated, or a switch that is not set right. And many other obvious things.

You can listen for any unusual sounds. The only sound from your computer should be the noise of your drive motors and the fan in the power supply.

If you have ever smelled a burned resistor or a capacitor, you will never forget it. If you smell something very unusual, try to locate where the smell originates.

If you touch the components and some seem to be unusually hot, it could be the cause of your problem. It is always best to be cautious. Except for the insides of your power supply, the voltage should not be more than 12 volts in your computer, so it should be safe to touch the components.

How To Find the Problem

If it seems to be a problem on the motherboard or a plug-in board, look for chips that have the same number. Try swapping them to see if the problem goes away or worsens. If you suspect a board and you have a spare or can borrow one, swap it. Also, if you suspect a board, but don't know which one, take the boards out to the barest minimum. Then add them back until the problem develops. CAUTION! Always turn off the power when plugging in or unplugging a board or cable.

Wiggle the boards and cables to see if it is an intermittent problem. Many times a wire can be broken and still make contact until it is moved. Next, check the ICs and connectors for bent pins. If you have installed memory ICs and get errors, check to make sure that they are seated properly and all the pins are in the sockets. If you swap an IC, make a note of how it is oriented before removing it. A small dot of white paint or a U-shaped indentation should be at the end that has pin 1. If you forgot to note the orientation, look at the other ICs. Most of the boards are laid out so that all of the ICs are oriented the same way. The chrome fillers that are used to cover the unused slots in the back of the case make very good tools for prying up ICs.

You might also try unplugging a cable or a board and plugging it back in. Sometimes the pins may be slightly corroded or not seated properly. Before unplugging a cable, you might put a stripe on the connectors with a marking pen or nail polish so that you can easily see how they should be plugged back in.

The problem could be in a dip switch. You might try turning it on and off a few times. CAUTION! Again, always write down the positions before touching the switches.

Remember, always make a diagram of the wires, cables, and switch settings before you disturb them. It is easy to forget how they were plugged in or set before you moved them. You could end up making things worse. Make a pencil mark before turning a knob or variable coil or capacitor so that it can be returned to the same setting when you find out that it didn't help. Better yet, resist the temptation to reset these types of components. Most were set up using highly sophisticated instruments. They don't usually change enough to cause a problem.

If you are having monitor problems, check the switch settings on the motherboard. Some motherboards have dip switches or shorting bars that must be set to configure the system for monochrome, CGA, EGA, or VGA. Most monitors also have fuses. You might check them. Also check the cables for proper connections.

Printer problems, especially the serial printers, are so many that I will not even attempt to list them here. Many printers today have parallel and serial. The IBM defaults to the parallel system. If at all possible, use the parallel port. Parallel printers have very few problems as compared to serial printers.

Most printers have a self-test. It might run this test fine, but then completely ignore any efforts to get it to respond to the computer if the cables, parity, and baud rate are not properly set.

Sometimes the computer will hang up. You might have told it to do something that it could not do. You can usually do a warm reboot of the computer by pressing the Ctrl, Alt, and Del keys simultaneously. Of course, this would wipe out any file in memory that you might have been working on. Occasionally, the computer might not respond to a warm boot. (You could pound on the keyboard all day long, and it would ignore you.) In that case, you will have to switch off the main power, let it sit for a few seconds, then power up again.

Diagnostic and Utility Software

When IBM came out with the XT, they developed a diagnostic or set-up disk that was included with every machine. It checked the keyboard, the disk drives, the monitor, peripherals, and performed several other tests. When the AT was released, the diagnostic disk was revised a bit to include even more tests. You had to have the disk to set the time, date, and all of the other on-board CMOS system configuration.

Most of the newer BIOS chips now have many of the diagnostic routines built in. These routines allow you to set the time and date, tell the computer what type of hard drive and floppies that are installed, the amount of memory, the wait states, and several other functions. The AMI BIOS has a very comprehensive set of built-in diagnostics that allows hard and floppy disk formatting, checks speed of rotation of disk drives, does performance testing of hard drives and several other tests.

I mentioned these utility software programs in Chapter 16. Many of them have a few diagnostics among the utilities.

Norton Utilities—It also includes several diagnostic and test programs such as disk doctor, disk test, format recover, directory sort, system information, and many others.

Mace Utilities—It does about everything that Norton does and a few other things. It has recover, defragment, diagnose, remedy, and several other very useful programs primarily for the hard disk.

PC Tools—From Central Point Software, PC Tools has several utilities much like the Norton and Mace Utilities. It has a utility that can recover data from a disk that has been erased or reformatted. It has several other data recovery and DOS utilities. It can be used for hard disk backup and has several utilities such as those found in SideKick.

SpinRite, Disk Technician, OPTune, and DOSUTILS—These are utilities that allow you to diagnose, analyze, and optimize your hard disk.

CheckIt—From TouchStone Software, CheckIt checks and reports on your computer configuration by letting "you look inside your PC without taking off the cover." It reports on the type of processor, amount of memory, video adapter, hard and floppy drives, clock/calendar, ports, keyboard, and mouse, if present. It also tests the motherboard, hard and floppy disks, RAM, ports, keyboard, mouse, joystick, and other tests. It can also run a few benchmark speed tests.

Interrogator—Dysan, a branch of Xidex Corporation, has developed the Interrogator software. It can check a floppy disk drive for head alignment and performance and do several other diagnostic tests. If you are having trouble reading software on a certain drive, a quick test with this software will tell you whether it is the drive or the software.

Again, if at all possible, join a user's group and get to know the members. They can be one of your best sources of troubleshooting. Most of them have had similar problems and are glad to help.

Glossary

access time—The amount of time it takes the computer to find and read data from a disk or from memory. The average access time for a hard disk is based on the time it takes the head to seek and find the specified track, for the head to lock on to it, and for the head to spin around until the desired sector is beneath the head.

active partition—The partition on a hard disk that contains the boot and operating system. A single hard disk can be partitioned into several logical disks such as drive C, drive D, and drive E. This can be done at the initial formatting of the disk. Only one partition, usually drive C, can contain the active partition.

adapter boards or cards—The plug-in boards needed to drive monitors. Most monitor boards are monochrome graphic adapters (MGA), color graphic adapters (CGA), or enhanced graphic adapters (EGA). The EGA boards give a higher resolution than the CGA when used with a high-resolution monitor. The video graphics adapters (VGA) can give an even higher resolution than the EGA.

algorithm—A step-by-step procedure, scheme, formula, or method used to solve a problem or accomplish a task. May be a subroutine in a software program.

alphanumeric—Having both numerals and letters.

analyst—A person who determines the computer's needs to accomplish a given task. The job of an analyst is similar to that of a consultant. Note that there are no standard qualifications requirements for either of these jobs. Anyone can call themselves an analyst or a consultant. They should be experts in their field, but might not be.

ANSI—American National Standards Institute. A standard adopted by MS-DOS for cursor positioning used in the ANSI.SYS file for device drivers.

ASCII—American Standard Code for Information Interchange. Binary numbers from 0 to 127 that represent the upper- and lowercase letters of the alphabet, the numbers 0-9, and the several symbols found on a keyboard. A block of eight 0s and 1s are used to represent all of these characters. The first 32 characters, 0 – 31, are reserved for noncharacter functions of a keyboard, modem, printer, or other device. Number 32, or 0010 0000, represents the space, which is a character. The numeral 1 is represented by the binary number for 49, which is 0011 0001. Text written in ASCII is displayed on the computer screen as standard text. Text written in other systems, such as WordStar, has several other characters added and is very difficult to read. Another 128-character representation has been added to the original 128 for graphics and programming purposes.

ASIC—Application Specific Integrated Circuit.

assembly language—A low-level machine language made up of 0s and 1s.

asynchronous—A serial type of communication where one bit at a time is transmitted. The bits are usually sent in blocks of eight 0s and 1s.

autoexec.bat—If present, this file is run automatically by DOS after it boots up. You can configure this file to suit your own needs; it can load and run certain programs or configure your system.

.BAK files—Anytime that you edit or change a file in certain applications the program will save the original file as a backup and append the extension .BAK to it.

BASIC—Beginners All-Purpose Symbolic Instruction Code. A high-level language that was once very popular. Many programs and games still use it. It comes standard on the IBM BASICA. Some of it is in ROM.

batch—The batch command can be used to link commands and run them automatically. The batch commands can be made up easily by the user. They all have the extension .BAT.

baud—Bits per second. A measurement of the speed or data transfer rate of a communications line between the computer and printer, modem, or another computer. Most present-day modems operate at 1200 baud or 1200 bits per second.

benchmark—A standard type program against which similar programs can be compared.

bidirectional—Both directions. Most printers print in both directions, thereby saving the time it takes to return to the other end of a line.

binary—Binary numbers are 0s and 1s.

BIOS—Basic Input-Output System. The BIOS is responsible for handling the input output operations.

bits—Binary digits. A contraction of Binary and digITs.

boot or bootstrap—When a computer is turned on, all the memory and other internal operators have to be set or configured. The IBM takes quite a while to boot up because it checks all the memory parity and most of the peripherals. A small amount of the program to do this is stored in ROM. Using this, the computer pulls itself up by its boot-straps. A warm boot is sometimes necessary to get the computer out of an endless loop, or if it is hung up for some reason. A warm boot can be done by pressing Ctrl, Alt, and Del.

bubble memory—A nonvolatile type memory that is created by the magnetization of small bits of ferrous material. It held a lot of promise at one time, but it is rather expensive to make and is slower than semiconductor memory.

buffer—Usually some discrete amount of memory that is used to hold data. A computer can send data thousands of times faster than a printer or modem can utilize it. But, in many cases, the computer can do nothing else until all of the data has been transferred. The data can be input to a buffer, which can then feed the data into the printer as needed. The computer is then freed to do other tasks.

bug, debug—The early computers were made with high-voltage vacuum tubes. It took rooms full of hot tubes to do the job that a credit card calculator can do today. One of the large systems went down one day. After several hours of troubleshooting, the technicians found a large bug had crawled into the high-voltage wiring and been electrocuted, but it had shorted out the whole system. Since that time, any type of trouble in a piece of software or hardware is called a *bug*. To *debug* it, of course, is to try to find the errors or defects.

bulletin boards—Usually a computer with a hard disk that can be accessed with modem. Software and programs can be uploaded or left on the bulletin board by a caller, or a caller can scan the software that has been left there by others and download any that he or she likes. The bulletin boards often have help and message services—a great source of help for a beginner.

bus—Wires or circuits that connect a number of devices together. It can also be a system. The IBM PC bus is the configuration of the circuits that connect the 62 pins of the 8 slots together on the motherboard. It has become the *de facto* standard for the clones and compatibles.

byte—A byte is 8 bits or a block of 8 0s and 1s. These 8 bits can be arranged in 256 different ways (2^8). Therefore, one byte can be made to represent any one of the 256 characters in the ASCII character set. It takes one byte to make a single character. Because the word "byte" has four characters, it requires 4 bytes, or 32 bits.

cache memory—A high-speed buffer set up in memory to hold data that is being read from the hard disks. Often a program will request the same data from the disk over and over again. This can be quite time consuming, depending on the access speed of the disk drive and the location of the data on the disk. If the requested data is cached in memory, it can be accessed almost immediately.

carriage width—The width of a typewriter or printer. The two standard widths are 80 columns and 132 columns.

cell—A place for a single unit of data in memory, or an address in a spreadsheet.

Centronics parallel port—A system of 8-bit parallel transmission first used by the Centronics Company. It has become a standard and are the default method of printer output on the IBM.

character—A letter, a number, or an 8-bit piece of data.

chip—An integrated circuit, usually made from a silicon wafer. It can be microscopically etched and have thousands of transistors and semiconductors in a very small area. The 80286 CPU used in the AT has an internal main surface of about a half inch. It has 120,000 transistors on it, the 386 has 275,000, the 486 has 1.2 million.

CISC—Complex Instruction Set Computing. This is the standard type of computer design as opposed to the RISC or reduced instruction set computers used in larger systems. It can require as many as six steps for a CISC system to carry out a command. The RISC system might need only two steps to perform a similar function.

clock—The operations of a computer are based on very critical timing, so they use a crystal to control their internal clocks. The standard frequency for the PC and XT is 4.77 million cycles per second, or million hertz. The turbo systems operate at 6 to 8 MHz.

cluster—Two or more sectors on a track of a disk. Each track of a floppy or hard disk is divided into sectors.

composite video—A less expensive monitor that combines all the colors in a single input line.

console—In the early days, a monitor and keyboard were usually set up at a desk-like console. The term has stuck. A console is a computer. The command COPY CON allows you to use the keyboard as a typewriter. Type COPY CON PRN or COPY CON LPT1, and everything you type will be sent to the printer. At the end of your file, or letter, type Ctrl – Z or F6 to stop sending.

consultant—Someone who is supposed to be an expert who can advise and help you determine what your computer needs are (similar to an analyst). No standard requirements or qualifications must be met, so anyone can take the title analyst or consultant.

conventional memory—The first 640K of RAM memory, the memory that DOS handles. The PC actually has 1Mb of memory, but the 384K above the 640K is reserved for system use.

coprocessor—Usually an 8087 or 80287 that works in conjunction with the CPU and vastly speeds up some operations.

copy protection—A system that prevents a disk from being copied.

CPS—Characters Per Second. When referring to a printer, the speed that it can print.

CPU—Central Processing Unit such as the 8088 or 80286.

current directory—The directory that is in use at the time.

cursor—The blinking spot on the screen that indicates where next character will be input.

daisy wheel—A round printer or typewriter wheel with flexible fingers that have the alphabet and other formed characters.

database—A collection of data, usually related in some way.

DATE command—Date will be displayed anytime DATE is typed at the prompt sign.

DIP—Dual Inline Pins. A DIP refers to the two rows of pins on the sides of most integrated circuit chips.

disk controller—A plug-in board that is used to control the hard and/or floppy disk drives. All of the read and write signals go through the controller.

DMA—Direct Memory Access. Some parts of the computer such as the disk drives can exchange data directly with the RAM without having to go through the CPU.

documentation—Manuals, instructions, or specifications for a system whether it is hardware or software.

DOS—Disk Operating System. Software that allows programs to interact and run on a computer.

dot matrix—A type of printer that uses a matrix of thin wires or pins to make up the print head. Electronic solenoids pushed the pins out to form letters out of dots that were made when the pins pushed against the ribbon and paper. Older printers used seven pins which gave rather poor quality print. Newer 24-pin heads can print in near-letter-quality (NLQ) type.

double density—At one time, most disks were single-sided and had a capacity of 80 to 100K. Then the capacity was increased and technology was advanced so that the disks could be recorded on both sides with up to 200K per side double-sided, double-density. Then quad density was soon introduced with 400K per side. Then of course, the newer 1.6Mb high-density disks. All of the above figures are before formatting. Most double-density is the common 360K formatted. The quad ends up with 720K formatted and the high density is 1.2Mb. The new $3^1/2$ disks standard format is 720K. The high-density $3^1/2$ inch disks hold 1.44MB.

dumb terminal—A terminal that is tied to a mainframe or one that does not have its own microprocessor.

duplex—A characteristic of a communications channel which enables data to be transmitted in both directions. Full duplex allows the information to be transmitted in both directions simultaneously. In a half duplex, it can be transmitted in both directions, but not at the same time.

ECHO—A command that can cause information to be displayed on the screen from a BAT or other file. ECHO can be turned on or off.

EEPROM—An Electrically-Erasable Programmable Read-Only Memory chip.

EGA—Enhanced Graphics Adapter. Board used for high-resolution monitors.

EISA—Extended Industry Standard.

EMS—Expanded Memory Specification. A specification for adding expanded memory put forth by Lotus, Intel, and Microsoft (LIM EMS).

EPROM—An Erasable Programmable Read-Only Memory chip.

ergonomics—The study and science of how the human body can be the most productive in working with machinery. This would include the study of the effects of things like the type of monitor, the type of chair, lighting, and other environmental and physical factors.

errors—DOS displays several error messages if it receives bad commands or there are problems of some sort.

ESDI—Enhanced Small Disk Interface. A hard disk interface that allows data to be transferred to and from the disk at a rate of 10 megabits per second. The older standard ST506 allowed only 5 megabits per second.

expanded memory—Memory that can be added to a PC, XT or AT. It can only be accessed through special software.

expansion boards—Boards that can be plugged into one of the 8 slots on the motherboard to add memory or other functions.

extended memory—Memory that can be added to an 80286 or 80386 that will be addressable with the OS/2 operating system.

external commands—DOS commands that are not loaded into memory when the computer is booted.

FAT—File Allocation Table. This is a table on the disk that DOS uses to keep track of all of the parts of a file. A file can be placed in sector 3 of track one, sectors 5 and 6 of track ten and sector 4 of track 20. The file allocation table would keep track of where they are and will direct the read or record head to those areas.

fonts—The different types of print letters such as Gothic, Courier, Times Roman, Helvetica, and others.

format—The process of preparing a disk so that it can be recorded. The format process lays down tracks and sectors so that data can be written anywhere on the disk and recovered easily.

fragmentation—If a disk has several records that have been changed several times, there are bits of the files on several different tracks and sectors. This slows down writing and reading of the files because the head has to move back and forth to the various tracks. If these files are copied to a newly formatted disk, each file will be written to clean tracks that are contiguous. This will decrease the access time to the floppy disk or hard disk.

friction feed—A printer that uses a roller or platen to pull the paper through.

game port—An Input/Output (I/O) port for joysticks, trackballs, paddles, and other devices.

gigabyte—One billion bytes. This will be a common-size memory in a very short time. In virtual mode the 80286 can address this much memory.

glitch—An unexpected electrical spike or static disturbance that can cause loss of data.

global—A character or something that appears throughout an entire document or program.

googool—A very large figure, 1 followed by 100 zeros.

handshaking—A protocol or routine between systems, usually the printer and the computer, to indicate readiness to communicate with each other.

hard disk—A disk drive that can usually store a large amount of data. It has one or more magnetically coated platters that spin at 3600 RPM in a sealed casing.

hardware—The physical parts that make up a computer system such as disk drives, keyboards, monitors, etc.

Hayes-compatible—Hayes was one of the first modem manufacturers. Like IBM, they created a set of standards that most others have adopted.

hexadecimal—A system that uses the base 16. The binary system is based on 2, the decimal system is based on 10. The hexadecimal goes from 0, 1, 2, 3, 4, 5, 6, 7, 8, 9, A, B, C, D, E, F. 10 would be 16 in the decimal system, and it starts over so that 20 would be 32 in decimal. Most of the memory locations are in hexadecimal notation.

hidden files—The files that do not show up in a normal directory display.

high-level language—A language such as BASIC, Pascal, or C. These program languages are fairly easy to read and understand.

ICs—Integrated Circuits. The first integrated circuit was the placing of two transistors in a single can early in the 1960s. Then ways were found to put several semiconductors in a package. It was called SSI, or Small-Scale Integration. Then LSI, or Large-Scale Integration, then VLSI or Very-Large-Scale Integration were developed. Today we have VHSIC or Very-High-Scale Integrated Circuits.

interface—A piece of hardware or a set of rules that allows communications between two systems.

internal commands—Those commands that are loaded into memory when DOS boots up.

interpreter—A program that translates a high-level language into machine-readable code.

kilobyte—Roughly 1000 bytes, also known as 1K or more exactly, 1024 bytes. This is 2^{10}.

LAN—Local Area Network. Where several computers might be tied together or to a central server.

laser printer—A type of printer that uses the same type of "engine" used in copy machines. A laser beam electronically controlled sweeps across a drum. It charges the drum with an image of the letters or graphics that is to be printed. The charged drum then picks up toner particles and deposits them on the page so that a whole page is printed at once.

LIM-EMS—Lotus-Intel-Microsoft Expanded Memory Specification.

low-level format—Most hard disks must have a preliminary low-level format performed on them before they can be formatted for DOS. Low-level formatting is also sometimes called *initializing*.

low-level language—A machine level language. Usually in binary digits that would be very difficult for most people to understand.

LQ—Letter Quality. The type from a daisy wheel or formed type printers.

macro—A series of keystrokes that can be recorded, somewhat like a batch file, then be typed back when one or more keys is pressed. For instance, I can type my entire return address with just two keystrokes.

mainframe—A large computer that can serve several users.

megabyte—Roughly 1,000,000 bytes, also known as 1Mb. More precisely, it is 2^{20} or 1,048,576 bytes. It takes a minimum of 20 data lines to address 1Mb, a minimum of 24 lines (2^{24}) to address 16Mb, and a minimum of 25 lines (2^{25}) to address 32Mb.

menu—A list of choices or options. A menu-driven system makes it very easy for beginners to choose what they want to run or do.

MFM—Modified Frequency Modulation. The scheme for the standard method of recording on hard disks. See RLL.

MHz—Megahertz, a million cycles per second. Some older technicians still call it CPS. A few years ago, a committee decided to honor Heinrich Rudolf Hertz (1857-1894) for his early work in electromagnetism. So they changed the cycles per second, CPS, to Hertz or Hz.

mode—A DOS command that must be invoked to direct the computer output to a serial printer.

modem—A contraction of modulator-demodulator. A device that allows data to be sent over telephone lines.

modes—The 80286 and 80386 will operate in three different modes, the real, the protected, and the virtual. For more details, see Chapter 9.

mouse—A small pointing device that can control the cursor and move it anywhere on the screen. It usually has one to three buttons that can be assigned various functions.

MTBF—Mean Time Before Failure. An average of the time between failures, usually used in describing a hard disk or other component.

multitasking—The ability of the computer to perform more than one task at a time. Many of the newer computers have this capability when used with the proper software.

multiuser—A computer that is capable of providing service to more than one user such as a server for a local area network (LAN).

NEAT chipset—New Enhanced AT chipset from Chips and Technology. Chips and Technology combined the functions of several chips found on the original IBM motherboard into just a few very large scale integrated circuits (VLSI). These chips are used on the vast majority of clone boards.

NLQ—Near Letter Quality. The better formed characters from a dot matrix printer.

null modem cable—A cable with certain pairs of wires crossed over. If the computer sends data from pin 2, the modem might receive it on pin 3. The modem would send data back to the computer from its pin 2 and be received by the computer on pin 3. Several other wires would also be crossed.

OS/2—An operating system that allows the 80286 and 80386 machines to directly address huge amounts of memory. It removes many of the limitations that DOS imposes. OS/2 does not benefit the PCs or XTs to any great degree.

parallel—A system that uses 8 lines to send 8 bits at a time, or one whole byte.

parity checking—In the computer memory system, parity checking is an error detection technique that verifies the integrity of the RAM memory contents. This is the function of the ninth chip in a memory bank. Parity checking systems are also used in other areas such as verifying the integrity of data transmitted by modem.

plotter—An X-Y writing device that can be used for charts, graphics, and many other functions that most printers can't do.

prompt—The > sign that shows that DOS is waiting for an entry.

protocol—The rules and methods by which computers and modems can communicate with each other.

QIC—Quarter-Inch Cartridge tape. A width of tape used in tape backup systems. Some standards using this size tape have been developed, but still several nonstandard systems are in use.

RAM—Random Access Memory. This is computer memory that is used to temporarily hold files and data as they are being worked on, changed or altered. This volatile memory can be written to and read from. Any data stored in it is lost when the power is turned off.

RGB—Red, Green, and Blue. The three primary colors that are used in color monitors and TVs. Each color has its own electron gun that shoots streams of electrons to the back of the monitor display and causes it to light up in the various colors.

RISC—Reduced Instruction Set Computing. A design that allows a computer to operate with fewer instructions allows it to run much faster.

RLL—Run Length Limited. A scheme of hard disk recording that allows 50 percent more data to be recorded on a hard disk than the standard MFM scheme. ARLL or ERLL, for Advanced or Enhanced RLL, will allow twice as much data to be recorded on a hard disk. The older MFM system divided each track into 17 sectors of 512 bytes each. The RLL format divides the tracks into 26 sectors with 512 bytes each. The ARLL and ERLL divides them into 34 sectors per track.

ROM—Read-Only Memory. This memory is not lost when the power is turned off. The primary use of ROM is in the system BIOS and on some plug-in boards.

SCSI—Small Computer System Interface, pronounced scuzzy. A fast parallel hard disk interface system developed by Shugart Associates and adopted by the American National Standards Institute (ANSI), the SCSI system allows multiple drives to be connected. It supports a transfer rate of 1.2 megabytes per second. Because a byte is 8 bits, this is about the same as the ESDI 10 megabit per second rate.

sector—A section of a track on a floppy or hard disk. A sector ordinarily holds 512 bytes. A 360K disk has 40 tracks per side. Each track is divided into 9 sectors.

serial—The transmission of one bit at a time over a single line.

SIMM—Single Inline Memory Module.

SIP—Single Inline Pins. Many small resistor packs and integrated circuits have a single line of pins.

source—The origin, or the disk to be copied from.

spool—Simultaneous Peripheral Operations On Line. A spooler acts as a storage buffer for data which is then fed out to a printer or other device. In the meantime, the computer can be used for other tasks.

target—The disk to be copied to.

time stamp—The record of the time and date that is recorded in the directory when a file is created or changed.

tractor—A printer device with sprockets or spikes that pulls the computer paper with the holes in the margins through the printer at a very precise feed rate. A friction feed platen might allow the paper to slip, move to one side or the other, and not be precise in the spacing between the lines.

Trojan horse—A harmful piece of code or software that is usually hidden in a software package that will later cause destruction. It is unlike a virus in that it does not grow and spread.

TSR—Terminate and Stay Resident. When a program such as SideKick is loaded in memory, it will normally stay there until the computer is booted up again. If several TSR programs are loaded in memory, there might not be enough left to run some programs.

turbo—Usually means a computer with a faster-than-normal speed.

user-friendly—Usually means bigger and more expensive. It should make using the computer easier.

user groups—Usually a club or a group of people who use computers. Often the club will be devoted to users of a certain type of computer, but in most clubs anyone is welcome to join.

vaporware—Products that are announced, usually with great fanfare, but are not yet ready for market.

virtual—Something that might be essentially present, but not in actual fact. If you have a single disk drive, it will be drive A, but you also have a virtual drive B if your DIP switches on the motherboard are set properly.

virus—Destructive code that is placed or embedded in a computer program. The virus is usually self-replicating and will often copy itself onto other programs. It might lie dormant for some time, then completely erase a person's hard disk or cause other problems.

volatile—Refers to memory units that lose stored information when power is lost. Nonvolatile memory would be that of a hard disk or tape.

windows—Many new software packages are now loaded into memory where they stay in the background until they are called. When called, the program will pop up on the screen in a window. The Microsoft company has a software package called *Windows* that provides an operating environment for many DOS programs.

Index